THE ABBEY
UP THE HILL

~

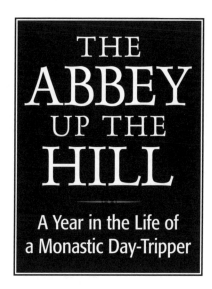

THE ABBEY UP THE HILL

A Year in the Life of a Monastic Day-Tripper

Carol Bonomo

MOREHOUSE PUBLISHING
HARRISBURG, PENNSYLVANIA

Morehouse Publishing
P.O. Box 1321
Harrisburg, PA 17105

Morehouse Publishing is a division of The Morehouse Group.

Design by Corey Kent
Cover art: Lee Snider/Corbis

Library of Congress Cataloging-in-Publication Data

Bonomo, Carol, 1952–
  The abbey up the hill : a year in the life of a monastic day-tripper / by Carol Bonomo.
    p. cm.
  ISBN 0-8192-1912-6
    1. Bonomo, Carol, 1952- 2. Oblates of St. Benedict—Biography. I. Title

BX4705.B57675 A3 2002
271'.97—dc21

2001054639

Printed in the United States of America
  02 03 04 05 06   6 5 4 3 2

For the old abbot

Those that be planted in the house of the Lord
Shall flourish in the courts of our God.
They shall still bring forth fruit in old age;
They shall be fat and flourishing;
To shew that the Lord is upright:
He is my rock, and there is no unrighteousness in him.

Psalm 92:13–15

CONTENTS

ACKNOWLEDGMENTS

If there's one thing I'm learning, it's that we are all part of communities, no matter how apart we may feel on some portions of the road. One special little community to acknowledge here is the October 27 Birthday Club: Marion Reid, Jamie Nelson, Sylvia Payne, Professor Deborah Small, and I. We celebrate 2002 with a joint fiftieth birthday party (if one of us has to be fifty, *all* of us have to be fifty). Hanging around such terrific once-a-year birthday buddies has helped me recognize what I'm capable of achieving in this world.

Five people formed a community to support me after I finished writing the draft of this book and looked around in panic to say, "*Now what?*" Keith Butler, Jamie Nelson, Sylvia Payne, and Richard Riehl read the draft, claimed to love it, and told me it only needed "a little bit of work" to become better. Father Larry Doersching, Society of Mary, Marianists, also kindly read the manuscript and worked it over from his perspectives as both English teacher and priest. Jeannie Ponessa graciously lent me her uncle, Father Larry, when I didn't have an uncle Catholic priest of my own. That's community.

The monks of the St. Augustine's Abbey put up with my day-tripping ways with their usual hospitality; most of my early discomfort was my own to claim. The oratory was always open. My fellow oblates, especially Gregory and Hildegard, are a very special community; we are all on the road to the New Jerusalem together.

Debra Farrington is an editor like no other; she is full of joy and took me on a whole new journey with this book.

My husband Felix is a skeptic, but hardly skeptical, at least with me. He always knew something good would come out of "all your out-of-body experiences to Pluto."

And for Blessed Joanna Mary Bonomo, St. Benedict and his Rule, and especially St. Paul: they are a community of saints I will never escape. Nor would I want to.

Carol (Joanna Mary) Bonomo
October 1, 2001

AUTHOR'S NOTE

Anonymity is at the heart of Alcoholics Anonymous. Tradition 12 of AA states that "anonymity is the spiritual foundation of all our traditions, ever reminding us to place principles before personalities."

Although the monks and oblates of St. Augustine's Abbey are highly personable and distinct individuals, they are also anonymous in their communal understanding of following the principles of the Rule of St. Benedict. Out of respect for the humility that underlies these principles, names and some identifying features of individuals have been changed. Their insights and teachings, of course, are as real today as the Rule was to St. Benedict when he wrote it in the sixth century.

JANUARY
If Ye Will Hear His Voice

Today if ye will hear his voice,
Harden not your heart . . .
Psalm 95:7, 8

January 7, 2000: Epiphany

Jubilee Year—and now that the frenetic shouting of "millennium madness" is over (and at some point, "millennium madness" seemed to have married the Y2K bug), it's time to make a unique kind of resolution this unique Jubilee Year.

I am not an expert on things Catholic, so the fact that I had never heard of a Jubilee Year before was no surprise. But, besides my lack of expertise, I had never lived through one either. The Pope declares Jubilee Years only every fifty years. Pope John Paul II has thrown open the Holy Door at the Vatican to symbolically let us in this year, to experience a renewal of our faith. Not only have I never known a Jubilee Year before, it is unlikely that I will ever know another.

All I would like to do this year, I think, is spend some time with myself—not the best company sometimes, but not the worst either—and the Rule of St. Benedict and think about how the two can work together.

I've been the sum of many labels up to this moment in my life. I'm one of those "seekers" who doesn't know what she's looking for and wouldn't recognize an answer to the meaning of life if she tripped on it in the dark on the way to the bathroom. "Artist," "crafter," "diarist,"

"Secular Franciscan," "recovering alcoholic," "Catholic," "Episcopalian," "spiritual gypsy," and now "Benedictine oblate" have all been identities I've inhabited.

Throughout all of it, my heart has remained stubbornly unattached. The label fits for a while, but then I get bored or the label stretches too tightly—or I do—or it gets too hard. And then I'm off again, my feet trailing my restless heart, which has never found its place in this world, and especially not since moving from small-town New England to the official "paradise" this side of heaven: San Diego.

I cried for two years after I moved to San Diego to join Felix's work and dream. I thought it would be the same as Boston, only with better weather.

"I hate it here," I sniffed. "The people are different. Nobody stays put, and nobody bothers to get friendly because they'll all just move on again anyway, and there are too many to start with. The houses are different and they're stacked together like pink boxes. The ocean's on the wrong side, and the sun comes up over the mountains. I get lost all the time, and I can't tell east from west. The strawberries bloom in February, and everybody makes fun of my accent and my hair."

"This isn't exactly the slums we've moved to," Felix would say carefully, baffled by my experience of paradise. He loved every perfumed-air, crinkly palmed minute.

After two years of crying in the shower so he wouldn't hear me, I decided that I was never going to get to go "back." I was stuck calling this "home." One of the earliest poems a cranky New England fellow, Robert Frost, wrote was no longer mine to claim:

> I do not see why I should e'er turn back,
> Or those should not set forth upon my track
> To overtake me, who should miss me here
> And long to know if still I held them dear.[1]

On the Feast of Christ the King, just six weeks ago, I became a Benedictine oblate—a secular "prayer friend" of the monks of St. Augustine's Abbey. This happened after a year's novitiate, or "practice run," where I fluctuated wildly between the clean peace of being a Benedictine and the wild and woolly freedom of being an artist. It was a close call. Benedict won, but most likely only because that's where the pendulum was on the day of my oblation.

I signed a paper promising to keep the Rule of St. Benedict to the best of my ability and as my station in life allows. Becoming a Benedictine oblate alleviated some of the long-standing homesickness for me. The monks had moved here from somewhere else too.

Now, having signed off my spiritual life with less thought than bringing a house cat to the vet for neutering, I want to take advantage of Pope John Paul II's generous opening of a Jubilee Year to figure out what I've done and whether or not—if I don't like it—I can turn it in for something else.

I think I was maybe fourteen when I figured out there wasn't any life decision I could make that I couldn't reverse, except for having children. Jobs, careers, college, majors, relationships, marriages, apartments, houses—I could undo them all. Short of abandoning a child on somebody's doorstep, I couldn't undo children.

So I never had any children, and I did and undid everything else as needed or desired. But this Benedictine thing is about stability as much as it's about prayer practices, or so the Franciscans who sent me here have told me. I'm willing to give it a try. I can always do something else if I don't like stability.

That was the reasoning behind the most ordinary of seekers turning into a Benedictine oblate. I am hardly one of the holy ones. I work at a university in a midlevel management position as a lobbyist and speechwriter. ("Say 'advocate'!" hisses my husband Felix. "Nobody likes lobbyists!") I work out in a health club four or five times a week, never eat my vegetables, have trouble remembering if I'm a Republican or Democrat or if it even matters. I like to spend free time with Felix and stitching baby quilts that I give away to new parents. I'm not sure if that last one is fraught with psychological significance or if I just like bright colors and easy cross-stitch patterns. I am thoroughly ordinary for somebody who's lived her life like a "lost" looking for a "found."

I have a plan for this Jubilee Year. I love making plans. I'm taking two days of vacation time each month and spending it at "my" monastery, St. Augustine's Abbey in San Diego. The schedule will be:

11:00	Mass at the abbey church
Noon	Lunch in the retreat dining room
12:30–1:30	Reflect: walk the prayer walk, digest lunch, wait for things to open

| 1:30–5:00 | Study: Rule of St. Benedict, read the commentaries on the Rule, monastic library |
| 5:00–5:30 | Vespers |

This is my plan then, this Jubilee Year 2000.

~

It is shockingly cold this winter in San Diego County. I say "shockingly" because when I moved here, I thought the weather would be consistent year 'round. I thought that's what a "moderate" climate meant. I gave away all my sweaters and sweatshirts when I moved here.

But now my blood is thin and my New England perspective of "cold" has mutated considerably. It is thirty degrees at 7:00 A.M. today, with another frost delay at the golf course. I am glad my monastery has a heated church at least. It is the first day of the Jubilee plan. I feel a little decadent, taking a vacation day just four days into the new working year. But I'm ready to see what the Rule looks like, and what I've gotten myself into this time.

I dress all in black, to better blend in—as if I am going to somehow be mistaken for a monk! I carry a notebook to write in, two commentaries[2] on the Rule that I have bought and read or am reading. The commentaries illuminate the Rule and try to "modernize" it. This little Rule—just sixty pages of text in my edition—was written nearly fifteen hundred years ago. But abbots, monks, and nuns write the commentaries. No matter how charmingly they describe life and the Rule, it is not my life, of pizza, politics, and promotions. But Benedict says his Rule is written for me too, right up front in the third sentence of the Prologue—*My words are meant for you, whoever you are*[3] . . .

Abbot Antony gave a copy of the Rule to me after our first meeting. He showed off the new bookstore still under renovation at the abbey, and while I ogled the how-to books, he handed me this little red-covered paperback with his hands as ancient as any desert father.

I have a second copy of the Rule he gave me, along with a St. Benedict medal, when I pledged myself as an oblate novice three months later. I sewed the medal into a bookmark I stitched for myself and put away the spare Rule, reading from the one he took (presumably "on account") from the yet-to-open gift shop.

I read the Rule four times through, a chapter or so a day, during my novitiate. I did one of those read-throughs chapter by chapter with *A Commentary on the Rule of St. Benedict for Oblates*, which I thought would help me relate to the Rule better. It did not. It was all a mystery to me. When I reached chapter 58 a few months into my reading, I learned that Benedict had the Rule read to newcomers three times in their first year. At the first reading, the candidate is told, *Behold the law under which you wish to fight. If you can observe it, enter upon the life; if not, you are free to leave.* I completed the fourth reading the week before my oblation. Mostly all I can remember from those readings of the Rule is silence, humility, no grumbling, and don't eat any quadrupeds. Felix had to tell me what a quadruped was or wasn't. For the rest, my signature making me an oblate was either my first genuine act of faith, or more likely, the usual headfirst plunge before deciding whether or not I can swim.

The Catholic bishops from Region 9 are at the monastery today for their annual retreat. Region 9 encompasses Kansas, Iowa, Nebraska, and Missouri—genuinely cold places. Abbot Antony told me last year that they came once for this early January retreat and liked it so much they have been coming ever since. It is an extraordinary sight to watch the procession at Mass beginning with black-robed brothers, continuing with white-vested fathers, and concluding with fifteen ruby-capped bishops, like exotic snowbirds come to visit. It is delightful. We are grateful for their presence here at the edge of the country, where the desert crashes into the sea. The bishops are grateful for their retreat time, the company of one another after a year spent as the only bishop in their district, the sunshine and the moderate temperatures, the ordinary faces of white, Hispanic, and Filipino hues that fill a Friday late-morning Mass.

Unfortunately, I learn from Brother John Climachus, the retreat master, the ruby-caps have taken over everything on the retreat center side. That includes the retreat dining room (lunch!) and the oblate library (study!). I instantly contemplate not the great mysteries of the Rule of Benedict—but rather, giving up. Going home to stitch or read, anything but this illusion of coming to an understanding with the Rule. Who do I think I am anyway?

It is still early in the century—just seven days. And early in the liturgical year—just Epiphany. In the church calendar's way of looking at things, the Wise Men have barely gotten off their camels, and I'm already looking to bail out to follow another star. I am usually more disciplined than this early on, at least with diets and exercise. Why not with study? My favorite quote from reading St. Paul's letters last year: "It is for discipline that you have to endure" (Hebrews 12:7). Or, as the athletic shoe company says, "Just do it."

I drive to Burger King (quadrupeds and fries to go) and then to the new branch library in Pacific Beach across the street from where I used to live, and I find a study carrel.

Rule of St. Benedict: Prologue

The desert fathers (and a few desert mothers) told stories in a rich, unique tradition.[4] These fourth- and fifth-century hermits fled the corruption of the crumbling cities of the Roman Empire and lived solitary lives in the deserts of Egypt, Syria, Palestine, and Arabia. In their individual cells, they became examples and teachers of Christian practices rich from their lives of isolation and self-denial. The folk traditions that developed around their sayings are some of the oldest in Christian literature.

St. Benedict drew on their traditions and habits in forming his Rule, either by borrowing their traditions or by reacting against them. We do the same with our parents. We either copy them or slavishly become something artificial in our attempts *not* to be like them.

I like the way the desert fathers expressed themselves. Their stories do not have the overly familiar sound of the biblical parables I grew up with. They have a surprising freshness and tartness around the edges. Okay, they remind me of me. I get done talking and get to the point I want to make, and the person listening suddenly blinks and says, "Are you from the East Coast?" This is rarely a compliment. It means I got to the point faster and with less prettiness than expected. The desert fathers did that too. Their stories are tangy. They speak to the wilderness in my soul and the wildness of this place of desert at the edge of the Pacific Ocean.

Abba Poemen, of blessed memory, has a great many stories and sayings attributed to him. One in particular strikes me as appropriate to beginning this study project.

> Abba Poemen said, When a man prepares to build a house, he gathers together all he needs to be able to construct it,

and he collects different sorts of materials. So it is with us; let
us acquire a little of the virtues.[5]

It takes one week to read the Prologue following the prescribed
daily pieces the monks use that give them exactly three complete readings of the Rule each year. When Abbot Antony gave me the Rule, he
opened it up, flipped past all of the historical introduction pages—
something I still tend to do—and said, "Here is the first word of the
Rule—'Listen.' It's the most important thing to remember."

After one week of reading the prologue slowly, "Listen" is still
pretty much all I ever remember of the Prologue. Benedict weaves the
psalms, proverbs, gospels, and letters of Paul into his text, which for
some reason bifurcates it into two voices talking at the same time, one
Benedict, one biblical. *Therefore, let us arise without delay, the Scriptures
stirring us:* "It is now the hour for us to awake from sleep" (Romans
13:11); *Let us open our eyes to the Divine light and attentively hear the
Divine voice, calling and exhorting us daily*: "Today if you shall hear his
voice, harden not your hearts" (Psalm 95:7–8), for example. Of
course, Benedict hears just one voice, and threads it together into a
Rule the way I take blue, purple, and gold threads, and piece them
together into one stitched bookmark.

My other problem besides bifurcation is that the biblical quotes
don't resonate in my memory. My translation of Benedict's Rule, still
the one given to me by the abbot, uses The Jerusalem Bible when-
ever Benedict quotes Scripture. I don't have Benedict's enormous
facility with Scripture, or any reasonable evangelical's command of
scriptural references. But I grew up going to the Episcopal Church
weekly, with an Old Testament reading, Gospel, Epistle (one of the
letters in the New Testament), and psalm each week. As a choir member and choral singer, I inadvertently committed goodly chunks of
Isaiah to memory via Handel's *Messiah* and selected psalms via
Brahms's *Requiem*. All of these were in the "king's English" of the
King James Version of the Bible, originally published in 1611, which
sounded a lot like Shakespearean English in its poetic quality and also
in its obscurity. The modern, accepted translations like The
Jerusalem Bible that I now hear in church and in the abbey and in the
daily office we use for saying prayers have the vague, slightly familiar
taste of a leftover meal. The King James is my mother tongue.

Modernizing the texts has undoubtedly provided greater access and understanding of Scripture for ordinary people like me, but it has done so at the cost of a common, collective language. I assume older born-Catholics must feel the same way about the loss of Latin in the Mass. For my study, I return to the King James version of my Protestant past to make my way as a Catholic in this Jubilee Year. Sometimes listening is best done with the ear of memory.

~

The patchwork sky of winter in San Diego. Brief bits of pallid pink set into a muddy baby blue sky. You would not put these together into any self-respecting baby quilt, and yet here they are, the handiwork of God, as I wait for Vespers next to a fine set of Nativity figurines. The piney smell of the Christmas trees is now so faint that you notice it only when you first walk in. After that it fades, like discipline, as the time wears on. The bishops are congregation now, not ruby-capped snowbirds after all. They sit, scattered, in sagging sweaters, fumbling through the chanted psalms of Vespers, as ordinary as any of us.

January 14, 2000: Baptism of the Lord

It is suddenly summer in January. At 10:00 A.M., it must already be seventy degrees, and the air that lies so still over the abbey is full of twittering (if confused) birds. Early for Mass—and a crime to be indoors—so I pour a coffee in the retreat lounge and sit outside. The retreat center seems to be doing a brisk business in solitude today (there are even cookies out next to the coffee pot). But no bishops, so I should have access to meals and the oblate library today.

One of the regulars to daily Mass, an old lady in a wheelchair, gets pushed into the abbey church when I cross the parking lot. She seems quite excited to see me, waves enthusiastically from her bent-over crippled position. I have seen her at past weekday services, but didn't realize she might have seen me, or that I might stand out in her mind. Maybe she is just friendly with everybody?

Usually the older couple that brings her keeps the wheelchair in the back of the small church, but for some reason, this time they push her right to the front. I realize she is blocking half the center aisle when the candidate-monks cannot walk past her double file to retrieve the

Eucharistic gifts. How will my side get by her to take communion? I wonder. The Gospel reading (Mark 2:1–12) we've just heard reverberates in my mind. First, Jesus forgives the man's sins. Only then does he give what he considers to be the easier gift: "I say unto thee, Arise, and take up thy bed, and go thy way into thine house. And immediately, he arose, took up the bed, and went forth" (Mark 2:11–12). I look at the old lady in her wheelchair, her head bowed low, exposing a bare skull under her wig. What does she think when she hears this? I wonder.

And now, how will we get around her to receive communion? There is no way around. The path to Christ must line up behind her. We will wait until she is received first.

The great fir trees, greens, and red poinsettias of Christmas and Epiphany are gone. The Wise Men have moved on, following their star and leaving us behind. It is just the first week of Ordinary Time, a few weeks of it stuck here in the calendar between Epiphany and Lent, and the hard work of ordinary begins again. "Listen," says the Prologue.

How hard can it be to listen? We are rapidly becoming an oral culture again, says the *San Diego Union-Tribune* in one of its endless "end-of-the-millennium" summations on life. "Forget about reading and writing," the article begins. "When we communicate in the middle of the twenty-first century, visionaries believe it will be through speech."

I am a speechwriter for a university president. I think I know all about listening, since I put words into some people's mouths that other people listen to.

But I suspect that's more about hearing than listening. Hearing is the rush that flows by my ears: words, music, airplanes, birds, loud interruptions, soft murmurs, computer modem dial-ups, and ATM machines spitting up money while gagging on my bank card.

Listening is the reverse, the ability to hear the inner flow, the song of God, the heart of Christ, the breathless spark of the Holy Spirit. That is what Benedict asks as Prologue. And once I have that attitude of listening, well then, commence.

⌒

The retreat center's dining area is open—and deserted! I find a corner table, clutching my luncheon companion, a book of Thomas Merton's diaries, and wait for the bells. There is one lay worker from the abbey on the other side, plus two monks. Brother Matthew is very business-like and very quiet.. His family stayed in the room next to mine during my novitiate retreat during the Holy Days, very nice, noisy. The other monk is a Franciscan friend of Matthew's, from Assisi, no less.

"What are you reading?" the Franciscan asks.

"The journal of Thomas Merton," I say. "I like his voice. He's a convert like me."

"Oh," the Franciscan says, totally losing interest. He turns to Brother Matthew. "How do I get to Fullerton?"

The bells clang their dull, Asian-gong sounds, as if far away. Brother Bernard, on kitchen duty for retreatants, closes his eyes and begins the *Angelus. The Angel of the Lord declared unto Mary.* . . . The four of us chime in . . . *and she conceived of the Holy Spirit.* . . . Brother Matthew, who, unlike me, knows this simple prayer by heart and does not need the cheat sheet, responds and crosses himself while bent over the *Thomas Guide to Orange County*, trying to find Fullerton. Brother Bernard rolls up the sliding door between us and lunch. The real retreatants begin to pile in and fill up the place.

Cream of mushroom soup with a strong dose of basil and baked cheddar potato chips for me. One cookie. Thomas Merton as lunch companion.

After lunch, I walk the prayer walk that starts along the side of the abbey church where the first seven brothers have been buried. "For twenty-five years after we got here, there was not a single death," Abbot Antony told me once. "And then, they all went." The prayer walk pushes out along the edge of the bluff, past Brother Cosmas's beehives, with great ocean views a few miles away, before turning back and winding along views of highways, traffic, malls, and, further off, the Franciscan Mission, where I spent a great deal of time in the past and purchased funeral niches for Felix and me for the future. Everywhere along my path there are marvelous great and little rocks: orange, white, and crystalline, many placed on the wooden altar markers for the Stations of the Cross. I decide this Jubilee Year to make a prayer walk of my own at home to remember always these days, to have a part of this place in my home. I select a handsome, nearly pure white rock to begin that project.

The porter has disappeared. Brother Paschal, who has suddenly been pressed into service, does not know anything about a key to the oblate library. He is quite abrupt about it, and dials Abbot Antony. "A young lady here [I am not, but don't mind being called young] wants the oblate library. She has an armful of books already." And Abbot Antony, who glides with the silence of a Benedictine, but stiff as an old crow from two hip replacements, must leave his cell and let me into his pride and joy, the oblate library.

Twenty minutes later, I am changing plans. Much as I like the idea of studying the Rule in our own oblate library, in reality it does not work. There are chairs to sit in while reading, watching videos, or listening to audiocassettes. But there is no surface on which to write comfortably. The room is unbearably stuffy from being closed up most of the time. It is probably seventy-two degrees outside—in January!—but the window will not open. A regretful, silent goodbye, and I relocate to a private, enclosed garden on the other side of that stubbornly shut window. My oblate novice classmate, Hildegard, from Germany, has spent a great deal of private time in meditation in the garden, she has said. It is pleasant: two full-flowered Easter lilies, some off-season agapanthus, some pale violets, and a gaudy bush of frenetic pink azaleas, plus one nameless tree in the middle, all walled off from the world. A single sparrow flutters in, routs around the ground cover for lunch, and flutters off again.

It will certainly do nicely as an open-air study—unless I get kicked out, since I have not asked permission to be here in the "retreatants only" section of the monastery. Or until I need my other notebook, which is in the car.

Chapter 1: The Kinds of Monks

There are four kinds of monks, says Benedict, and he describes them this way: The Cenobites are the best: they live in a monastery. The Anchorites are hermits who have lived and matured spiritually in a monastery. The Sarabites are the worst—unschooled, undisciplined, and they follow the law of the pleasure of their desires. The gyratory monks are even worse than the Sarabites, restless and wandering. Benedict's Rule is written for Cenobites. But I feel a real kinship with and sorrow for the gyratory monks, so quickly and brutally dismissed by Benedict—*It is better to be silent as to their wretched life-style than to speak.*

The gyratory I was listens and remembers. I remember years of searching hard and the amazingly cruel responses that clearly indicated

I was not wanted. Other times, the cruelty and not-wanting was on my side. What comes first: the stability of the Cenobites or the wild fluctuations of faith that cause the gyratory to move along, not even aware of what faith looks like? "If ye will not believe, surely ye shall not be established," says Isaiah (7:9).

The Benedictines, being Cenobites, vow stability to one particular monastery. As oblates, we too affiliate with one particular monastery where we make our vows. But what comes first, the vow of stability or the belief, securely established? Without belief, we are surely rootless, and will shift and loosen and blow across the land, a gyratory, like those Benedict so clearly disliked.

In my own wanderings, like those who are *restless, servants to the seduction of their own will and appetites*, as Benedict says, I sporadically reached for religion, went out and bought bibles during drunken, lonely years, and tried to capture their essence, like pinning beautiful butterflies. But pinned, they were dead to me; the bibles remained closed. In college on the late-night shifts working during the summers, I prayed the Episcopal Book of Common Prayer and tried to find the roots I had as a child, to no avail.

I became AA's "recovering alcoholic" without belief in AA or in their diagnostics. I journeyed into being an artist, a writer, a graduate student, a perpetual careerist, a devoted workaholic, a convert to Catholicism, a Secular Franciscan, and finally a Benedictine oblate novice. I felt no particular call, no claim to become a Benedictine.

"Just do it," said Abbot Antony.

That rare and lovely creature, the desert *amma* (mother) Syncletica could have been speaking of this chapter when she said:

> If you find yourself in a monastery do not go to another place, for that will harm you a great deal. Just as the bird who abandons the eggs she was sitting on prevents them from hatching, so the monk or the nun grows cold and their faith dies, when they go from one place to another.[6]

My beloved Abbot Antony, "retired" from his position as abbot, is now the oblate master. I may not have felt called to the Benedictines, but I made a call—literally. And Abbot Antony both listened and heard. My life as a gyratory was ending, to be replaced with the stability of the Cenobites. And from that stability, belief has come to flower and grow. I had grown very tired of abandoning the eggs before hatching. My faith has grown weary of growing cold.

I love the first full line of Psalm 150 where we are called "to praise God in his sanctuary," because I always think his sanctuary is the same as mine—St. Augustine's Abbey atop the bluffs, above the Pacific, where these monks arrived to establish a monastic community and take root. I have followed by a different route, but have found them and settled here too.

~

I hurry into the abbey church in anticipation of Vespers. It is cooling off outside, but the church is still warm. A very lively group of women from one of the large downtown San Diego churches have arrived for their weekend retreat. There is something about a retreat that makes for a lot of talking and not much listening. I provide directions to the rooms, the chapel, and the cafeteria. I hurry to the church to escape them as soon as I can. It seems funny to remember that this is Friday afternoon and the weekend is arriving, all giggles and talk. My time here begins to end with the setting sun, and concludes with Vespers.

Funny. I never sing at Mass here, but I almost always sing at Vespers. Perhaps that's because if you don't sing Vespers, there is very little else to do.

"Please move to the other side," says the lady dusting down the pews. "I do this once a week. It's my prayer work."

I have no idea what that means, and have never seen her before. Obviously, her "prayer work" takes precedence over anybody else's prayer work if they are in her way. When I move, the sun is a gauze-drenched ball, diffused and jagged, ready to slide away into the ocean after its long day. It is a beautiful visual send-off to end my day here. But as soon as the prayer-work lady leaves, I move back to "my" seat, left end, row three, right center.

Chapter 2: The Qualities of the Abbot

Although St. Benedict scatters references to the responsibilities of the abbot throughout his Rule, this is the only chapter aimed at the abbot himself. The abbot is the highest authority on earth to his monks. As

Benedicts puts it: *He is believed to hold the place of Christ in the monastery, since he is addressed by a title of Christ.* Being the CEO of men's souls is a heavy responsibility, and Benedict offers guidance on how to manage those responsibilities—not through a "helpful hints" guide, but by describing the qualities the individual needs to succeed.

I was too unaware of these details to be confused by an abbot who was also the oblate master. He introduced himself simply as "Abbot Antony."

"Abbit?" I asked. "What is that? I once had a cat named Abbit."

"And did you like the cat?" he asked mildly.

"Oh, yes!"

"Well, that's good then. I'm the old abbot." A joke on his advanced age, but St. Augustine's Abbey may be unique among Benedictine monasteries in that it has two abbots. Abbot Henry carries the responsibilities that Benedict enunciates in his chapter on abbots—*to care for and guide the spiritual development of many different characters.* Abbot Antony retired as abbot at the age of eighty-five. Now he has similar responsibility—at a lesser degree—for our two hundred-some oblates. He is amazingly modest, the way some of the old desert fathers probably were:

> To one of the brethren appeared a devil, transformed into an angel of light, who said to him, "I am the Angel Gabriel, and I have been sent to thee." But the brother said, "Think again—you must have been sent to somebody else. I haven't done anything to deserve an angel." Immediately the devil ceased to appear.[7]

Some of the commentaries on this chapter, especially as they apply it to oblates, talk of the family roles. This makes sense, especially since "abbot" is from *abba,* or "father." (A familiar usage translates it as "daddy.") It was a great gift that Abbot Antony came into my life during a grief-stricken time, just five months after my own father had died at the end of a short, terrible fight with cancer.

But whether it should be or not, family metaphors are tough to work within a *school for God's service.* Although I grew up in a church-going family that was active in parish life, religious activity and spiritual growth were two very separate activities. And spiritual growth, when I went seeking it, seemed to require guidance from those who had traveled the path I now wanted to take.

In AA, they're called sponsors, and although they infrequently "sponsor" a membership, they are the people chosen for their "good sobriety" to guide you through the hurdles of early sobriety. "Read the Big Book." "Ask for help." "Go to meetings." Standard sponsor guidance.

As a convert to Catholicism, I found my "sponsor" to be anybody who would stand with me in the various rituals of RCIA (Rites of Christian Initiation for Adults), the "convert class" for adults becoming Catholics. My next-door neighbor did the honors. I learned quickly not to ask the real questions of salvation, because most sponsors in my group were more interested in determining at what point in Mass a "late arrival" still "counted" as going to Mass. Nor did I want to impose my doubts or issues on the deacon supervising the effort. I was afraid I wouldn't pass the class, that I would be left behind.

"So do you like to read?" Abbot Antony asked as he steered my elbow toward the lunchroom for retreatants at our first meeting. *Now that's an odd question,* I thought, but assured him of my scholarly interests. He was less than impressed, I think, when he asked what I read—popular books about spiritual life, biographies of religious authors, journals and letters by authors, rarely the actual books of the authors themselves. "Too hard for me," I explained.

He lent me a copy of *The Imitation of Christ* from the oblate library. "Read it slowly," he urged. (I peeked inside. "Go where you will, but you will never find rest except in humble obedience to the rule of your superior," I read.[8] There was little danger of speed reading.) "It is my favorite book," he said. That was when he also gave me my first copy of Benedict's Rule.

Homework! As an academic (even the fast-food kind), I could handle homework. But when I read chapter 2 of the Rule and learned that abbots are accountable for their teaching and the obedience of their charges on Judgment Day, I was horrified and called him to ask, "Even us? Oblate novices?"

There is surely nothing less praiseworthy or fun than imparting spiritual direction to oblate novices *of many different characters,* as the Rule says. In my tiny novice class of three, Gregory asked many questions and took many notes. Hildegard made many solitary retreats and prayed many prayers in the abbey church. I continued to read spiritual-lite books, write long letters full of new "self-understand-ings" to Abbot Antony, and show up for lunch and Mass so he could see how spiritually evolved I was becoming. (I had to do those things. I missed four out of my first six oblate meetings due to business travel, got bored easily, and left early even when I did show up.)

Abbot Antony persevered with me as he did with all of us. He embodied the listening commanded in Benedict's Prologue. When I came to the notion of *lectio divina* (sacred reading, practiced by Benedictines daily) and announced that it was too hard for me, he found copies of lecture notes on the topic, given to his monks over the years by visiting retreat speakers. When I finally got the smallest pos-sible version of the Divine Office (the "Liturgy of the Hours" prayed by priests, nuns, clerics, lay persons, and even the Pope each day) and announced I couldn't figure it out, he spent an afternoon showing me how the canticles, psalms, and prayers fit into life, like bookends, morning and night. Over the year of my novitiate, like a patient spi-der, he wove a sustaining web of the Word, the Rule, and the Office around me, his reluctant charge.

And still I poured out more for him to guide. Like Isaiah says, "And he shall snatch on the right hand, and be hungry; and he shall eat on the left hand, and they shall not be satisfied" (Isaiah 9:20). Spiritually, I must have been starving, and I made my way up the hill frequently for Mass, for questions of my abbot. "Should I run for political office, Abbot?" "Should I have spoken up when I was attacked unfairly at work?" "When I take a saint's name at my oblation, whose should I take? I don't know any saints."

He answered the barrage of letters that continued as well as the questions asked. And I began to understand what being a spiritual child (even a spiritual brat) is like. In order to gain knowledge, you need a spiritual guide, an *abba* or abbot.

Abbot Antony even found me my very own saint, an obscure Benedictine Abbess of Vincenza, Italy, from the early 1600s. Blessed Joanna Mary Bonomo probably echoed the sanctity of my abbot when she responded of her difficulties: "These trials are priceless treasures; tell me rather how to offer them at the foot of the Cross than to resent them."

Excited by this finding in the Benedictine martyrology, Abbot Antony wrote, "You may be following in the footsteps of a relative! I hope so!" And that was the name he gave me at oblation.

My spiritual advisor takes the responsibilities entrusted to him as seriously as Benedict would wish. But he still despairs over my reading material.

Chapter 3: The Counsel of Brothers

Decisions must be made that assure the success of any endeavor, says Benedict. Although power and responsibility reside in the abbot, and ultimately, all decisions are his, Benedict calls the entire community together for advice. From the humblest novice to the most senior members, they give their best consideration to the problem before them. For less important matters, the abbot may consult with just senior members. Even the abbot will learn from others.

Benedict's words on seeking counsel could come right out of a "consensus-building" handbook on leadership written today. I am no abbot—and not much of a consensus-builder either, for that matter—but I can clearly understand this chapter from my own experience of seeking counsel.

The matter was not insignificant to me at that moment of my life. When I moved to California, I was just three years sober, saying goodbye to groups who had nurtured me since I first walked defiantly into their meeting halls.

"Find a home group fast," my former sponsor Lucille said.

"They seem to have AA clubs out there," I said, having visited Felix, who was already in San Diego. "Alano Clubs, they call them, with monthly membership dues."

"Well, that's not *real* AA then," Lucille said severely. "No dues or fees in AA. You know that. Stay away from the other stuff."

I stayed away from the Alano Club near my new apartment, inviting as it looked, and went to "regular" meetings in church halls instead, ones that Lucille would have endorsed from her New England perspective of AA.

"They all tell stories about drug use," I complained to Joanie, my other sponsor, by mail. "I can't relate."

"Those stories belong in Narcotics Anonymous," Joanie wrote back firmly. "Keep going to meetings. *Don't compare—identify!*"

All good AA advice, unoriginal, but certainly effective for thousands and thousands of drunks, and I knew I wasn't a special kind, just an ordinary sort of drunk. I went to meetings. I listened. I tried to identify with bikers and beachcombers. I wanted to say, "It's not your New England sort of AA in a smoky church basement. For one thing, California doesn't have basements."

I wasn't happy, but I followed the counsel of my old community of AA elders. The consequences of going astray were still too terrifying to me. After a year of attending regularly, sharing the pain and frustration of the losses incurred by moving to San Diego, April was rolling around—my sobriety date.

"How do you know to celebrate?" I asked someone. While New England AA might be horrified by AA clubs with dues, the San Diego AA groups were horrified at the thought of sign-up sheets with first names and telephone numbers and anniversary dates.

"You tell that month's secretary a week in advance," this month's secretary said.

"Okay, I'm sober four years next week," I said.

"A day at a time!" she snapped at me.

"Oh, good grief. I'll make it seven more days."

And I did. I showed up the following week, expectantly and best-dressed, listening to the drug stories, the biker stories, and waited . . . through adjournment. "Keep coming back! It works!" everybody chanted after the Lord's Prayer.

No, I don't think I'll be coming back, I thought. I made it all the way to the car before I started to cry. Who would I see for counsel now? I didn't want to drink, and AA and the Big Book made it pretty clear that I *would*, if I didn't go to meetings. But I just couldn't. Not anymore.

I lived on eggshells for a month, the longest I'd ever gone without meetings. I was heading back to New England to surprise my mother for Mother's Day. I decided to call on the counsel of the social worker who rescued me and sent me to AA in the first place. *All are to follow the teaching of the Rule*, says Benedict, *and no one shall rashly deviate from it*. The "rule" I lived under in early sobriety was failing me in southern California, but I did *not* want to rashly deviate from it. The desert fathers know about seeking counsel.

> The old men came to see Abba Anthony, bringing with them Abba Joseph. To test them, Abba Anthony gave them a text from the Scriptures and beginning with the youngest, asked what it meant. Each gave an opinion. But to each, Abba Anthony said, "You have not understood it." Lastly he

asked Abba Joseph to explain the saying. Abba Joseph replied, "I do not know." Abba Anthony said to the rest, "Indeed, Abba Joseph has found the way, for he alone has said, 'I do not know'."[9]

I poured out my experiences to Ron, fully expecting the usual AA advice when you land yourself in a "bad" meeting or find yourself in "bad" AA: find another meeting. I'd been following that counsel for a year, turning into the gypsy AA, trying to make it work and wondering what was wrong with me.

"What do *you* want to do?" Ron asked.

"Stop putting myself through those awful meetings," I said.

"Then you should stop going to them."

"Will I get drunk?"

"Not necessarily. It's not either/or, you know." It used to be either/or the way he spoke to me in the beginning of sobriety, but this was four years later. Maybe the best counsel changes over time.

"How do I not get drunk and not go to AA?"

"Just don't get isolated," he said. "Drunks isolate themselves. Find a community. It doesn't have to be AA, but find yourself a community."

I returned home relieved of a great burden of fear, and called my next-door neighbor, whom I knew just slightly. "I'd like to go to your church with you this Sunday. Would you mind taking me?" And Paul became my sponsor into the Catholic Church, which ultimately brought me to the door of St. Augustine's Abbey, where, still a spiritual orphan, I began at last to find the way home.

January 25, 2000: The Feast of the Conversion of St. Paul

The rain comes—much anticipated as it sweeps in from the Pacific and swirls down the coast of California. The weather here rarely takes us by surprise. But this winter has been exceptionally dry, and the hills have not lost their barren brownness yet. The rain is a welcomed guest here.

You know you're an oblate when you anticipate feast days like the Conversion of St. Paul the way the secular world takes to a civic holiday like Presidents' Day. Two days ago, plodding through a major "to-do" list for work, I saw this feast day on my abbey calendar and suddenly became very happy that I could join "my" monks in celebration—even in the middle of a workweek.

The Conversion of St. Paul isn't one of the fanciest or most popular of feast days, but I like it. Paul, called Saul originally, was a well-educated Jew of the highest ranks, and also a Roman citizen. He was also one of the most zealous persecutors of the initial Christian community.

And then, on the road to Damascus, came the dramatic call that threw him to the ground and blinded him, and the voice saying, "Saul, Saul why persecutest thou me?" (Acts 9:4). Christianity received its greatest apostle when Saul converted, heard that call, and became Paul the missionary and theologian, who went off to convert the world with the same fervor with which he had tried to kill off the early Christians. Paul was one of those all-or-nothing types.

The abbey church is quieter than usual. Perhaps the rain has kept the day-trippers (like me) away from Mass today. The consecrated Host (communion wafers already blessed by the priests) is exposed on the foot-high stand in front of the altar used for such days. A small framed work of art depicts Saul on that road to Damascus—*Saul, Saul why do you persecute me so?* A fat orange flower sits in front, mysterious and foreign to these parts. A small candle burns brightly against the chill gloom of rain and the ignorance we all pursue until Christ calls and saves us from ourselves.

I had wanted to take the name Paula as my oblate name before the abbot found Joanna Mary for me. Paul is just about the only saint I feel like I know as a friend, or perhaps as a stern mentor. And, as one convert to another, who better to lead me out of my own blindness or misdirected zeal?

Paul is also the only saint who has directly spoken to me. At 2:00 A.M. on April 25, 1998, I woke up with his words: "I have fought a good fight, I have finished my course, I have kept the faith . . . "

Is Daddy dead now? I wondered. I was in my parents' house on the death watch for my daddy, just turned sixty-six years old and dying.

There was no call from the hospice. I went back to sleep. At 7:00 A.M., I thumbed through a bible I borrowed from my mother. I did not know Paul. It took a while to find Second Timothy 4:6–8. I copied the whole thing down, and we left for the hospice.

There, two hours later, Daddy died. The last words he may have heard on this side were Paul's, read by his tear-choked daughter:

For I am now ready to be offered, and the time of my departure is at hand. I have fought a good fight, I have finished my course, I have kept the faith: Henceforth, there is laid up for me a crown of righteousness, which the LORD, the righteous judge, shall give me at that day . . .

And now, this much-anticipated feast, like the rain sweeping down to soak the barren hillsides. It was an opportunity to say thank you in the company of my new community: For God brought me to my Abbot Antony just five months after I met Paul on my own road to Jerusalem.

"The God of our fathers hath chosen thee" (Acts 22:14), we hear during Mass. I wanted a great call, to be another Paul. My abbot chose Joanna Mary, an obscure abbess of whom little is known, a small call indeed. I could have chosen my own oblate name, of course, but I wanted the gift of my abbot's choice. Blessed Joanna Mary, shrouded in obscurity, now burdened with mine. "And now why tarriest thou? arise and be baptised, and wash away thy sins, calling on the name of the LORD" (Acts 22:16).

The heavy sky falls seaward, creating a perfect gray shroud around the abbey church. No longer to tarry, it is time to return to work.

FEBRUARY
Your Goal Is Jerusalem

Keep your way without halting;
and remember that your goal is Jerusalem,
that is what you want, and nothing else . . .[1]

February 2, 2000: The Feast of the Presentation

Santa Anna winds howl with their strange, edgy heat today. It is the dead of winter, but the temperature will hit eighty degrees. It is a mean sort of heat, blasting in from the deserts east of San Diego. When I read the desert fathers and their stories, the "desert" seems like such a great, silent, clean metaphor for the soul striving toward God.

In reality, when the Santa Anas blow the desert into the sea, my highest goal is worrying what my hair looks like and trying not to get nosebleeds from the winds, which is a common side effect of Santa Annas. I think about my hair as I careen up the canyon today, mid-week. And I also wonder, *What is this feast day?* We have just celebrated the birth of Jesus, and his temptation by the devil lurks a month ahead. We barely have time for this celebration before the Lenten and Easter seasons begin. Then comes Ordinary Time again; we catch our breath, tell the old stories, and ask what it all means to us.

The dull clanking bells begin and the desert winds roar. Father Jerome whirls in first in his motorized cart, priestly robes fluttering. Brother Robert usually whirls in last, the coda. Father Stanislaus has been in a wheelchair before, but today he is in his seat and does not march in with the others.

We thank God for the thirty-year anniversary of Brother Patrick's presentation before God as a monk.

The Presentation of Jesus in the Temple is the feast that celebrates the time when Jesus' earthly parents brought their firstborn son to the temple in Jerusalem the way all observant Jews did, to offer him to God, along with the sacrifice of birds. Although I do not know the fine points of the meaning of this feast, I know the words of the Gospel by heart: *Nunc dimittis* in Latin, *Lord, now lettest thou thy servant depart in peace, according to thy word. For mine eyes have seen thy salvation* (Luke 2:29–30). As a young choir member in the Episcopal Church, I sang Evensong. I have chanted these words as dutifully as any monk. Even then, I thought the words were richly appropriate for evening, for the "good death" we wish for as adults. *You promised me, Lord,* Simeon might have said. *You promised me that before I die I will see the Christ, the Consolation of Israel.*

And of course, God fulfills his promise, and Simeon acknowledges receiving the promise and releases his life's hold in these four short verses of haunting beauty and holy resignation.

And then he probably croaked right then and there, I used to think irreverently in my choir stall. The story was so vivid to me, laced with the plaintive chant of Evensong, filled with magical promises and the certain sudden death after their fulfillment. A ten-year-old, dreamy-eyed Episcopalian choir kid just *knew* these things.

The magic of that story echoed in my own "presentation" just months ago when I became an oblate. I made an offering of myself, as Jesus' parents did of their firstborn. I only stumbled once—could barely remember my baptism name as I spoke:

> I, Carol Joanna Mary Bonomo, offer myself to Almighty God through the Blessed Virgin Mary and our Holy Father Benedict as an Oblate of St. Augustine's Abbey, and promise to dedicate myself to the service of God and mankind according to the Rule of St. Benedict insofar as my state in life permits.

My classmate Hildegard sobbed with deep emotion as she offered herself. Gregory—the one who studied so hard—was the best prepared. I stood there proudest, mostly of myself for having managed constancy, somewhat, over the year of novitiate.

Hildegard was worried for Abbot Antony, worried he would not be here in another year for our final vows. "Perhaps he could do our vows with the earlier group in June," she fretted.

"It doesn't work that way," I said, just as serenely as the abbot discussing his heavenly future. Simeon had his promise. For some magical, childish reason, I thought I had mine: he would be there for the presentation of these spiritual gifts of his old age.

At one of our oblate meetings months later, Michelle, the first oblate I'd met when I joined, expressed concern that the abbot wasn't at Mass that morning. "I got hysterical and called him in his cell," she said. "He wasn't feeling well."

I'd be hysterical too. I realized my vain "certainty" that the abbot would live to my presentation was a child's whistling in the dark.

But like Simeon, he stayed on, sailed past his ninety-first birthday and met us at the altar of the chapel on the Feast of Christ the King. In the week before we made our final oblation, he sat with us—one day in the middle of a crazy workweek—to discuss what we were about to undergo. It was hardly what I expected. Abbot Antony stood before us, hands clasped.

"Do not allow anything that you may see, hear, or feel on the road to delay you," he began, consulting his notes. "Do not stop for it, look for it, take pleasure in it, or fear it. Remember that your goal is Jerusalem; that is what you want, and nothing else." His ancient voice grew ragged at the effort of his words. *Keep your mind constantly on Jerusalem.*

I did not know if he was speaking from his thoughts or from a book he had read or what was happening. In fact, weeks later, I was walking through the university's library and a volume in the medieval history section seemed to jumped out at my eye: Walter Hilton's *The Ladder of Perfection.* When I opened it up, there were the words the abbot had spoken, now laid out before me like a perfect gift.

But I didn't know that then, and his evident emotion scared me. I was pretty sure he would die of a heart attack right then and there.

"While I am here," he continued, no longer using his notes, "I will do everything I can for you. And when I am no longer here, I will continue to do everything I can for you."

He met us at the little chapel altar on the Feast of Christ the King, and we offered ourselves, the prideful, the studious, the tearful, as our dispositions called us. Afterwards we ate cookies, told tales, took pictures, and waited for Vespers, then had supper together.

An hour after we left, Abbot Antony had a seizure and fell, breaking his front teeth, bruising his face and hands. I began to wonder if my vanity about him staying around for me was not frighteningly close for comfort. But the magic was faulty, and thankfully he did not die.

Today we celebrate the Presentation. The desert wind howls. I return to work.

February 18, 2000: Sixth Week of Ordinary Time

The winter lasts forever, even in southern California. I am only at chapter 4 of the Rule. I decide to strive for legitimacy of presence at the monastery on these study days, rather than skulking about.

Brother John Climachus is the cheerful retreat master, a convert like me. "There's no suggested donation for something like that," he says of my day plan. "Just call me ahead of time to see if the retreat cafeteria can handle a guest. If so, we'll just add a little water to the soup and everything will be fine."

Suddenly it is cold again after a week's burst of intemperately warm weather and nearly a tenth of an inch of rain. Everything greens up quickly at the merest spot of rain in this region. We are a land of hope in St. Paul's best sense—faith in the unseen. "For we are saved by hope: but hope that is seen is not hope: for what a man seeth, why doth he yet hope for? But if we hope for that we see not, then do we with patience wait for it" (Romans 8:24–25). The ridiculous rainfall of this desert coast is more unseen than anything else, an idea of greenness more than measurable outputs.

We have our first camellia of spring. Shy, it turns in toward the stucco white wall of the house, gaudy bold pink in coloration. I've had those kinds of days myself. I want it to be Easter already, but the season of Lent is still before us.

Thinking I will have a quiet lunch, I enter the cafeteria to hear Abbot Antony say, "Join us!" His one relative, a niece, and her husband, are visiting him from the Midwest. Instead of quiet, I have social, but it feels okay.

Chapter 4: The Tools for Good Works

Without preamble, Benedict lists seventy-two items on his "to-do" list for achieving good works. When we have used these tools, says Benedict, *our wages will be the reward the Lord has promised.* The Ten Commandments are in the list, as is the "great commandment" Jesus gave in the Gospels (love one's neighbor as oneself) and the corporal works of mercy (comfort the poor, clothe the naked, visit the sick). Just about any command of biblical significance or else valued by Benedict for its effect on community life has been gathered up in chapter 4.

The first time I read this chapter, I was overwhelmed. This year as I have been "studying" the Rule (versus gulping it down with my post-breakfast third cup of coffee). I am reading the Rule in daily segments that approximates its reading three times yearly at the monastery. ("How many times you figure you've heard the Rule?" I asked Abbot Antony once, trying to figure three times a year times the sixty-five-plus years he's been a Benedictine. "Oh, a lot," he answered.)

Read over four days, the way the monks read this chapter, the tools are not as intimidating. Besides the biblical repeats, there are several that look like my New Year's resolutions over the last ten years or so. ("Refrain from too much eating" is the noble way my New Year's resolution "Lose ten pounds" would read.)

As with any set of tools, some seem more useful than others. I am sure the thrice-yearly review is helpful just as a private review before confession might be (if I ever actually did that). For me, the "action" tools ("clothe the naked, visit the sick, bury the dead") held the highest importance when I was younger and my energy level was a dangerous, edgy thing. I had to do those things to convince myself of my own worth, not necessarily seeing it in the eyes of the "needy"—and certainly not understanding that my need to "do" and recognize my "doing" to give self-validation was at least as strong as the needs I was attending to.

I began the process of becoming a Secular Franciscan exactly because the tools of doing were so prominent in my hands. The Franciscans never seemed still, and California is dotted with the results of those busy, bustling, brown-robed mission-builders. So "out there," as Abbot Antony once described the Franciscans with a wave of his hand, indicating energy "outwards."

The Franciscans sent me here, to the Benedictines, who seem to pray a lot, read a lot, and shut up a lot. Some of my tools are changing as a result.

"I know how it feels to read the obituaries now that I'm sixty," Felix said a few weeks ago. "It's like you know what's coming for you, but it's still out there. I wonder what it feels like when you're seventy. Or eighty."

His mother is ninety. She does not read obituaries at all. I am forty-seven. I read them every day because Benedict says, *Day by day remind yourself that you are going to die* (#47). For some reason that is the tool that gives perspective to *all* my works, good, temporal, paid, heartfelt, whatever. Each night as I go to sleep, my last prayer is, "May I sleep with You, and rise with You in glory." And with that, I know that each night could be my last, that in the end, neither good works nor bad will matter in the world we leave behind. The radiance that lies before us will matter much more. I used to jog the city streets of Brookline and Boston, Massachusetts. As the plodding miles passed, my mind frequently lit on the Big Topic: Why are we here? And what is the meaning of all of this? And does jogging four miles five days a week matter any more than losing ten pounds, or am I really supposed to abandon it all and become a nurse in the Peace Corps? And if I'm supposed to abandon all worldly gods and worldliness, how come I've never known anybody who's done it?

Somewhere in the middle of this mental monologue, an actual, physical funeral hearse would slowly crawl into my line of sight. I lived just blocks away from the mortuary, so this wasn't Divine Providence. But it certainly was enough of an answer to put a damper on my meaning-of-life soul searches.

Years later, in California, I took up jogging again. As I jogged along, lost in thought over a graduate school problem, a hearse rolled up alongside me.

"Oh dear," I thought. "Even here."

The driver rolled down the window. "Do you know how to get to St. John's Church from here? We're lost."

We? There was nobody in the hearse except the driver and the casket. Lost for the poor guy's own funeral.

Abbot Lot came to Abbot Joseph and said, "Father, according as I am able, I keep my little rule, and my little fast, my prayer, meditation and contemplative silence; and according as I am able I strive to cleanse my heart of thoughts: now what more should I do? The elder rose up in reply and stretched out his hands to heaven, and his fingers became like ten lamps of fire. He said, "Why not be totally changed into fire?"[2]

I know where I'm going. I keep the destination before my eyes once a day before I close them in sleep. This tool is the most powerful one in St. Benedict's kit for my middle-aged times. Practice makes perfect.

~

As I drove up the ridiculous hairpin turns that lead to the abbey up the hill this morning, I remembered the one time Felix came here, the Feast of Christ the King, when I took my vows as an oblate.

"How did you ever *find* this place?" he asked as the road kept falling away from under the car. He knows I am not a brave driver.

There was an article about the abbey's retreat center that somebody once gave me, knowing I "did" retreats with the Franciscans. The description of the fifties polyurethane furniture and the doubled fee for overnight guests left me unimpressed and uninterested. Years later when my father was dying, I visited the abbey for a mental health day. If it hadn't been for a cell phone in my car and a patient monk on the other end, I would never have arrived. Once there, I didn't find a soul around, not even the one on the phone who talked me up the hill. It seemed cold, forbidding. I left, untouched.

And now it is my spiritual home, and I have pledged myself to try to grow here in a wonderful, mysterious sort of pact that has stilled my anxious, restless heart, and forced my feet to stay put.

Some tools are totally unrecognizable as help the first time around.

The lilies have sprouted everywhere since my last visit!

The big chair in the abbey library is "mine" for oblate meetings. It is a bear of a chair, a gift from someone, Abbot Antony tells me. Carved from an enormous single piece of wood, perhaps the trunk of a big sturdy tree, it is big enough to make me think the library was built around it. An old sheepskin seat cover sets off the fiery-brown wood. Most of the oblates avoid it because, once in it, it becomes impossible to get out of and leave with any dignity intact.

At less than five feet tall, with no dignity ever, anywhere, to be seen, I climb in, tuck my legs under me and become embedded, like the arms of Christ have taken me up. I use the one wide arm as a mini desk or wet bar for my coffee during meetings. I fall asleep there when the oblate meeting is dull. Today I surround myself with my notebook, Rule, Bible, two commentaries on the Rule, and a cookie from the retreat dining hall, and write. The quiet is deafening, even with another woman here, also working on some sort of project. Hers involves artwork and looks more interesting than my study project, but I have a cookie and a Bear Chair. I am fine here until I either fall asleep or begin prowling around for more coffee.

Chapter 5: Obedience

Obedience. Not my strong suit, to say the least. Not for lots of people, especially we rugged individuals who came West. But Benedict doesn't beat around the bush on this one. Unhesitating obedience is the first step of humility, Benedict says, and it *comes naturally to those who cherish Christ above all.* For those for whom it comes less naturally, Benedict offers examples of what such obedience looks like and how it feels to those who practice it. Obedience is only acceptable to God and agreeable to men when given gladly without secret grumbling.

I dote on St. Paul, and spent months reading his letters as my first lectio (sacred) readings. But when he says, "Wives, submit yourselves unto your own husbands, as unto the Lord" Ephesians 5:22), all us ladies of the church bristle and some of us more recent graduates of political correctness begin mumbling "misogamy." It is really obedience that makes us bristle, whether we are male or female. It is not American. It is not natural. But it has been part of spiritual practice since Christianity's earliest days.

> Abba Hyperechius said, "Obedience is the best ornament of the monk. He who has acquired it will be heard by God."[3]

Choosing to obey is certainly a big difference from being forced to obey. There are rules. There is slavery. There is overt power played out in the workplace. I don't think Benedict has anything like that in mind here.

In religious circles—at least some of the ones I am familiar with—we love to talk about being "Called." "Call" in this usage should always be capitalized. My mother was Called to be a church bell-ringer, she says, but Not Called to bring the Eucharist to the sick (which she also does, and with great care and thoughtfulness). When my father was dying and discussion topics were few and far between, my mother asked him if she should be his substitute in taking communion to shut-ins.

"You'd have to take a course first," he warned her, ever practical.

"I know," she said. "That's not the problem. The problem is that I don't feel Called to do this particular ministry."

He thought it over as best he could, dying in a hospital bed with advanced lung cancer that had branched out and was just beginning to invade his brain.

"Just do it," he said finally.

She did.

That's obedience. I like to say—frequently, fondly, maddeningly often—that I never did get no stinking Call to *nothing*: not to become a Catholic, stay an Episcopalian, sing in the choir, carry the crucifer, give out the Eucharist, or even feed the hungry, clothe the naked. *No Call, No Way*.

And it's a funny thing about the Call. It never looks like something you would want to do at any level of your awareness.

But there *was* a time, one sense of a Call, despite all the years when God could have yelled Himself hoarse for all I could have heard. I felt a Call to become a Secular Franciscan. They were my kind of people. They had my energy level. They were "out there" in the world like me. They had their own radical call to poverty that the poverty of my soul resonated to nakedly. Early in my formation as a Secular Franciscan, I stood in a strong, unlovely Catholic church in a Washington, D.C., neighborhood and experienced a moment of complete "transparency" before God, which I took as a sign of the Call to Francis—as well as immanent proof of my rapidly accruing holiness.

But Call or No Call, transparent before God or not, it didn't work out between the Secular Franciscans and me. "Run, don't walk, to the abbey up the hill," a professed Secular told me. I knew it wasn't working. I prayed before the same sort of San Damiano cross that had spoken to Francis, asking it to speak to me, and it said *No Call, No Way*. But I cried anyway because they didn't want me, and I had wanted them so badly.

I obeyed. I made an ordinary old telephone-type call to the abbey and asked for the secular order master or whatever the Benedictines called them. A firm, elderly voice answered. "Come for lunch and we'll talk," he said. As I tried to calculate the time away from work to find that cold, forbidden abbey again, "do lunch," and then return to work, he added, "Come for Mass, too." I was suddenly on Benedictine time.

I obeyed. It wasn't what I wanted, the Benedictines. It was what I got. "I wanted to be a Franciscan!" I howled early on to the abbot.

"You're too prayerful for them," he said serenely. "What are you reading these days?"

"But the Franciscans are doing things. I want to be doing things."

"You can't give away what you don't possess," Abbot Antony said. "Are you saying the Divine Office in the morning, by the way?"

I obeyed. It was an amazing experience, truly the first step of humility as Benedict told me later it would be. I prayed the Divine Office morning and night after I made Abbot Antony sit down to help me figure out the system of my little book. I read the Rule. I gave up the self-indulgence of a lifetime of diary keeping to attempt sacred reading when the abbot suggested it. Obedience is about the first word of the Rule. I began to listen.

Two months later, Abbot Antony said it was time to move from candidate to novice. I hadn't known I was officially anything. The Franciscans had clear steps in the book for these things. "I'm not sure I'm ready," I said apologetically, trying to be honest.

"That's okay," he said. "You don't have to be ready. Just do it."

And with this new spiritual father, appearing in my life unwanted so soon after my earthly father died, both of them good men, both of them echoing the hard Nike shoe ad of pragmatism and promise, I obeyed.

⌇

Vespers. An ordinary Friday in Ordinary Time. Down the hill, people are heading home from work, thinking about their weekend plans, anticipating their "freedom" from the everyday, the ordinary.

Here it is not ordinary at all. The four raw, solemn candidate monks, who suddenly showed up at Mass about two months ago in my observation, are becoming novice monks.

The dull bells clang. The family members of the candidates sit and watch. I can talk about being empty-handed, but they are about to see their sons and brothers into a cloister with no exit except the row of little crosses that mark the cemetery out the left window.

The candidates prostrate themselves before Abbot Henry. Like a lot of Protestants, I can barely bring myself to kneel, so prostration affects me strongly. I want to cry. I don't know much about obedience at all.

Chapters 6 and 42: Silence

Chapters 6 and 42 both deal with the spiritual discipline of silence. In chapter 6, Benedict says that *so important is silence that permission to speak should seldom be granted even to mature disciples, no matter how good or holy or instructive their talk.* Chapter 42 adds to the importance of silence to monks by saying that they should especially cultivate it at night. Only for guests who need attention—and even then, *with the utmost seriousness and proper restraint*—are exceptions allowed.

What can I say? I have known, and probably loved too well, the sullen kind of silence when I am crossed or hurt or punished. This silky kind of silence, a silence born of listening, is new to me. It reminds me of when I was exploring the idea of quilting. My plan was to make a quilt entirely out of white squares, with perhaps a single green strip imposed somewhere in the design.

"Oh, yes, your Zen side," my secretary laughed when I told her.

Benedictine silence looks like that quilt would, I think.

"I was going to write a book about Franciscan spirituality," I told Abbot Antony. "But then I became a Benedictine. I can't write a book about Benedictine spirituality."

"Why not?" he asked.

"Because the page would be all white."

"That's right," he said, looking quite pleased.

That's what the silence that comes from listening looks like.

Dear old Isaiah, my current morning lectio reading, and the kind of prophet who always believed in just laying it *out* there says,

    e drought in a dry land
    u will repress the clamour of the proud;
    ke heat by the shadow of a cloud,
the singing of the despots will be subdued. (Isaiah 25:5)

That's the Jerusalem Bible translation. My sturdy King James Version says of God: *Thou shalt bring down the noise of strangers. . . .* According to Isaiah, God is always going to get even with great vengeance. He uses the sort of language that makes televangelists rich and the Old Testament so hard to read first thing in the predawn darkness.

But this could be a nice commentary on silence for oblates, to bring down the noise of strangers. It is a horribly noisy, maddening, deafening world. The desert fathers sought to escape such a world nearly two thousand years ago.

> Abba Isidore of Pelusia said, "To live without speaking is better than to speak without living. For the former who lives rightly does good even by his silence but the latter does no good even when he speaks. When words and life correspond to one another, they are together the whole of philosophy."[4]

> Abba Pastor said, "Any trial whatever that comes to you can be conquered by silence."[5]

> Abba Poemen said that a brother living amongst them asked Abba Bessarion, "What ought I to do?" The old man said to him, "Keep silent and do not always be comparing yourself with others."[6]

As an oblate, I do not pray the Compline mentioned in chapter 42 ("No Talk After Compline") except for my once-a-year retreat here at the abbey. Hence I do not have to honor the "grand silence," as they call what follows Compline.

And, truthfully, retreatants don't necessarily honor it either, despite the request on our retreat schedule. Last year, Brother Matthew's family was having quite a good time next door to me a half hour after Compline. Torn between charity to others and the cold, cranky necessity of getting up the next morning at 4:45 to attend Vigils at 5:30, I chose cranky, and pounded the wall between us to induce quiet.

It worked. And I took only a little unchristian glee at 5:00 A.M. using my hairdryer and assuring myself that *everybody* was up getting ready for Vigils (or soon would be).

Not talking is a scary luxury. I get silence at home at night when Felix is traveling, but it comes with the reminder that someday he will be gone for more than a trip, and the silence will be filled with the echoes of eternity. Sometimes silence holds the reminder of being unwanted, of being shut out, forgotten, passed over.

Silence, embraced, is the marvelous gift. Benedict knows what I resist: the humility that underlies silence, when there is no longer any prop of self-importance. If all I can do is bring down the level of my own noise, then I have accomplished something good and Benedictine in this world. Benedictine silence is a glorious sinkhole. Others who come in contact with it are pulled into it also.

There is clamor even at the monastery, let alone in the city. There are chatty, noisy "retreatants" who cannot listen and cannot bear silence. The monks listen to them respectfully, even as intrusions to their own silence, the way wind chimes capture and swirl the quiet air with their contrast.

The silence tends to win out at some point. Silence ends up heavier than noise, and carries it away, away from the soul, which takes its nourishment in silence.

Chapter 7: Humility

The chapter on humility is the longest in this short Rule. Benedict lists twelve steps to perfect humility: (1) keeping the fear of God before your eyes; (2) not satisfying your own desires, but doing the will of God; (3) submitting to your superior in obedience; (4) obeying even when it is difficult to do so; (5) confessing all sinful thoughts to your abbot; (6) accepting with content the lowest and most menial treatment; (7) believing in words and mind that you are inferior to all others; (8) doing only what is endorsed by rule and example in your monastery; (9) remaining silent unless asked a question; (10) not laughing easily; (11) speaking gently and seriously; (12) manifesting humility with head bowed and eyes cast down.

There used to be a joke in AA circles about the member who received her group's highest honor—a pin honoring her humility. The first time she wore it, of course, the group confiscated it since it was no longer applicable to her. Even St. Benedict could have smiled at that one. Humility is of such importance in his Rule that he spends more time on it than on any other chapter. On a daily reading schedule, it takes sixteen days and twelve steps to reach what Benedict describes as "simple and natural"—a perfect love, which casts out fear.

Reading this chapter in one gulp is overwhelming. Reading it over sixteen days can easily get you confused or discouraged. Confused because Benedict uses the "steps" to humility to go *up*, when they would seem to naturally need to go down instead of "elevating" you. Much is made in commentaries about the ladder being modeled on Jacob's ladder full of ascending and descending angels in the Old Testament. For me, the image of *climbing* to humility, step by step, is still an odd one, Jacob's ladder or not.

Discouragement comes not only from the impossibility of achieving for ordinary people (*only speak when asked a question*), but also from the sheer unwillingness as a citizen of the world in this millennium to even *desire* humility (*contentedly accepts all that is crude and harsh and thinks himself a poor and worthless workman . . .*).

No way, Buster!

I first met humility at an AA meeting. I didn't like it much then either. AA has twelve steps its founders label as a "group of principles, spiritual in their nature . . . practiced as a way of life," to bring about not merely sobriety but quality to the sober life. Although they were not modeled on Benedict's steps (or Jacob's ladder), they put some meat on the bone of humility long before I became a Benedictine. And if I was not wildly enthusiastic about the path, at least I had sampled parts of the route before.

Deep into the steps of AA, after admitting powerlessness, accepting God, turning a life over to God, inventorying sins and admitting them to ourselves, to another individual, and to God, come the "forgotten steps," numbers six and seven:

Number 6: "We're entirely ready to have God remove all these "defects of character."

Number 7: "Humbly ask him to remove our shortcomings."

Which seems to say, if I can at least get to an attitude of willingness about humility, God might assist in the rest. I asked my old abbot once how he managed to carry out the exhausting, humiliating, soul-wrenching role played by the abbot during the liturgy of Holy

Thursday through Easter. He looked at me, surprised, and the mured, "Well, through the gift of grace, of course."

Humility is the gift of grace, regardless of the steps we ordinary people may take. It is not humiliation, although that may be one of the more unfortunate ways we arrive there. The author of AA's twelve steps writes, "We heard story after story of how humility had brought strength out of weakness."[7] That is a modern-day echo, not only of Benedict, but of the great apostle Paul, whose words still comfort me on bad days: "And he said unto me, 'My grace is sufficient for thee: for my strength is made perfect in weakness'" (2 Corinthians 12:9). AA founder Bill W goes on to say:

> In every case, pain had been the price of admission into a new life. But this admission price had purchased more than we expected. It brought a measure of humility, which we soon discovered to be a healer of pain. We began to fear pain less, and desire humility more than ever.

Benedict's steps deal more with achieving humility as a desired state than with the gift of grace that heals pain, but both roads arrive at the same destination. Humiliation is what is inflicted upon us. It is not holy. Humility is about *acceptance*, including acceptance of what is inflicted upon us. To use Benedict's reverse imagery, humility can be the highest order of holiness we ordinary people can achieve.

"He shall smite and heal it: and they shall return even to the Lord," says Isaiah (19:14). Healing comes in the humility. The smiting is part of the humiliation. I have known both in my year as oblate novice.

Subjected to incessant and frightening harassment by a fellow employee, I complained and complained to no effect. Finally we sat in a human resources office for conflict mediation. Like bookends, the Scriptures bore me through a horrible, humiliating experience. *For many bare false witness against him, but their witness agreed not together* (Mark 14:56). The attack was unbelievably personal. My tormentor suddenly had not only a target, but also an audience for his abuse. "All the work I've had to do to fix her own abominable work . . . " "I don't like her and I have to work with her . . . " "She's a liar, . . . " "And all her false civility . . . "

But he held his peace, and answered nothing (Mark 14:61). My silence was construed as weakness, and unlike Paul, I could not find in it my strength. Silence was construed as a tacit agreement with the charges. The mediator couldn't mediate if I didn't respond.

I returned to the abbey the next day and told the abbot of my experience.

"Good!" he said, after listening intently. "You did not respond. It was beneath you."

"But, Abbot, I shook from head to foot!" Indeed, even the muscles of my face had trembled as if from physical blows.

"Good! The Spirit conquered the body."

> One of the elders was asked what was humility and he answered, "If you forgive a brother who has injured you before he himself asks pardon."[8]

> Another brother asked the elders, "What is humility? The elder answered, "To do good to those who do evil to you." The brother asked, "Supposing a man cannot go that far, what should he do?" The elder replied, "Let him get away from them and keep his mouth shut."[9]

The healing call of humility came slowly, but it did come. I did not work any steps, AA or Benedictine. I went to the monastery, asking forgiveness for my sins and confirmation from my abbot, accepting communion as my desire to change, to those "sanctified in Christ Jesus, called to be saints" (1 Corinthians 1:2).

No wonder victimization is so popular in our culture. Point at the smiters instead of climbing to humility. No wonder this is the longest, most impossible chapter of the Rule. The steps Benedict lays out cannot be grasped intellectually, but our human or natural partners can certainly force the issue. Broken by the vicissitudes of our humanity, we begin to understand and become open to the grace of humility. Firm, like the everlasting blue skies of San Diego, we would never learn or green up or grow.

MARCH

For Discipline You Endure

It is for discipline that
you have to endure.
Hebrews 12:7

March 3, 2000: Blessed Katharine Drexel

"How are you?" I ask politely, when I call Brother John Climachus about availability for a "day-tripper" on Friday.

"Going crazy, as usual," he responds cheerfully.

"Oh dear. Maybe I'm doing better than you today?"

"But it's okay to go crazy for our Lord," says Brother John Climachus. "You should have the place to yourself until dinnertime," he warns. "Then it will be mobbed."

How nice. I leave right after Vespers and *before* the dinner mob.

As I drive up to the monastery from a legislation action committee breakfast meeting downtown (talk about commuting between two worlds equally connected by Interstate 5), the weather is a patchwork of uncertainty. Along the coast—actually beyond it, over the Pacific—are bold, small packages of blue sky, stitched into the light gray we call the "marine layer." Along the highway and a mile or two inland, the sky is a patchy mix of gray and white. Completely inland—but plainly visible at the coast—fierce black skies punctuate the low-slung mountains, threatening or delivering rain that is rare in this winter of La Niña.

San Diego's weather is finely tuned by inches of geography and single degree differences. Living in New England's blunt climate, I could approximate temperatures by the decade—it was in the fifties, sixties, or seventies. Here we look around, as if the temperature is a visible thing, scowl, and ask, "So is it seventy-two degrees or seventy-four? I can't decide."

We expect this conversation to be taken seriously by whoever is in earshot—hopefully not a New Englander. The coast is cooler by ten degrees than inland in spring and fall, twenty degrees cooler than inland summer, rainier in winter. Two miles in, subtract two degrees from everything I just said. The weatherman calls them "microclimates." I know that the absence or presence of the sun changes everything. I also know that the sun visits New England but it seems to regard San Diego as its permanent place of residence.

It is really amazing that the clash of such topographic extremes—ocean and desert—produces such a moderate climate for those of us who live here. I would like to think my journey to the New Jerusalem has similarities, that the land created between the harshness of sin and the glory of redemption can become the moderation "in all things" Benedict preached. I know that the presence or absence of the Son changes everything in a life's landscape.

Mass in the last days of Ordinary Time before Lent. The new monk novitiates no longer have the shorn look of visitors now that they are in their new scapulars. It is First Friday, explains Father Aloysius of the most resonant voice, which is why they wear robes of white with gold one last time before Lent. First Friday is one of the real mysteries of faith to me, a convert. Periodically I read about what it is supposed to be, and promptly forget. It has something to do with one of the requests the Blessed Mother made in an apparition, but I can't peg it tighter than that, and I always get the apparitions of Mary mixed up in my mind anyway. It's all very foreign to my New England Protestant way of upbringing.

There is a row's worth of my fellow oblates. Nancy is the surrogate mother of us all. Milan is the exotic Vietnamese, usually dressed in ankle-length silk, clanking when she prays in all her pieces of religious jewelry. At some point, Father Aloysius prays for "our oblates about to spend the weekend in retreat." Now I know why the place will fill up by supper. There are too many of us for one retreat and some of us need to wait until August. Out of a rare burst of consideration for those who cannot come here as often as I, I signed up for August—and promptly forgot about this one.

The abbot has old friends in for lunch. "Join us!" he insists, pulling on my elbow. "You shouldn't be alone."

"They're enjoying your company," I say reluctantly. "Let them enjoy." He smiles and returns to his table. Giving him up is harder than anything I could do in Lent. But there are so many who cling to the few opportunities left to be with him. I have been blessed by his generosity in my most fatherless time of need.

"There's plenty for supper, so please stay," says Brother John Climacus, checking out the full, noisy cafeteria lunch crowd.

"Quite honestly, I'll be tired of the place by then," I admit. This delights him.

Father Stanislaus walks by. "Father Stanislaus, you're moving well since surgery," I say.

"Yes, thank you," he says in his difficult, Eastern European accent. He keeps moving, clearly not wishing to engage in small talk.

"I made you a bookmark," I say, wistfully, wishing I did not have this need to make myself *known* to these people, who do not suffer the same attention-getting disorder as I do. "When you were operated on."

"Oh, yes. It was quite beautiful. I put it in the library on display."

"It was the least I could do. You radicalized my prayer life."

"That is good," he says with the ghost of a grim smile, and he abruptly departs. It must be so hard for them to balance sociability with the work of God and the admonitions of the Rule to silence, brevity, and solemnity. These are not "out there" Franciscans, after all. But I feel awkward in my need to make contact with them. I am shy around all of them, except by pen. Dear St. Paul, the grand apostle, is my soulmate in this. "For his letters, say they, are weighty and powerful; but his bodily presence is weak, and his speech contemptible" (2 Corinthians 10:10).

The sense of isolation is an old one for me. Here it is understandable: I am not part of this cloistered community, but I am permitted to be a partner. To establish some equilibrium, I walk the prayer walk, under the overcast, cool skies, seeking out a rock, representative of this day's visit, for the tiny rock garden I will eventually make. The Easter lilies are blooming furiously in the graveyard with its seven identical wooden crosses, and the flaming gladiolas are a suitably gaudy touch. The violet-red bougainvillea is in full winter flower.

Still, some days it just doesn't work for me. Today being one of those days, I can either be crabby and stay, writing in the retreat lounge and saying hi to my fellow oblates as they arrive, or go home and call it a day.

I pack my books and my new rock and head home under leaden skies. My angel, Gregory, who became an oblate with me, is just arriving as I depart.

Chapters 8–19: The Divine Office

These short chapters lay out which psalms and readings are to be used in the various offices of prayer, how the times of those offices are affected by the liturgical seasons, and how many offices are to be said daily. Although Benedict approaches the liturgical structure with care and attention, he urges anyone who finds his arrangement unsatisfactory to rearrange to suit their needs.

When you're reading the Rule a chapter a day, these are the "wasteland" chapters you skim. If they were the *first* twelve chapters of the Rule, Benedict's Rule would never have lasted fourteen centuries. But by now, you're committed. The how-to's of the Divine Office—what the monks pray each day—and how many psalms and which psalms and when the alleluia is chanted—does not make fascinating reading. Nor does much of what is in today's Divine Office resemble any of Benedict's suggestions anyway. If it does, I am failing to make the necessary connections. For an oblate, however determined, these chapters aren't very useful. I like the desert story better than Benedict on this score.

> Abba Poemen thought that Abba Paphnutius was great and he had recourse to short prayers.[1]

But these chapters do remind me of a part of my life that many people might not relate to the Rule. I think of weight and resistance training when I read Benedict in this section of chapter 18: *The remaining psalms are to be divided among the seven Night Offices, the longer ones should be divided in half, and twelve should be permanently assigned to each Night Office.* I'm reminded of the number of repetitions I'm supposed to do when I lift weights, what order I do them in, how much weight or resistance I use. Like Benedict's suggestions, I do these to become stronger and to acquire the discipline to push past obstacles ("resistance") to growth. "It is for discipline that you have to endure," says St. Paul

(Hebrews 12:7) in the way of the Revised Standard Version, Catholic Edition. Or, as my King James Bible puts it, more severely, "If ye endure chastening, God dealeth with you as with sons . . . " "Physical exercise is good for the health," says Clement of Alexandria, "while it stimulates the desire to care for the bodily vigor, it stimulates the same desire for vigor of soul."[2]

I am not very disciplined. I'm sure there are novice monks who are not very disciplined when they arrive at the monastery either. If discipline were easy, it would be called something else. I remember Abbot Antony not feeling well and also not wanting to give in to illness. An oblate asked him how he was feeling, and he said, "I persevere." When I first began weight training, I could see, and certainly feel, the results of my efforts in short order. Forearms filled out, shoulders padded with muscles, legs reshaped and thinned. I imagine it's much the same when I first start a particular prayer practice. There's novelty, there's mastery, and there always seems to be some great benefit right away. Then it gets old and boring and stupid. Results are subtle or seem to disappear altogether.

At about six months of adding reps or weights, seeing no discernible improvement in body shape, and thinking, *Is this all there is?* I went to our track coach at the university.

"What's the point?" I asked Steve, who was once an Olympian and U.S. record holder, but focuses on coaching his best today rather than on his past glories. "I'll never be buff. I'm not going around trying to catch a guy. All this work isn't even particularly making me look any different. Why bother?"

Steve smiled and shrugged and said, "You work out now so when you're old and fall out of your wheelchair, you'll have the upper body strength to drag yourself to the telephone to call for help."

Oh, great. I wanted sleekness now, not self-sufficiency in my old age. But that's what this painful accumulation of instructions about when to pray what amounts to: predictability. Perseverance.

That's a value I want to acquire as a Benedictine oblate. Otherwise I'm back to being a Sarabite, or worse, adopting that gyratory life again. Resistance training is about pushing the boundaries of spiritual strength, one practice at a time.

Chapter 20: Reverence at Prayer

Benedict asks again for humility, this time as part of one's prayer life.

Prayer should be short and pure, he says, since God sees our hearts and not our many words.

This part of the Rule is frequently lumped with the previous group as part of how to say the Divine Office. But my experience of it came separately, earlier than when I began studying the Rule itself.

In one of the first lunch-after-Mass meetings I had with Abbot Antony, he asked, "So what did you think of the homily?"

Well, let's face it: nobody became a Catholic because of the quality of the sermons. Leave that to the Protestants for whom the spoken Word is the centerpiece of worship like the Eucharist is for Catholics.

"At least I didn't read during it," I offered. "I usually bring a book and read during the sermon."

The abbot was horrified at what was clearly not liturgical reverence. Listening, he suggested, might sometimes bring God's words to me through a messenger I might not greet any other way.

Norvene Vest, an Episcopalian oblate and writer, introduced me— through the book I was reading during a sermon at my parish Mass— to the Benedictine notion of silence of the body. "We may take for granted that the body is silent," she writes, "but in fact, it can be very intrusive . . . the monks slip into their seats so quietly that we may not even be aware anyone else is present."[3]

I began to watch my abbot during Mass, my living laboratory of Benedictine virtues. Indeed, during the homilies he seemed nearly dead, or else asleep, which I considered the natural consequence of getting up at 4:30 A.M. when you are ninety years old. I have a ways to go to achieve that kind of reverence. But letting the words soak into me instead of combating them with ones of my own choosing is definitely a start.

March 5, 2000: Fifth Week of Ordinary Time

It rained us awake this morning—fat, plentiful drops on the enormous skylight we had opened in the dressing room next to our bed. Quite the novelty, waking to rain. We lay in bed, savoring the sound as well as the knowledge that since it's an early Sunday morning, there will be no need to fight the elements—combined with kamikaze freeway drivers—anytime soon.

They really drive like crazy people here in the rain, unable to recognize or acknowledge any change in braking-to-stopping ratios or visibility modifications. The drivers' flaunt-the-devil attitude is compounded by the denial that builds our roads in southern California. Assuming the sun will always be with us, our roads are not banked, so rain falls and forms moving sheets on the roads, ideal for hydroplaning. The side streets don't have drains, and half the roads between me and the university I work for—just three miles away—are under water if we get more than a tenth of an inch of rain.

I should have known what I was getting into when I came out from New England, where I was selling a house, to visit Felix, who was already working in San Diego. Because of heavy snow run-off and spring rain, everyone who came to look at my Boston house rushed first to the cellar to see if we were "taking water." We were not, but the stampede mightily annoyed the dog, who was banished to the cellar during real estate visits.

Sitting in sunny southern California in the apartment, I heard rain start hitting the slider door. Felix rushed over to stare. "It's *raining*!" he finally explained.

I should have known it was different here by his obvious excitement over something as constant, I thought, as rain. But I moved to California during a prolonged drought, which led to certain understandings of "weather" and "seasons" I might never see again, but would always assume were the norm. Still, by the second year I had lived in this coastal desert, I must have acclimated. Like the morning I woke up to the sound of rain pounding on my windows and thought, "Well, I can't go to work today. It's *raining*." This in 1988 from a woman who survived the Blizzard of '78 alone in a basement apartment with two cats to scrounge food for.

But it does rain in the coastal desert, normally a whopping nine inches a year, which is about a month's worth in Boston—a respectable, well-behaved month at that. What they don't tell you is that most of those nine inches come one storm after another. Take this latest storm, for instance. Until two weeks ago, we were living on a desperately dry, brown-parched earth. I will live here forever before I reacclimatize my New England mind to the backward sense of brown summers and green winters. But this winter, La Niña, after the "enormous" winter last year with sixteen inches of rain, has been as dry and brown and dusty as an old dog bone.

Suddenly two weeks ago, a storm rolled in. "Good. We *need* the rain," the locals said with sovereign understanding and forbearance, as if a tenth of an inch of rain, or even the whole nine-inch magilla, will fill our taps and tubs and swimming pools. It's been overcast, windy, cold, or rainy ever since. As of today, San Diego is at 4.29" of precipitation for the season. Normal for this time of year is 7.32" of rain. But two weeks ago we were at one inch of rain for the season. Three inches of rain—one-third our yearly total—in two weeks! The natives get restless, for all the "need the rain" bravery. Especially when it rains on the weekend, which is explicitly forbidden by the Rule of Camelot we *really* think we live under.

"A big cold storm is heading this way," says our sodden Sunday paper. "Rain will become heavy; snow levels lowering to 3,000 feet." The temperatures will hover in the mid-fifties all day, ten degrees below average and considerably below the record for this day established the year I moved here—eighty-five degrees.

My poor fellow oblates are on retreat in more ways than one. The abbey is high on a hill that juts out into the Pacific and is considerably cooler and wetter than the rest of the county. I stayed there on private retreat the first weekend of April last year. The temperatures hung in the forties and the wind whipped off the ocean and howled into its first point of resistance, the abbey. The cheaply made retreatant rooms rattled and shook in the cold rain as much as the retreatants did. A candle on my desk blew out during one of the gusts, and at night I huddled, fully dressed, complete with shoes and socks, under all the blankets I could find, including those I stripped off the twin bed I wasn't using. Plus both bedspreads. I spent most of my days "retreating" to the church—too dark to read in, but at least it was heated. It was difficult to feel prayerful. My heartfelt sympathies are with my retreating oblates.

The wind is picking up again. "Our umbrella looks like it will pick up and go," says Felix, looking out the kitchen window to our tiny backyard. I ignore his remark, since the umbrella is plopped into a heavy concrete stand.

A booming sound. "The umbrella!" Felix says and goes outside to retrieve it. It is nowhere in the backyard. How can you lose a table-sized umbrella in a backyard barely bigger than the table? He stands on the short cinderblock fence, looking up and down the ninth fairway of the golf course that runs the length beyond our backyard. "Check the front yard," he tells me.

And there it is, this enormous umbrella. First, it freed itself of its concrete mooring. Then it flew over our roof and landed in the juniper trees, site of its first resistance.

Like the abbey, and those who live there, those who visit. The abbey is the first thing the bad weather hits when it comes up off the ocean, and the last hit with the blasting Santa Ana winds that come up out of the east, the desert.

> A brother asked Abba Poemen saying, "Can a man put his trust in one single work?" The old man said to him that Abba John the Dwarf said, "I would rather have a bit of all the virtues."[4]

I hope my fellow oblates are gaining a bit of all the virtues as they button up an extra sweater or two today.

Chapter 21: Deans at the Monastery

For large orders, Benedict recommends deans, who are subordinates of the abbot and manage smaller groups of monks. If one of them becomes arrogant with his supervisory duties, he should be replaced with another.

It is not a chapter particularly useful to oblates and others who only visit a monastery. The commentaries regarding these "organizational chart" chapters suggest caution and avoidance of self-importance if you—like the deans at a monastery—receive some delegated authority.

Exercise prudence in serving *under* such delegated authority, I would add. Deans, like deacons in a parish church, must be capable of sharing the duties of their abbot, says Benedict. If they do not and are not responsive to correction, they are to be removed, and another is to take their place. It is very possible that those under supervision will be the ones to discern suitability.

I found myself in that unenviable role as a catechumen, preparing for confirmation as a Catholic. For his many fine, Christian leadership qualities, our deacon had become a church leader, but our catechism experience was a disaster in his hands. We drifted loosely in a sort of Bible study for a while. Bible study—like preaching—is part of the mastery and magnificence of the Protestant tradition I had grown up in, and I was less than impressed with his touchy-feely, "how this story made me feel" approach to Bible study.

What about the Eucharist? I asked. How does confession work, and why oh why would I ever want to do it? What's the rosary about anyway? Where do I get one? First Friday? The deacon would smile earnestly and let our sponsors take over with a rousing discussion on what part of Mass must you be present for in order for your attendance at Mass to "count."

Those were the weeks he showed up. Three out of four weeks he was missing, and a well-meaning, totally unprepared sponsor would be pressed into service. "So how did the Gospel make you feel this morning?" Oh, dear. We were presented as candidates to the bishop. We were presented to the congregation. We had no idea of what or why anything was happening. We were led out and then led away. Our sponsors gamely struggled along.

I didn't want to make waves and maybe flunk catechism and not get to be a Catholic, but finally I wrote to the deacon. *Where are you?* I cried out on paper. *This is important. We need guidance.*

He showed up that week, suddenly confessing to us the distraction of many personal problems that were "put in perspective by a cold dose of reality I got in a letter this week."

I got quiet, afraid of being singled out or expelled. Not that he would have known the author of the letter, even sitting in front of us. He didn't know any of his flock by then. But he took control and began explaining the mysteries of the Eucharist that would become part of our lives on Holy Saturday. He was a masterful teacher, informed, humbled, sharing greatly.

I never saw him again.

We fumbled along with sponsors thrust "in charge" each week. I wrote a note to the deacon's supervisor that was not answered. I gave up and bought a book called "Everything Catholics Should Know"— and read it while my catechumenates struggled with how today's Gospel made them feel.

She appeared like an angel on Palm Sunday, Paula, director of catechumate ministry. "The deacon is no longer with us," she said in a clear, clean voice that brokered no questions, "and I will walk the rest of the way with you."

Which she did, magnificently, like a rainstorm in a San Diego drought, swift and merciful, overflowing. And my soul flooded over and greened up as the designated authority evaporated and the owner took charge. Had I not been so fearful of that designated authority's power over my desire to become Catholic, I would have gone to its source more quickly. But even Benedict gives the dean chances to improve. Without improvement, however, the authority disappears, as the new appointee picks up and keeps the work of God moving forward.

Chapter 22: How Monks Sleep

Monks are to sleep in separate beds, clothed, and under the watchful eyes of their superiors, says Benedict. Their communal work of prayer will be supported if they will quietly encourage each other, *for the sleepy like to make excuses.*

I don't sleep in a dormitory now, nor did I when I was in college. Perhaps it would have helped foster a sense of community if I had. Certainly it would have cut some of my sleep time down.

I love to sleep. "You were always a sleepy baby," my mother says. The idea of subsisting on less than eight hours of sleep per night—just the *idea* of it—makes me crazy with anxiety. The issue of sleep and early morning wake-ups would be a serious detriment to my ever choosing to live a monastic way of life.

On sleep, the spiritual fathers seem to have plenty to say, and it is rarely as positive as my mother's spin. "Falling asleep is a bit like the fall into death," Clement of Alexandria cheerfully notes in his writings.[5] "Emptiness of mind, loss of feeling." Since we are children of light, he wants us not to sleep too much, "especially when the days are short." Those are the *best times* to sleep! I want to say. "Sleep is like the tax-collector; it robs us of half our life." And the desert fathers are regular spoilsports too.

> Abba Arsenius used to say that one hour's sleep is enough for a monk if he is a good fighter.[6]

Phooey.

When I first moved to San Diego, Felix would get up at 5:30 A.M., go jogging, return and make coffee, read his newspaper, commune with the slow rise of the sun over the eastern mountains outside our kitchen window, and finally, at 7:00 A.M., shake me out of bed.

"Five more minutes," I would plead, sometimes successfully.

Somehow my clock crept backwards in the years that followed. I took up jogging when I quit smoking and had to get up at 6:00 A.M. Then I became an oblate novice and began to say the Divine Office in the morning—5:30 A.M. Finally, with terrible reluctance, I began the practice of *lectio divina*—5:00 A.M. wake-up call!

What helps me is the same thing that helped Benedict's monks. *When they arise for the Divine Office, they ought encourage each other*, says Benedict in his Rule, *for the sleepy make many excuses*.

You ain't just kidding on that one. My husband still gets up at 5:30, and we go work out together at the gym. But the 5:00 A.M. alarm is mine. I think of "my" monks, "my" community, arising in the same inhospitable dark. Abbot Antony has already been up half an hour by then. We are children of the light, together, at 5:00 A.M. And in the medium of shared purpose, we somehow encourage each other.

Chapters 23–30: The Punishment of Apartness

These chapters review all facets of discipline in community: what acts merit discipline (including stubbornness, disobedience, pride, or grumbling, according to chapter 23), degrees of punishment (including taking meals alone, per chapter 24, to working alone without a blessing in chapter 25, to corporal punishment, being prayed for, and if all else fails, being banished from the monastery in chapter 28). The abbot's role as disciplinarian and its balance with saving souls is dealt with in chapter 27. How to act around those being disciplined is covered in chapter 26, and children's punishments are covered in chapter 30. Finally, there are rules on receiving back a brother who, *following his own evil ways, leaves the monastery but then wishes to return*. Three opportunities to return must be granted him, says Benedict.

The punishments St. Benedict mentions in these chapters—whipping, enforced fasting, or flogging—sound terrible to our enlightened minds. But the worst possible punishment Benedict can list has a very postmodern air about it—excommunication. To be cut away from the community one is part of is the awful, existential "otherness" and apartness so many of us suffer today. Having experienced it, I would not wish it on another.

When I first found a folder on the Secular Franciscan Order during a retreat at a Franciscan mission, I was beside myself. *There was a place for people like me*, committed to the world, but not necessarily worldly, desirous of a community of like-minded souls. "We come together to pray, to retreat, then return to the world in the spirit of Francis," the brochure practically sang. I no longer have the brochure, but I must have memorized it. I carried it around in my pocketbook for almost a year before I got up the courage to call. How could I be worthy?

Is *anybody* worthy? I wondered weeks later. I became a candidate, along with a husband/wife team, and a few months later, the group stumbled through a meaningless mouthful of ugly ritual, somebody played a guitar, and everybody talked about themselves, and lo, we were suddenly novitiates, heading down a seemingly endless path to becoming *real* Secular Franciscans.

It reminded me of my catechumenate classes, meandering and directionless, both candidates and lay instructors struggling to understand a prepackaged curriculum. The husband and wife were nice people and eager to "share" in that oh-so-sweet tone I have always labeled as "Jesus voice."

I didn't have a Jesus voice. I had anger and plenty of it at the uncertain mess made of beautiful ideals.

"You don't have to stay," the formation leader said one day after I sniped more than usual.

"You're right. I don't." I left, all *stubborn, disobedient, proud . . . scornful* as the Rule describes people who are really like me. Alone, I tried to say the Divine Office regularly anyway. *He shall work alone, remaining in penance and sorrow*, says Benedict. I couldn't figure out the Office on my own.

> An old man said, "Judge not him who is guilty of fornication, if thou art chaste: or thou thyself wilt offend a similar law. For He who said, 'Thou shalt not fornicate', said also, 'Thou shalt not judge'."[7]

My father suddenly got ill. Five months later he was dead. As I drove his car home to San Diego from Rhode Island, I thought of Francis and of the story of his last words before he died: "I have done what was given me to do. May you find what it is given you to do."

The Secular Franciscans called in my mind on the long journey back. I had read Kathleen Norris's book *Cloister Walk*. If she could make the Benedictines sing, I could make the Franciscans dance, I decided.

I returned to the Seculars. Nothing had changed in my nine-month absence. The husband-and-wife team were still nice, still "sharing," still oh-so-sweet, and they stayed far away from me. Mary was still the formation director. "You'll have to start at the beginning again," she said, an unknowing echo of Benedict's chapter on readmittance (chapter 29)—*in the lowest rank so his humility may be put to the test.*

I wanted to talk about my father, about the experience of death I'd recently witnessed. They wanted to talk about tomorrow. I wanted to live in yesterday. I was a misfit, unable to become humble in my return, unable to forgive them for not being what I wanted or needed.

"Run, don't walk, to the Benedictines," one of them said in a whispered telephone call to me after a particularly frustrating meeting.

"I don't *want* to be a Benedictine. I want to be a Secular Franciscan. I want to dance."

"Maybe this isn't about what you want. Maybe you should leave."

I did leave, one last time, feeling the bitter taste of excommunication once more before I called the monastery and asked for "whoever does new secular friends."

"Come to lunch. Come early to Mass," he said. And I did. My abbot comforted this transgressor, *to keep him from being overwhelmed by sorrow,* as the Rule says. My old abbot stooped to place the sheep on his shoulders and return it to the flock.

March 20, 2000: Second Sunday of Lent

We have spent seven hours crossing the sandy, flat deserts of Tucson, Arizona, through the mountain passes and into the oceanic desert of San Diego. "What will you do when you're finally home?" Felix asks cheerfully, glad to be heading in the direction of San Diego at last.

"Go to church," I say mournfully. As I get back into the car to drive the thirty miles round trip to the monastery, he thoughtfully waits for me to leave before getting into the golf cart to go hit a few.

Driving isn't exactly what I feel like doing. Since arriving home, I have received a $1,800 overdraft notice from the bank and lost the prescription for Felix's glasses I just had my hands on one week ago—and Felix just lost his glasses this weekend in Tucson. Maybe Vespers is the safest place for me to be right now.

I go to church every week no matter what, not because I am good, but because I am not. If I don't make a once-a-week rule for myself, I will make excuses. If I were a good Catholic, it would have to be Mass every week. But I am a Catholic made of bits of the Episcopal Church, AA, and a bad RCIA program. Vespers "count" in my book.

Even this early in the year, the late sun burns the ocean below, creating halos of glare around the monks. As soon as they begin singing, the marine layer settles over the coast, shrouding them all in ordinary, flat light.

There is much singing in Latin tonight—nothing I can sing as a post-Vatican II convert.

Abbot Antony waylays me as I leave. "I *thought* I saw you, finally," he says. I have missed the last two oblate meetings due to my business travel schedule. It has obviously been noticed. Abbot Antony always appears to be praying or has his eyes closed. How is he noticing? Is he sneaking peeks? He talks about the Internet review I did on a Benedictine book and asks what I am reading.

"Come back so we can talk!" he says as I head out, back to my car, oddly peaceful for the additional driving.

Chapters 31–34: The Sanctity (and Horror) of "Stuff"

These chapters deal with the necessities of life in the monastery and those who take care of the necessities. Chapter 31 is a job description of the cellarer, who maintains and purchases the goods used, like a combination purchasing agent/warehouse supervisor. *He will regard all utensils as sacred altar vessels*, says Benedict. In chapter 32, Benedict asks for an inventory of goods and tools. Chapters 33 and 34 talk about monks owning no personal property. Rather, they should *look to the father of the monastery for all their needs.* Brothers receive according to their needs.

"Nothing so defiles and ensnares a person's heart as the undisciplined love of created things," says Thomas à Kempis.[8] It is that "undisciplined love," I think, that Benedict really sees as the evil, more than the created things themselves. He bans private ownership (chapter 33), which might lead to undisciplined love or even idolatry of "stuff" instead of love of God. The chapters on the sacredness of property and treatment of goods are really some of the nicest words I've seen on the created goods around us.

We live in a consumerist society and engage in orgies of unbridled spending and acquiring stuff. We know this—and maybe regret it sometimes—but still flash the credit card more often than a smile. I certainly know how important the stuff is. When I moved to San Diego, my home in New England stayed on the market for a long time, filled with our furniture, my "stuff." I grieved the absence of my stuff—my books, my diaries, my photo albums—nearly as much as the absence of family, friends, and the familiar way of life I'd left behind.

Unlike the rest of my grief list, my stuff eventually got packed into a moving van after the house sold. When I saw that same van approach my new address in San Diego, I cried. If my stuff was here, I was home. I was never going back.

But stuff has its dignity and its use too. Benedict's "cellarer" will think of the monastery's properties *as if they were consecrated chalices* (chapter 31).

When my dear grandmother died, I hopped on a plane from San Diego to Boston and chartered the path of loss. The phone call took away the essence of a person I loved: "This is the call you didn't want—Nana died last night." And then there were the calling hours, where we stood next to Nana's body and left behind her friends and her history. Then we lost even her body and the person we recognized as we committed her to the earth.

The next day we cleaned out her apartment. I had never done that before. We respectfully and silently sorted out the unusable, the give-away, the throwaway, all the things she used faithfully in life, now becoming consecrated in death. Things were all that remained. I wore her old-fashioned silver-plated watch with the wristband too big and sliding around for months because I had seen it on *her* arm my whole life. Finally Felix said, "Give Nana a break. She's busy getting settled in her new life now." This from a non-believer. He was right. It had become an amulet, a way of stubbornly hanging on to *her*, not her "stuff" being respected and used. I gave it a rest.

> When the abbot Macarius was in Egypt, he had gone out of his cell: and returning found someone stealing whatever he had in his cell. So he stood by as if he himself had been a stranger and helped load the animal with all stealth and led him out, saying, We brought nothing into the world. The

Lord gave, and the Lord hath taken away: and as He willed, so it comes to pass. Blessed be the Lord in all things.[9]

In *The Re-Enchantment of Everyday Life*, Thomas Moore says it so well. "The soul craves ordinary pleasures, depth of feeling and relatedness, worldly delight that is not inimical to a spiritual practice, human scale in the making of culture, and exposure to the magic that lies just beneath the surface of familiar things."[10]

Sometimes my stuff is just stuff. Sometimes I get too attached and I lose all perspective about what it was meant to be. And sometimes an old watch, worn long and serving well, holds the magic of God's creation just beneath the surface of its created silver face.

March 21, 2000: Passing of Our Blessed Father St. Benedict Feast

Abbot Antony writes so very much like he speaks:

Our Lord would be pleased, our Holy Father Benedict would be pleased, and the monks would be pleased if there would be a good representation of the Oblates at the Holy Mass. Afterwards we would also be pleased to serve refreshments and sandwiches . . .

On the drive from work to the abbey, a freeway sign catches my eye: "The school of character is in daily living—PureFlo Water." I would like to think that sentiment would please our Holy Father Benedict. When I arrive at the abbey church, there is a statue of him before the altar, candles, and fresh flowers—Easter lilies unfolding their promise now, in the deepest of Lent—and, in front, the Holy Eucharist, exposed to us like the heart of Christ, the bold beauty of redemption on this glorious late winter, Lenten workday. The day is a magnificent one on which to celebrate a passing. Considering that our San Diego weather is so nearly perfect, we spend quite a bit of "daily living" obsessing about the perfect weather. Would that we could obsess so completely in praising God.

But that is for monks to worry over, not lobbyists taking a few hours off to please our Holy Father Benedict. The abbey church fills slowly, inevitably.

I know very little about this man named Benedict. I am arrogant enough to think if I know his Rule, I know the Ruler. We sing.

Laeta dies magni ducis,
Dona ferens novae lucis,
Hodie e recolitur.

(We celebrate this day,
the happy day of our great leader,
which brings us the blessings of new light.)

There are many of us, perhaps fifty, for refreshments in the library afterwards. Pleasing. The bells clang and Abbot Antony raises his old voice against the din: "And the angel of the Lord . . . " By the third verse or so, we are all zoned in to the *Angelus*.

"I'm sorry we have so little to give you," Abbot says, pointing to the tables set with fruit, vegetables, yogurt, and sushi. "The good part is waiting in heaven."

For a lifelong outsider, a lifelong gyratory, I leave feeling like I *belong*, to a company of saints as well as sinners, for the first time.

Chapter 35: Weekly Kitchen Service

Benedict dictates that all monks will serve on kitchen duty, *for such service increases reward and fosters love*. In this chapter, he spells out the duties of the week's server and the prayers said for the incoming and outgoing servers.

I was pretty reluctant to look at this chapter. Food, kitchens, and eating carry baggage with me.

My thoughts on this chapter were principally focused around the abbey's cafeteria for visitors. The food is nearly uniformly terrible. I blame Benedict. At the Franciscan mission's retreat house just a little bit from here, the food is quite tasty and—as one joyous Father Rusty used to remind us—"you don't have to cook it yourself! It just appears!" For many of the tired older women on retreat, this was like being tended by the angels.

The Franciscans hired people who could cook to cook. And then there's Benedict. "The brothers shall wait on one another." I have never seen a priest-monk stuck with kitchen duty at the retreat cafeteria here, but whoever is cooking is making various menus out of brown. Everything cooked is brown. Everything tastes brown.

Still, I can hardly complain. Unlike the tired ladies on retreat at the Franciscan mission, I don't cook, never did, and don't intend to start now. My food has always appeared magically, as if by angels.

"You're a princess," grumbles Felix, stirring the sauce he's making from scratch.

"Who made me one, huh?" I usually respond ungraciously. "And what am I supposed to say about Benedictine kitchen duty, huh?"

He snorts. "Tell it from the point of view of the one being served, ha ha."

Dammit, he's right. It is not about cooking, really, but about love and care that Felix puts into that sauce—and everything else that comes out of "his" kitchen. When he's traveling I have attempted to duplicate his menu, but even my ham sandwich does not taste like his ham sandwich. Where I have thrown the lettuce atop the ham and stuck it all between bread, he has chosen the freshest leaves, rinsed them clean, and laid them down with deliberation on the bread. Where I feed myself thoughtlessly, he brings great thought and love. He finds a blessing in the work of his hands, the feeding of his life companion. Unless he is traveling, I take all of this for granted. I sit down and nourishment appears. I complain if it is not to my liking. Otherwise I eat in silence. When I am feeling particularly thoughtful, I praise the creator and server of my sustenance.

> A brother said to Abbot Pastor: If I give one of my brothers a little bread or something of the sort, the demons spoil everything and it seems to me that I have acted only to please men. The elder said to him, "Even if your good work was done to please, we must still give to our brothers what they need."[11]

It is too much a parallel to my response to God's grace—taken for granted until it is gone, the complaints, the rare praise. In kitchen duty, we have the opportunity to give as well as to receive service. Without both, the one quickly loses flavor.

March 31, 2000: Third Week of Lent

We are deeply into spring as well as Lent. The combination is an ironic one. Last year, Lent was early and Easter was a cold promissory note. This year you want to get the promise of the Resurrection before you have suffered your winter soul. The ocean desert climate that jars the liturgical calendar once in a while: mild, but not hot; breezy, not windy—"shaken, not stirred," as James Bond would have said about his martini.

It seems like a long time since I have been here on a vacation day— the very beginning of the month, the days before the start of Lent. Next month I get to stay here for a few days of retreat. I reserved my room eleven months in advance for the Easter weekend celebration. Every time I visit, I walk by room #26—facing the back of the retreat area, even quieter than the courtyard area where my room was last year—and breathe a prayer of gratitude that I am allowed to be part of such a community even peripherally, even for only a day or an hour at a time.

Chapters 36 and 37: The Sick, The Elderly, The Children

In chapters 36 and 37, Benedict tells us to care for the sick, the elderly, and children. Although he asks the sick to be respectful to their caregivers, he demands greater respect from those tending these groups no matter what their behavior, and grants the sick, the elderly, and children special dispensation from rules about eating meat and prohibiting baths.

There is a sameness to my community that reflects a few big choices I made in my life: the decision not to have children (made when I was younger—perhaps sixteen years old—and never revisited); the decision to move to southern California that separated me not only from the growing children of my sister, but also from the aging and illnesses of the rest of my family; the decision to buy our last residence—after four moves in eight years in California, amid the chant of "never again!"—at a retirement community. The sum of those decisions equals a community without family or intergenerational mix, a community of more sanitary sameness than the monks' community here at the abbey.

For my ordinary life in this part of the Rule to be understood, I need to talk about my "borrowed" sick and elderly, an odd sort of ministry I found within the Franciscans. It is a type of caring for the sick and elderly you find in the pages of the history of the monks of Egypt, not in current periodicals on "caregivers":

> One by one they abide in their cells, a mighty silence and a great quiet among them: only on the Saturday and the Sunday do they come together to church, and there they see each other face to face as folk restored in heaven. If by chance anyone is missing in that gathering, straightaway they understand that he has been detained by some unevenness of his body, and they all go to visit him, not indeed all of them together, but at different times, and each carrying with him whatever he may have by him at home that might seem grateful to the sick. But for no other cause dare any disturb the silence of his neighbor.[12]

I am a big believer in my privacy, and as a result, it's the biggest gift I can give to others. It is partly the value I place on privacy that makes me a stranger to the monks here. I do not want to intrude, particularly since St. Augustine Abbey is one of the most cloistered monasteries in the country. But the needs of the sick, the frail, the elderly, may be different from my gifts of privacy, and I try to heed Abbess Matrona, a desert mother,

> It is better to have many about thee, and to live the solitary life in thy will, than to be alone, and the desire of thy mind be with the crowd.[13]

How the sick and elderly found me: the weekly church bulletin at the Franciscan Mission listed two Franciscan nuns or brothers and two parishioners who were ill or housebound, with a suggestion about sending a card or prayer. "I can write notes," I told Father Rusty. "I write good notes. And it's an anonymous ministry. Nobody has to know I'm doing it." He agreed that it made sense for me. As a former classical singer, now lobbyist, who seems to suffer sometimes from excess personality disorder, I have to reach back deep for humility—it rarely finds me.

I chose the Franciscan religious to write to since I aspired to become a Secular Franciscan then. Each week I offered up a rosary for each of the Franciscans listed in the bulletin, wrote them a note, and enclosed a counted cross-stitch bookmark with Bible verse and design. Each bookmark took about three or four hours to make, because I stitch like a lunatic on fire—nothing about serenity *there*—with hours of busy work and manual labor of sorts that was consecrated by prayer and dedicated to someone else. I had stitched "stuff" for years, but never given it away. I had done the same with writing. I kept a diary for me, but had never given writing away in little notes.

The first written thank-you came as an unpleasant shock, bursting *my* anonymity, *my* prayer work for the sick and dying. But as thank-you's trickled in—maybe one a month—I began to understand that this virtual community was made up of real people.

> Thank you so much for your kind note and for the beautiful needlepoint. I just love it! I have a great devotion to my guardian angel, so it is received with much joy and gratitude.
> —*Franciscan Sister, Sacramento*

> From your handiwork and your writing, I know you are artistic and neat—nice combination. If you ever find yourself in Ohio, do stop in at Salem Heights.
> —*Franciscan Sister, Dayton*

> I deeply appreciated your kind letter and the beautiful bookmark. I have it in my Divine Office, marking Vespers, and every day when I begin that section of the office, I ask a blessing on you. I celebrated my 101st birthday on October 3, and have been a professed Sister of St. Francis since April 10, 1917, four days after the U.S. declared war on Germany. I remember it as if it were yesterday. Each day I pray, "This is the day the Lord has made, I will rejoice and be glad in it." And during these lovely spring days, I, like you, have many reasons to rejoice.
> —*Franciscan Sister, Santa Maria*

Visiting the sick this way was like those old desert monks, visiting at different times as able, carrying whatever we had at home "that might be grateful for the sick." And I, too, received of the bounty of these elderly, ill individuals—a prayer card, a drawing, a favorite story, an admonition, even a dried flower from the Holy Land.

I made more than two hundred bookmarks, each one as individual as its anonymous recipient. I received much, much more. It was the most rewarding ministry I could have ever imagined, for all its oddness.

I became too great in my own eyes for this prayer work. It went away from me when I departed from the Franciscans and their mission. At the local parish I began attending instead, I submitted a note to the priest: any shut-ins I could write to? The note was met with silence. It was time to listen, not to talk, time to go up the hill to the cold, silent abbey of the Benedictines instead of the "out there" exuberance of the Franciscans. It was time to go.

But in the long run, I will return to the Franciscans one more time since my burial niche is on the Mission grounds and my perpetual care will be under their care.

And, in a way, the elderly and ill continue to bless me in their comings and goings. At least twice a year, I get a letter from the head of the Santa Barbara chapter of Franciscans, giving me the sad news of the happy death of a religious brother or sister. "Your name and address were among the papers, and so we write to make sure you are aware of the death . . ." and a prayer card is enclosed for me, like a last gift and a last prayer for this very special community of the sick and elderly.

～

The retreat cafeteria is deserted when the noon bell chimes. Brother Cosmas, the beekeeper, comes out of the kitchen in his black habit and white apron. "The angel of the Lord declared unto Mary . . . "

"And she conceived of the Holy Spirit," I gulp, scrambling to my feet and grabbing my cheat sheet. I can hardly hear my own voice, the bell is so loud, but Brother Cosmas must have this timed to the nanosecond by now and doesn't miss a beat.

The retreatants and secular staff must have the *Angelus* tuned to a heartbeat too. As Brother Cosmas and I say, "Amen," they come pouring in.

"What's your name?" Brother Cosmas asks in his kindly voice as he walks past me to open the sliding door between retreatants and lunch.

"Carol. I'm an oblate here."

"How nice," he says, and kitchen service takes over.

I made you a bookmark at Easter last year, I want to say. *It was green and purple thread on a white bookmark and it had a honey bee on it, and it said,*

"Pleasant words are as an honeycomb, sweet to the soul, and health to the bones" (Proverbs 16:24). *And you wrote in the newsletter once that it was your favorite verse, but I never heard anything and maybe you didn't like it or get it, or maybe the vice of private ownership meant you couldn't keep it, but I felt like I'd done something wrong, not nice, and chalked it up to cultural differences I'll never understand about Benedictines and Franciscans.*

But instead, I sit in silence, respecter of privacy, shy around monks (except Abbot Antony).

Nancy sees me later and gives me a novena to the Divine Mercy to begin on Palm Sunday. Nancy is always pulling us together relentlessly, doing whatever she can, completely selfless. "I'm a doer," she says looking at my notebook. "Can't write my way out of anything. I'm a doer."

"I'm not," I say, aware of how very truthful I am being. If Jesus hadn't dignified "the better part" of Mary, I'd feel even worse in the society of doing-it-all's I am in. As long as I don't then go and feel superior from what I deem my "laziness." As the desert father Silvanius said:

> So Martha is necessary to Mary for because of Martha, Mary is praised.[14]

Prayer walk after lunch. We are all pagans, I think, as I observe the monoliths made from rocks everywhere. The fact that I am looking for today's rock for the prayer garden I'm going to make at home someday is completely different, of course. The silence of the vast Pacific beyond and the roar of the interstate below are modified by the soft songs of four elderly Filipina ladies as they walk to the next station of the cross and offer a prayer in Tagalog before moving on in song. Who needs to go halfway around the world to walk the *Via Dolorosa*, the "Sorrowful Road" in Jerusalem? The way of sorrows is every way.

The wooden rosary beads that Kathleen's father made for me suddenly break when they are caught on a bush and I keep walking. It occurs to me that I never see the Benedictines doing beads or chaplets or any of the gaudy, beautiful customs that have developed in Catholicism over the centuries. That's probably because the Benedictine way is so old it predates everything. As a Benedictine, I'm not a bad Catholic or a lapsed Protestant. I'm trying to follow a

Gospel-based Rule that came up out of desert traditions just a few hundred years after Christ.

I would not have chosen the Benedictines or called this wind-swept perch on the edge of the ocean home, but it is my journey and my destination now. Something about the moist blue sky reminds me of Kauai, where Felix and I hiked along the isolated gorge on the western shores. I went to the edge so Felix could take my picture, but my spirit continued on. A long time later, I heard the wild goats below and my spirit returned, and as I faced Felix, all I knew was that wherever I was during that time, the next time I returned, I could stay.

"What were you staring at all that time?" Felix asked. I turned back one more time to see, but the cliffs were shrouded in fog. Our tour book explained that this was the place where, in Hawaiian legends, the soul went for one last moment before it leaped to the other side.

And here I am, a Benedictine oblate, visiting this monastery as I can, practicing the Rule as I am able. And someday, I will get to stay.

I don't care *where* I am today, the "prayer lady" is fussing at something around me—*very* annoying. Both Marys and Marthas are probably burdens to these poor monks who thought they were getting away from *all* of us.

The breeze has turned to wind. The library groans its displeasure. I fall asleep with the Rule in my lap, not a doer at all.

Chapter 38: The Weekly Reader

Here, Benedict offers instructions on the blessing of and requirements for the weekly reader, who reads while the brothers take their meals.

I hate being read to. It's genetic. My mother hates being read to as well. She blames it on pace—she reads faster than the reader reads. I blame mine on being easily distracted, on not being really able to *listen*, at least to the level I can see when I'm reading.

Felix, on the other hand, loves being read to. I have read hundreds of rough draft poems and stories to him over the years to gauge response, to hear where the words fall flat, maybe to push Benedict's idea that *listening* is done with mind, body, and soul, not ears or eyes alone.

In AA, sober a week and none too happy about it, I walked into a step meeting. I didn't know what kind of meeting that was, but it was close in an area of far-flung meetings, and I needed a Monday night meeting.

They read to each other from an AA publication called *The Twelve Steps*. Every week they read aloud, round and round, a step a week, with two weeks for the twelfth step, and then start over again at step one, each person reading a paragraph. I hated it at first, but then, I hated everything in the cold, harsh light of early sobriety. Good readers, boring readers, stumbling readers, readers with all kinds of regional accents, we read and were read to as the words tried to carve their place in our souls.

John came in after I'd been there two years. He never read. Sometimes he passed, sometimes he forgot his glasses, sometimes he forgot his book. But his eyes were bright and his hunger "for what you people have" was plainspoken.

One day when it came to John's turn to read, he put the book down and said, "I've got to be honest with you people. I don't know how to read." And he put his head down on the book, and his bright eyes filled up and he cried in a shame I couldn't imagine.

The next week he was gone. Arrested for drunk driving again, he hung himself in a jail cell in Concord. And we picked up the reading where we left off and we went round and round, because, unlike Benedict, we let everybody read, not by *their ability to benefit their hearers.*

> Someone asked Abba Anthony: "Father, how can you be so happy when you are deprived the consolation of books?" Anthony replied, "My book is the nature of created things, and any time I want to read the words of God, the book is before me."[15]

Listening is part of reading. When I do my own reading, it is not communal but solitary—which is fine in itself, and I do enough of that. Being read to is a form of community, and the union takes place in the medium between where the reader's words leave off and the listener's heart begins. It is in this dry moment of air that I imagine the spark of the Holy Spirit may ignite. Ironically, Brother John Climachus is probably the best reader of lessons at Mass here at the abbey. A recovering alcoholic, he puts spaces between each word and gives the Holy Spirit room to strike between him and us.

I should know all this well by now. As a speechwriter, my medium is not the page on which I write, but the space between the words my speaker speaks and the audience who hears them. When I write, I "hear" my speaker, his idiom, and place those rhythms onto paper, reminding myself of the old joke: when a speechwriter dies, his last words are those of his speaker.

When I drafted my university president's inaugural address, he was anxious to read it. "Sit down and listen instead," I said. "Nobody else is going to read it. They're going to hear it."

And he did, with great intensity. Between reader and listener, the speech was born, like a performance or a dialogue, or exchange of ideas. Until that moment, it had been *my* words on paper. Spoken and heard, the words ignited into community.

And so it can be of any work worth a good reader and good listeners.

~

By 4:30 P.M., the only safe place is the abbey church. The library is closed now, and I fell asleep in there anyway. The retreat center is filling up. At one point, the prayer work lady and I were giving directions, Brother Matthew and Brother Micholas were carrying luggage, and Brother John Climachus, undoubtedly "crazy for the Lord," was letting two ladies who locked themselves out back into their rooms.

And now it is too cold and blustery to sit outside.

These days here are a bit rootless. I can only half-blame the monastery. I am here, on the fringes, not unwelcome, but with no place to really light. And I have a spirit that still doesn't want to take root.

APRIL
The Parched Ground Shall Become a Pool

And the parched ground shall become a pool,
and the thirsty land springs of water . . .
                                    Isaiah 35:7

April 9, 2000: Fifth Sunday in Lent

I think this is only the second time I have come to the monastery for Sunday Mass. Felix is very supportive of my weekly attendance at Mass—and quietly grateful that I normally attend a Saturday night vigil Mass. Sundays are our day free together, and church-going, for me, is a solitary activity.

The monks do not do a Saturday vigil Mass. For monks, I think, their whole lives are vigils, and daily Mass here simply moves from weekday 11:00 A.M. to Sunday 10:30 A.M. The only other difference between their weekday and Sunday Mass is that all the folding chairs are set up. Sunday Mass is performed to a packed house.

I went once before on a Sunday when we also had our oblate meeting at 2:00 P.M. The plan was to attend Mass, snag something to eat in the cafeteria, study for an hour, and then join the oblate meeting— a retreat for a few hours before the crush of the weekday schedule began again.

What I would rather not repeat is the awful isolation I worked myself into that Sunday. I had gotten the idea of this mini-retreat schedule from the first oblate I ever spoke to at the first meeting I ever attended. She stood when Abbot Antony introduced the newest oblates and I went over afterward to introduce myself and ask about her experience as an oblate novice. Old AA training at work. "I come here from Fullerton," she said. "I take the train to Oceanside and Abbot Antony picks me up in time for Mass. I stay for lunch and the meeting, and then he drives me back to the train station before Vespers."

It seemed a lot of Abbot Antony's responsibility to get her and her two friends to an oblate meeting, but I wasn't up on the rules of Benedictine hospitality, so I didn't comment on it. "I was a Secular Franciscan novice for a while," I said. "I wonder if this is similar?"

"I did the Carmelites before," she said. "This is better. The monks themselves are involved. And you can get spiritual counseling and it's free."

All that and donuts after Mass. What more could you want?

I showed up a month or so later for the Mass/lunch/oblate combo when Felix was off in Asia. It sounded like a comfortable, communal thing to do on a Sunday afternoon. The Mass was crowded and uninspired. I saw the oblate I'd spoken to at the donuts and social time. She was with her Fullerton friends. The cafeteria was empty and I didn't know the rules. I ate a cookie and visited the gift shop, which was mobbed.

Abbot Antony materialized at my elbow out of nowhere. "What are you reading?"

"I was looking at these daily reflections based on the writings of St. Thérèsè de Lisieux," I said, trying to stay levelheaded when it was all just *not* working.

"It's a good book!" said the abbot vigorously. And he was gone, silently. I didn't buy the book (alas, I also never saw it again in the bookstore), and stayed only a short time at the oblate meeting, wondering what was wrong with me, and why was I such a misfit all the time.

Today is a hazy, coolish day with the sky full of the lazy drone of planes swooping in and out of San Diego's airport. The monks file in for Mass, and the priests wear the gaudy purple of Lent. Because of Lent, they process out silently. The retreat hall fills up with donut eaters, and a sign at the door reads, "Because of the large number of retreatants this weekend, the cafeteria is closed to non-retreatants."

I stumble down the hill for fast food, trying to practice praise for the steamy gray ocean and the blooming ranunculus fields, stretched out like rainbows that have fallen to earth. It does no good. I am crabby and displaced again.

The Franciscans knew hospitality. The Benedictines know how to leave me alone. Funny how Divine Providence—the abbot's favorite destination—gets you what you need.

When I return to the monastery it is to a wondrous little sight: Brother John Climachus is processing carefully and with great dignity, trying to keep a candle lit as he walks across the parking lot. Father Ignatius follows with the Sacrament covered under his golden shawl like eagle wings. They march, unobserved, toward the prayer chapel, where (presumably) there will be Exposition of the Blessed Sacrament.

"I spoke to Brother John Climachus," says Abbot Antony when the library opens for the oblate meeting. "Maybe we shouldn't have retreats when the oblates meet, so everybody coming in from a long way can have lunch together."

I feel guilty for my ugly comparative thoughts about the hospitality of the Franciscans . . .

Chapter 39: Food Apportionment

In this chapter, Benedict takes care that there is enough food, in both quantity and variety, to satisfy hunger. Overindulgence should be avoided because it brings indigestion. None but the sick should eat meat.

I didn't come to St. Benedict looking for diet advice. In retrospect, I don't know why I didn't: I certainly looked everywhere else. Like the gyratory of chapter 1, I have been all over the map trying to achieve the "right weight" (my definition, not the insurance company's fat version of same). I started with Weight Watchers in my twenties, but quickly moved left or right of "balance": Atkins, calorie counting, carbo counting, fat gram counting, Slim Fast, Healthy Choice. It's like my husband says, "Try enough diets, and you'll get to eat everything."

The goal: no gain, no pain. In my twenties, every diet worked, and my weight crashed. In my thirties, I discovered that if I smoked enough cigarettes and drank enough coffee, I could maintain that weight crash, probably due to a nervous stomach and nicotine-crazed metabolism.

In my forties, being smoke-free with an aging metabolism, no diets work. I think I ran my entire repertoire of diets over six months, finally settling on Atkins, where I could at least eat half a cow with a side of bacon and never be hungry again.

Then I became a Benedictine oblate. I wasn't planning on changing my diet for *spiritual* reasons. That seems somehow un-American. But reading this chapter about "cooked food," fruit, vegetables, and bread began to weigh on my mind. Finally, I said, "Okay, no quadrupeds," because it sounded funny and at least it was *something*—something clearly not Atkins, either. By ruling out one thing, I began to approach moderation—which is all Benedict really asks, and far more than I'd been able to achieve until now.

> Abba Poemen was asked how to fast. "For my part," he said, "I think it is better that one should eat every day, but only a little, so as not to be satisfied." Abba Joseph asked, "When you were younger, did you not fast two days at a time, Abba?" The old man said, "Yes, even for three and four days and sometimes the whole week. The Brothers tried all this out as they were able and they found it preferable to eat every day, but just a small amount. They have left us this royal way, which is light."[1]

I will never be a desert saint, much as I admire and resonate to the old disciplines. While some of those men and women of the desert would look like they had eating disorder, most of them preached moderation. I no longer curse my large appetite. I do try to redirect *some* of it to prayer—an activity I could never do full of food (or full of myself). And I stopped looking at the scale. It does not measure what needs to be measured.

April 14, 2000: Fifth Week of Lent

There is barely any warmth in the patches of clearing sky today. The ocean below us has a clearly defined "edge" and the color of a deep metallic blue.

We've had several cloudbursts already, and it strikes me how unusual that is in San Diego. We either get rain or we don't. Usually we don't. It is a temperate climate, but not a moderate one in Benedict's sense of a balancing act. The bad weather is usually brief and fully bad. The sunbursts are not enough to warm today, and I am chilly in my new "uniform"—white stretch pants and white tee shirt lettered black with "St. Augustine's Abbey" and Benedictine medal.

When I arrive, I realize it's pretty much the outfit the prayer work lady wears. I am becoming one of the abbey groupies. For some reason, this bothers me, since I know I don't really "belong," and my days here are full of the sheer angst of finding a quiet tabletop to write on.

Mass is said between a split reality. To the left, toward the city, the windows are blue with calm skies. To the right, toward the north, the windows are full of angry and gray, with the bougainvillea bending in the wind. Eventually the angry gray skies take over, even here. But of course, it is still Lent.

Prayer walk: It is a little cool for the walk the way I am dressed, but I am prayer walking briskly for reasons more fearful than getting a chill. At Sunday's oblate meeting, the serious, studious young man who made his final vow just before I first came told Abbot Antony, "There was a rattlesnake along the prayer walk."

"Where was it?" the abbot asked, looking quite interested.

"The Twelfth Station."

"And was it a baby snake?"

"I didn't stay to find out!"

"Ah, well, they won't harm you if you don't harm them."

I have no intentions of ever harming a rattler, no matter what its age. I walk in the middle of the path now, all cautious and fearful where before my prayer walks had been an unfettered romp, praying, and looking for suitable rocks for the fledgling home prayer walk. One rock per visit. I am up to a grand total of five rocks so far. I think I forgot one the day I left early and kind of huffy.

The monoliths and dead flowers have all been swept clean for the first time since I've been coming here. The Stations look ready for prayer now, ready for Holy Week—but not as full of passion as they did when littered with their human touch.

I have decided to try returning to the oblate library for afternoon work. Partly this wandering, not-belonging, has begun to turn into not wanting to be here at all, and I need to stop those thoughts before I go into full gyratory mode. Partly, for some reason in Mass today, I am given the brief discernment—a Franciscan word, and painfully wonderful when it is given—that my "place" here is, indeed, in the oblate library that Abbot Antony so lovingly prepared for us.

The discernment has in it echoes of the Gospel of John, words I repeat to myself in times of sorrow, the basis (for some reason) of most of my faith on the bad-faith days: "In my Father's house are many mansions; if it were not so, I would have told you. I go to prepare a place for you" (John 14:2). Imagine answering, "No thanks on that place. It doesn't meet my requirements and I don't like the view. What else do you have?" Abbot Antony prepared this place for us just as I arrived on the scene, so we would have "our" place at the abbey to study, to read.

I ask Brother Paschal, filling in as porter again, for the oblate library key. He has it, and is quite cheerful about lending it. The room is cleaner than I remember it, plainer too, and there is a crucifix on one bare wall. The glorious mantel clock on the bookcase still does not work, and the room becomes timeless. Today the window opens easily onto the small courtyard that Hildegard has spent so much time meditating upon.

Sometimes accepting place is anything but confining.

Chapter 40: Drink Apportionment

Benedict prescribes *with some uneasiness*, as he notes, a half bottle of wine daily for each of his monks. Abstinence is its own gift, he says, but since monks will not tolerate a ban on wine, let them drink in moderation.

Ironically I am writing this the day after the seventeenth anniversary of my sobriety. I no longer "celebrate" it with cake or tokens as I once did. It's been years since I set foot into an AA meeting. April 13 will still always resonate for me—not for taking my last drink—but as a day when I faced the demon of my self-destruction square in the face. And realized the demon had won. "But they also have erred through wine," I read in Isaiah today, "and through strong drink are out of the way" (28:7).

I didn't use words like "sin" or "redemption" in those days, and certainly not words like "moderation" or "discipline" either. In the face of failure with a demon of self-destruction, I accepted the language of AA: "sobriety," "surrender," "Higher Power."

"You've got one week to establish a relationship with a Higher Power—whom I choose to call God," said Ron the social worker who'd watched me crash and burn and who was now picking through the wreckage of my former self.

"I don't go in for that crap," I sniffed.

"Better go in for something, or you'll never make it. One week."

It was a dreadful homework assignment for a self-declared artist and intellectual, living in a secular university city. But surely the God I had rejected, still waiting in the wings for me, sent me the substitute I could live with: the Virgin Mary.

"Odd choice for a nice Protestant girl," was all Ron said of my choice.

"I want a lady Higher Power," I muttered. Having grown up Protestant, I didn't carry the mental baggage about the Blessed Mother that I did about God. I only thought she must have nice eyes. And the words to the Hail Mary prayer ("Hail Mary, full of grace, the Lord is with thee . . . "), which I learned after I chose her, was a marvelous mantra for a frayed, splintered soul to use as glue during early sobriety.

I stayed with AA—a marriage I didn't much care for—until I entered the Catholic Church seven years later. AA was my first "rule," and it led me, nearly directly, to Benedict's Rule: seven years from AA to Catholicism; nine years from Catholicism to Benedict. There is no "moderation" for a drunk. Like sin itself, like the rain in San Diego, when you're a drunk, you either drink and be damned or don't drink. "Why can't you just drink a glass or two of wine like everybody else?" a former friend asked me in frustration. "Why does it have to be everything or nothing with you?"

I supposed Brother John Climachus would understand. People of immoderation, we fell in love with the Spirit the way we once immolated ourselves with spirits. Our dear Father Benedict gives us a special blessing in this chapter when he writes, *But those to whom God gives the strength to abstain must know that they will earn their own reward.*

> Some brothers told Abba Poemen of a brother who did not drink wine. Abba Poemen answered, "Wine is not for monks."[2]

Even with the all-or-nothing hellfire that drink poses to a drunk, some moderation can be reached. Last summer, laden low with misery of human cruelties, I escaped work for an hour and headed up this hill for Mass. As I watched my old abbot stand to give communion, I thought, *The Cup of Salvation is not going to get me drunk!* And for the first time I took both species of communion, the bread and the wine, from my old abbot's hands.

~

I say hi to the prayer work lady. She notices we are dressed alike and is quite pleased by this. "It's a uniform," she says, for when she comes here. "Like the monks," she adds, waving her hand toward the cloister.

The clock in the oblate library actually keeps time quite well. It just didn't get arbitrary about daylight savings time the way we did. I change it to match oblate time, since I'm going to be spending a lot of that here.

Chapters 41 and 47: Hours for Eating and Prayer

As the hours of prayer are spelled out at length in earlier chapters, in these, Benedict announces times for eating, based on the hours of daylight, and gives the abbot authority to announce the times for prayer *so that everything may be done at the proper time.*

> The abbot Moses asked the abbot Silvanus, "Can a man every day make a beginning of the good life?" The abbot Silvanus answered him, "If he be diligent, he can every day and every hour begin the good life anew."[3]

Regularity in all things seems to be the watchword for Benedict. It's not a bad thing, either, since regular times for sleeping and eating seem to curb abuses. Anybody who has had to keep a tiresome "food diary" at the beginning of a diet or a "smoking diary" before cessation of smoking knows that we can become creatures of habit, good or bad.

I happen to like habit and regularity, which can make discipline and even obedience a lot less troublesome. I have the feeling that these patterns of regularization, which Benedict takes such care to spell out, help curb the gyratory in me, the useless, restless spirit that will not let me take root.

Routine is freeing in a lot of ways. If you are doing what you're supposed to be doing when you're supposed to be doing it, a lot of wavering and mental "noise" can be eliminated, freeing us up for our "work of God" (*opus dei*), however that is designed for us.

"Designated hours" is interesting, of course. Designated by whom? If I were a monk, it would be the abbot or his prior who set the parameters of our hours. But I am not, so I receive instructions from multiple sources: my husband, my coworkers, my boss, my customers, even the gentle prodding of my Abbot Antony. ("*Lectio* is a fine thing to do—even for twenty minutes a day, more if you can.")

Right now, none of my dining hours have any regularity. My work as a lobbyist, and the resultant rounds of public meetings (chambers of commerce, economic development organizations, mayor and city manager luncheons, and four separate legislative action committees) have me on the "moonlit highway," traipsing down to downtown San Diego at 6:30 A.M. today, returning from up north in Temecula at 8:00 last night.

The best I can do is to follow the rest of Benedict's advice here, regulating, scheduling, and arranging as much as I can ahead of time, posting my schedule to husband and office mates alike so that my "off" schedule does not promote problems with theirs, *and so they may go about their activities without justifiable grumbling.*

For the last year, my designated hour for the gym has been 5:00 A.M. This came about because Felix is a morning person, because the gym gets too crowded after that, and because I also need time for *lectio*, Divine Office, shower, breakfast, contact lenses, and getting ready for work *after* the gym.

Designated or not, the schedule has been unraveling. Ironically, it has been during this Lent that my self-discipline has completely eroded—which is good for humility, but not much else. After much thought, much guilt, and many mornings of battering the snooze alarm into submission, I finally concluded that I needed to reset those designated hours myself. I am now exercising at 8:30 at night, taking the three-hour routine of my morning and breaking it out between morning and evening to accommodate my body rhythms and energy.

I would never succeed as a monk with my 6:30 A.M. wake-up now (and there are no good psalms to praise the virtues of the sleepy not-so-morning bird), but in the sounding of my hours, there is now routine and rhythm.

There is also a longer-term meaning for me in this regularization of life's schedule. Benedict's words remind me that there are designated times for designated parts of my life. Because I live in a peaceful retirement resort community, the urge is strong to want to retire *now*, aged forty-seven. Benedict's Rule is telling me, *not now*, later, in retirement's time. We see nothing amiss in rearranging the times of life as easily as I changed my exercise schedule.

But where others are involved—as they are in Benedictine communities or in life phases, I think Benedict speaks clearly, even if counterculturally, to "having it all,' and all of it when we want it.

~

Vespers. I need this coda, the end part of my visit formally prayed and sung before I slip back into the world. If I do this enough, surely some of it will stick to me as I make my way down the hill.

The thick smoky clouds file in from the ocean as the monks file out.

April 20, 2000: Holy Thursday of the Lord's Last Supper

We older Episcopalians once called it Maundy Thursday. I didn't know what it meant, but it had a grand, poetic sound that lent solemnity to the speaker. I still call it Maundy Thursday.

I am so happy and grateful to be here, which is almost silly, since I remember a difficult time here last year, dreadful weather. Good omen today: the weather is so suddenly, abruptly perfect that it *tastes* like Easter.

But let us not rush the ending without paying our dues just a bit. It is still Lent, and the approaching hours ahead will be rich with intensity. I woke up repeatedly last night, my stomach in knots over the age-old story that would unfold around me real time in the days ahead. The feeling is identical to what I felt the night before I returned to the family home to be at my father's death—knowing, and yet not really knowing, what would have to transpire before I returned. Knowing there would be no escape, no avoidance, no looking away (*Take thou this cup away . . .*).

I got here early to settle in, unpack, try to stop vibrating from the pressures of a workday that began on the freeway at 6:15 A.M. Work pressures leave almost as soon as I unpack. There is a bigger story here today than my efforts to create a technology partnership between the university and a children's advocacy network.

Brother Robert is wheeled in to the abbey church half an hour before the bells ring the Mass's beginning. Usually he is the last in. I can understand *my* needing to get here early to get a seat—but Brother Robert has no such concern!

This Holy Thursday of the Last Supper—for all the foot washings and other attachments of authenticity—is a day on which the Eucharist (what I, in my Episcopalian language still refer to as "holy communion") is the central reenactment. I know some Catholics who feel "called" to daily Eucharist. I am not such a one, and I blame my non-Catholic upbringing for not understanding its centrality or appreciating those with such a call. Abbot Antony and I were heading for the cafeteria after Mass one day and a gentleman stopped him to say, "I'm here on retreat to celebrate ten years since I was first called to daily Mass. I haven't missed a day in ten years."

"That's *very good*," the abbot said, approvingly. As we continued our walk, he said to me, "So many good people in this world."

I thought it was icky, especially in a guy, but then the abbot radiates Christian holiness and I radiate impatience, intolerance, and too much caffeine as a general sort of rule. To Episcopalians of the fifties and early sixties, the Communion Service was just "the really long one" we got stuck with once a month—and with a sermon too. Even now, I can barely sit through the entire service, and sometimes even bow out before the "goodies" (communion) are distributed.

But not today. This is the day it's all based on, the Last Supper and first Eucharist . . .

Chapters 43–46: Latecomers, Laggards, Mistakes, and Their Satisfaction

Reflecting the importance of timeliness and order to Benedict, these chapters deal with tardiness and mistakes. Lateness to prayer or meals requires making amends. The way of making amends (prostrating before all) is spelled out. Mistakes in any part of the Office are to be corrected immediately.

Surely Benedict had monks like me! In the parish church I eventually settled on, I established "my" seating in a side wing of the magnificent church in an area I called L3: the lame, the lapsed, the late. Away from the main throng, and only in the peripheral view of the priest, the handicapped find their tortured way, the unfamiliar slip in hoping to be swallowed up, and the tardy rush in clutching children and coloring books. I have my own reasons for sitting there.

I arrive very early for Mass, usually forty-five minutes before it begins, frequently the only one there, except the priest, who is waiting in vain for confessions, and probably wondering when I'll get up my nerve to approach the confessional. In the cool, prayerful gloom, surrounded by some of the best modern religious art I have ever seen, and with St. Francis's San Damiano Cross for company (mine does not issue Calls, however), I read the "spiritual lite" books that make Abbot Antony try to upgrade my reading. ("St. Augustine's *Confessions* is good," he offers up. "You'd like him." "Oh, Abbot, that's too *hard* for me. Is there a book *about* his confession? Did his mother write letters to him I can read or something?") The church fills in the last minutes before Mass begins. L3 fills up in the ten minutes *after* Mass begins.

I usually read through the sermon. "If I wanted a good sermon, I'd stay Protestant," I say about the tepid tradition of Catholic homely homilies. And that's the real reason I sit in L3—so the priest won't see somebody in the front row reading a book, and highlighting madly while doing so. I share my row with children with coloring books, who are busy with their toys for probably the same reason.

So why would I sit in the front row if I'm going to be so noticeably doing something quite different from the rest of the congregation? *The attention they attract will shame them into mending*, Benedict says, hopefully (chapter 43:7). I don't want to mend, so I stay in L3. Besides, as soon as I receive communion, I turn around and instead of returning to my seat, walk out the door and zoom out of the parking lot before anybody else.

It's my horror of announcements about ham-and-bean suppers from the pulpit, I tell Felix. Not that this high-brow church with the gorgeous art has ham-and-bean suppers, but I grew up on ham-and-bean supper announcements and all kinds of money-making and community-making activities that needed pitching from the pulpit—usually from my father. I fantasized about Jesus overturning the tables of the money changers in the churches of Pawtucket, Rhode Island, someday, because I understood.

I never told Abbot Antony about leaving early. I had shocked him enough with my reading during the sermons. But telling him the bit I did and seeing his dismay has begun some change. As the Rule says (chapter 46:5–6), *When the cause of the sin lies hidden in his conscience, he is to reveal it only to the abbot . . . who know how to heal their own wounds without exposing them and making them public.* I don't honestly know the cause of my sin, only what it looks like. But the abbey church, not being a parish, has no announcement, no newsletters, doesn't even take up collections. Their community is their own, and I am allowed to merely visit. I am not troubled in spirit by this kind of community then, and so I stay until the end.

> The old ones told of a certain old man that when his thoughts said to him, "Let be today: thou shalt repent tomorrow," he would contradict them, saying, "Nay, but I shall repent today: tomorrow may the will of God be done."[4]

Most of the sermons here are a bore, but I practice listening and obedience at least, watching my old abbot sunk into his chair looking like a sponge soaking up the Word of the Lord.

It is a beginning.

~

The Lord's Last Supper. Abbot Henry, wearing a high white miter, like a bishop becoming an angel, is escorted in with great pomp, his magisterial shepherd's crook, and much incense. We cough immediately, unmagisterially. I suddenly realize that these days of the Easter Triduum—another grand word not much in our mouths anymore—are the only days on which the abbot presides.

This Abbot Henry, as a young man, used to dance Polish folk dances with his sister in Balboa Park on Polish Hospitality House days. He went to college at San Diego State University, and asked them at the Newman Center, "Where's a Benedictine monastery around here?" And they brought him here, overlooking El Camino Real—the King's Highway of the early Franciscans—to St. Augustine's Abbey. This is his sixth holy days as abbot since my old abbot retired.

The glory of his entry—with the taste of memory of Palm Sunday so recently celebrated—is in sharp contrast to what comes later in the service, the humility of stripping off his outer robe, putting on an apron, and washing the feet of the priests and monks. Even the newest, lowest-rank monks, who just weeks ago threw themselves prostrate on the floor of the abbey to move from candidate to novitiate, even they sit in the seats in front where only the priests normally sit, and their feet are washed too.

Nobody imitates Peter's boldness, however; he is reported to have said, when Jesus washed his feet: *Lord, not my feet only, but also my hands and my head!* (John 13:9). It is pretty hard to witness this humility. Much of the congregation sings endless verses of the anthem, never lifting their eyes from the page until the washing is over.

No, I don't have any particular call to the Eucharist and I'm not even polite about it most of the time. I don't miss it—until now, the end of this Mass, when it is all swept away under the eagle wings of Abbot Henry and his robes, and I hear in my head Mary Magdalene's words: *They have taken away my Lord, and I know not where they have laid him* (John 20:13). I find myself nearly in tears as the monks form an honor guard at the back of the abbey church, and the Sacramental Body is borne away.

⁓

A certain brother went to Abbot Moses in Scete and asked him for a good word. And the elder said to him, "Go, sit in your cell, and your cell with teach you everything."[5]

This is not last year's retreat, which is good, because as Abbot Antony would say, I am not last year's person either. Barely unpacked last year, I was writing notes to myself that read, "Remind myself, I can always go home if it gets too awful. What's going on? I have never *ever* had that thought at a retreat." I thought I liked retreats. I had been addicted to them as a Franciscan Secular and here I was, barely an hour into a retreat at a Benedictine monastery, comforting myself with thoughts of home.

I didn't feel comfortable, my room was awful, and the weather was even worse.

One year later, I light a candle in front of the small bas-relief of Our Lady of Lourdes done in glass that I inherited from a Catholic relative and brought with me today. I ignore the signs—"no food or drink in rooms"—and make herbal tea in the portable coffeepot I brought. (I did not travel light on this retreat, I will admit.) I am content to stay in my cell and eat my bread here instead of going to the cafeteria for meals as I did last year. Not only was I cranky with hunger since I was fasting, I was irritable at the noise from the other retreatants.

My cell will teach me everything. I was so disappointed nine months ago when I learned my room assignment for this retreat. It is isolated from the retreat center's core and faces the back wall of the cloister. I wanted to see stuff—and probably be seen in all my holiness as well. But this year there are Easter lilies planted right next to my door—the only ones in the retreat center area. And inside, these rooms are either newer or redone. Simple and plain, but not hideously decorated as my room was last year. The candle flickers against the faceted face of the bas-relief of Our Lady. The desk is enormous. I am so glad I get to stay here.

Compline. The sky draws black streaks against a dark blue background. There is a deeper hush now than during the day. People are sitting near the Blessed Sacrament, keeping watch. "Please leave room for us," Brother Stephen pleaded awkwardly early before Mass began. But we are looking to pay reparation for our terrible sin—"Couldest not thou watch one hour?" (Mark 14:37).

The sky goes all black, black-robed monks blur against an inky sky above the night-black Pacific. The blackness wins.

Magnum Silentium.

April 21, 2000: Good Friday of the Lord's Passion and Death

In a rare burst of consideration versus personal preference, I forgive showering and using my hairdryer until after Vigils at 5:30 A.M. Judging by our appearance, as about half the retreatants stagger in, I am not the only one who has made this choice. Frankly, we look like hell.

It is dark in a cloud-filled, soft kind of way at 5:00 A.M., and deeply silent, since even the birds have an hour or so left on their snooze alarm. Isaiah—my current *lectio* reading book, begun before Christmas—beckons appropriately: "For, behold, the darkness shall cover the earth, and gross darkness the people" (60:2).

Lectio: This seems fitting enough for Good Friday (which I always thought ironically named). It is not *supposed* to be a day of grieving, says the missal, but surely it was once a great day of darkness. I associate these days with my father's dying two years ago during Lent and Easter. To think of what we witnessed—the ugly, senseless death of a decent, God-fearing man—makes me wonder how *any* faith, except blind hope or denial, could flourish in such darkness.

Our souls are in their most endangered state just before the light. You think it will never come, the light. You forget the faithfulness of light and make plans under the cover of darkness. It is not a good thing to forget the light of the world.

So it is with Christ. Today we celebrate the brutal dying of the light. Others have died more brutal deaths, but others have not been God in their dying. Today we will lay our hopes in the tomb. We live our darkness daily in thousands of little ways, but today celebrates the darkness that spreads its stain across the earth.

There is nothing to do but to behold the darkness today, since, of our own accord, we cannot return the light. In our darkness we must hold on to some blind faith and *know* the light will come again as he promised, to renew the face of the earth.

~

Abba Theodore said, "Privation of food mortifies the body of the monk." Another old man said, "Vigils mortify it still more."[6]

Vigils, 5:30 A.M. Vigils, the Bore, and for *this* I got up so blasted early and stand here forever with clumpy hair? We sit, then stand, then sit again, surrounded by darkness. The psalms roll along, and the biggest discipline is not flipping ahead to see if we're nearly *there* yet to the end. It would lead to despair—I resist. The Lamentation of Jeremiah, which make Isaiah's rantings look like puff pieces for a ladies' magazine, are chanted, and chanted again. (Whatever the missal says to churchgoers about this not being a day of grief does not apply to the first thing in a Benedictine's day, listening to the Lamentations of Jeremiah.) "Mine eyes do fail with tears, my bowels are troubled, my liver is poured upon the earth, for the destruction of the daughter of my people" (Lamentations 2:11).

We are lamented into a dull, dusky dawn. We get there.

Thirty minutes round trip to shower, declump hair, blow dry, put in contact lenses, and try to look human. When I return to Lauds at 7:00, we go back to the same themes. Definitely darkness today.

~

My room may feel isolated and off the beaten track, but it is apparently part of the walkway between the cloister and the retreat chapel. Black robes and measured, solemn steps have been coming past my desk for a whole hour. Brother Robert and later Father Jerome zip by, beyond Benedictine speed limits, in their various motorized wheel chairs.

"Boy, that's how I feel," I hear one shrouded figure say. "Lamentations."

I look at the printed schedule for the weekend. They are heading into "Chapter of Faults [For the Monastic Community Only]." As I dimly remember Abbot Antony explaining last year, Chapter is the official airing of dirty laundry at the monastery, the aches and annoyances of these people living together. ("We can't escape each other," Father Vincent said to me once. "We can't come here to get away. It gets very hard." "Try marriage," I wanted to say. "Try in-laws.")

Chapter 48: Daily Manual Labor

Benedict arranges the daily hours of work in accordance with the seasons, and also encourages the assignment of specific times for prayerful reading. Extra reading is prescribed during Lent. If a brother is unwilling or unable to read, he is given additional work to keep from idleness. *Yet all things are to be done with moderation on account of the fainthearted.*

This chapter takes three days to read in the daily cycle of reading, which seems appropriate given its emphasis on both labor *and* reading. Although the *lectio divina* so associated with the Benedictines does not get discussed in its formal, complicated way anywhere in the Rule, commentaries take the opportunity to discuss it within this section on daily manual labor, and so shall I.

Like many people granted the luxury (and obligations) of a solid education, living as "information workers," I do not make my living by manual labor. Nor do I toil in the soil and weeds around my house as "chores." Nor do I find yard work particularly rewarding as a hobby. Here in southern California, such work can be hired out cheaply if you don't mind a language barrier (Spanish or Vietnamese), and that is what I do.

For some reason, I draw the line at housecleaning. Although I can also probably bring someone in cheaply to clean my house, I have only done so in my last year of graduate school.

Restoring a house to order and cleanliness can be tiring and time-consuming, even when there are only two rather neat adults and one comparatively neat pet bird—"comparative" in the case of a cockatiel compared to the shedding and shredding of cats, which I had for the years before I met Felix, who, despite his name, hates cats. For some reason, I am reminded of the prayer work lady as I write this, probably because I load up on paper towels, cleaning solutions, dusters, and the vacuum cleaner the way she does on Fridays when I am tackling my aging but graceful small house.

I would like to report that this mindless work somehow joins me to God, as Benedict assures me in the opening of this chapter: *Idleness is an enemy of the soul.* But the disturbing truth is that great quantities of anger and hurt from past and present sources almost always surface along with the physical dust, and I cannot count the times I have pushed the vacuum cleaner and my tears at the same time.

I don't know why this is, or if these things need to find expression until, like demons, they can be removed by time and grace. Perhaps I need to turn my "mindless" physical activity into "mindful" work.

In one area of my life, I have seen this turn, from mindless to mindful, and it is a turn of radical proportions. I started stitching (needlepoint, crewel embroidery, cross-stitch) when I first left home at twenty-one, and when I sobered up some years later, stitching became the furious salvation of my hands.

Sitting at a cafeteria lunch table, talking early sobriety with my sponsor, eating my lunch *and* stitching a piece of needlepoint, I must have looked like a portrait of black energy with the title, "Alcoholism Thwarted." It became my substitute for drinking, which had become my substitute for the dreamscape of reading that I lived in my childhood and adolescence. I must have looked like I was pulling my alcoholic weeds out by the roots the way I pulled those yarns through the stiff-backed needlework canvasses.

I made sixteen complete, full-size pillow-back pieces in the first three months of sobriety—more than most normal people would stitch in a lifetime. I had to throw them all away. They were a complete mess, each one of them, as was their stitcher.

Stitching quieted down to my "idle activity" after that, flaring to mania every time I quit smoking. Like Benedict, and Cotton Mather, and all my sturdy Protestant Puritan forbearers, I believe that idle hands are the devil's workshop, and I capped my idleness with large needle-pointed pillows.

As I noted earlier, at some point after one of many Franciscan retreats, I turned the mindless into mindful and began to make those book-marks to send to the elderly or ill Franciscans whose names appeared faithfully each week in the Mission's parish bulletin. Stitching became a wordless prayer act, or, as I put in the bookmark I made for Sister Pat, my Franciscan spiritual advisor, "My prayer life is in my hands."

I don't do that particular prayer work anymore, and I still miss it. But as I begin stitching my third baby quilt in nine months for some unsuspecting embryonic baby, I know how my fierce and favorite St. Paul could find God as he made his living as a tent-maker, and I have a sense of connection with the ancient desert fathers who weaved bas-kets in their cells.

> Abba Locus told of how to pray without ceasing: "I sit down with God, soaking my reeds and plaiting my ropes, and I say, 'God, have mercy on me according to your great goodness and according to the multitude of your mercies, save me from my sins.' Is this not a prayer?" They agreed it was. Abba Locus continued. "So when I have spent the whole day working and praying, making thirteen pieces of money more or less, I put two pieces of money outside the door and I pay for my food with the rest of the money. He who takes the two pieces of money prays for me when I am eating and when I am sleeping; so by the grace of God, I fulfill the pre-cept to pray without ceasing."[7]

But reading is another story, and *lectio divina* has been my bane as a Benedictine oblate novice.

"I don't understand *lectio*," I complained to Abbot Antony nearly every time I saw him for the first six months (where my spiritual des-peration must have looked as fierce and demon-driven as my early sobriety once did). He found me a lecture on the subject given to the monks to read. He implied that if I simply read the good books slowly, the Holy Spirit would do the rest.

Lectio divina can be quite a daunting practice to the uninitiated. Instructions I got from a Benedictine web site told me to find a quiet place where I would not be disturbed for twenty minutes. I would read slowly, stop when "inspired" and follow six easy steps: *lectio* (read), *ruminatio* ("chew" the text, mull it over), *meditatio* (reflect on text), *contemplatio* (reflect on how it can be applied to my life as a Christian), *oratio* (ask for assistance to enact these thoughts in my life), and *actio* (take action on the fruits of meditation).

I was not keeping it simple. I read books on the subject of reading books. I made collages of the phrases that caught my attention. I fell asleep at 5:00 A.M. a lot in boredom as I tried to *not* speed-read the psalms.

Finally I gave up the formal methodical approach. As a Franciscan moth, I think I could have burned brighter before extinguishing. The practices of the Benedictines seem to require a dimmer switch, and I possess only "on" and "off" ones. As a habitual diarist for years, I had learned to "think" through my right hand, my pen—to the point where I had to handwrite the entire draft of my graduate thesis if I wanted to say anything with depth. Perhaps *lectio* could become for me a right-hand activity.

In this last year, that is how it has worked—two or three pages per day "writing *lectio*" on the verse or phrase that caught my gyratory eye the night before. Sometimes the dry page before me ignites with the spark of the Holy Spirit. Most mornings, my whiney self grips the pen tightly. But the psalms of David, the letters of Paul, the tribulations of Job and now the sighs and furies of Isaiah have all been my teachers, forming me slowly in the meaning of the Word.

~

The sun finally climbs above the fog banks and the temperature becomes—well, if not warm, then "less cool." I need to clear some mental fog banks of my own, so I do a brisk (and wary) turn along the prayer walk.

The wildflowers have exploded along the bluff, thanks to this week's rain. Gaudy colors—yellow, orange, purple—are set against pale white columbines made more beautiful by their stark contrast to the gaudy ones. Franciscan colors, I think. Franciscan wildness. Not Benedictine tidiness or reserve at all. But just beyond the fog banks, on the other side of the highway, I can see the Franciscan Mission from the prayer walk. Their gardens and prayer walks are immaculately maintained. So much for stereotype and geography.

There is a stiffening ocean breeze, and I'm the only short-sleeved fool out here. The monoliths are returning, our deep (probably pagan) urge to "make something," like a shrine to our desires. Rocks are back, piling up, and wildflowers, plucked and mounted, are on most of the Stations.

I gather robin-egg-blue rocks for my collection, and then it is nearly time for Sext, one of the most interestingly named of the seven possible daily offices that monasteries may observe. Here at St. Augustine's Abbey, it is not one of the offices said daily, and is only being used during the Triduum because of the special services being held in place of the usual daily Mass.

Which is too bad, because this little Sext really *zips*, ten minutes start to done, my kind of office.

Chapter 49: Lent Observance

Although a monk's life should be like a long Lent, few have the strength necessary, says Benedict. So Lent must serve as a time to add to the usual measure of service to God in prayer and abstinence so as to look forward to Easter. All of these extra measures must be done with the approval of the abbot.

How appropriate and timely to get to study this chapter at the end days of my second Lent as a Benedictine under a rule.

More so than with most of the Rule, Abbot Antony's oblates live under this particular chapter. *A monk's life should always be like a Lenten observance, writes Benedict. Since few are capable of this, we urge that during Lent we conduct our lives with the greatest possible purity.* Perhaps Abbot Antony suspects that if few monks can live a life of Lent, then virtually no oblates can, so he tries to pack as much holiness as possible into our forty days.

We each receive a "Lenten Opera" sheet just before Lent, encouraging us to reread this short chapter of the Rule and also "The Royal Road of the Holy Cross" in *The Imitation of Christ*.

Then, prayerfully, we write the details of how we will add prayer or abstinence into our lives during Lent. The monks fill out the same form, Abbot Antony tells us, and all are submitted to Abbot Henry because *everything must be done with the abbot's approval*. This is eventually returned with a word or two of blessing from Abbot Henry.

Last year, Abbot Henry wrote, "May the Lord in his mercy deepen your joy of self-denial!" which I found comforting and saving on fast days. This year, he wrote, "May our Lord grant you the wisdom and strength to follow him more closely in this Lent," which looked like something fished out of a Benedictine fortune cookie—or I may have been acting my usual, irritable self. But I found the phrase, "in feast and in fast" from a book I was reading, and that became the blessing of this Lent.

While a monk's life ideally is lived in Lent, I am reminded of how St. Francis lived "four Lents" of fasting and penance—four times a year at forty days each. "Do the math," Father Rusty had said. "Malnourishment did him in." I am not a Franciscan anymore, although I understand the temperament, having once written a note in my prayer journal suggesting for myself "a great fast of forty days for humility." I saw the humor of that statement only much later.

There are only three lines to fill out on our Lenten Opera, certainly helpful in keeping us from "resumption and vainglory" as Benedict calls such "grandness." I think last year I chose to fast once a week on bread and water and say the rosary each day. As I have moved (however imperceptibly) "deeper" into Benedictine spirituality, I have also moved away from the rosaries, novenas, and other "goodies" that were so attractive to me in Catholicism, into some desert "basics"—the Rule, the Office, the Word. This year, I decided to fast two days a week, plus the Holy Days, and read *The Imitation of Christ*, since it is Abbot Antony's favorite book. I lined up the *Imitation* at three sections a day, so it wouldn't crush me as "too hard" to read.

> Abba Isidore said, "If you fast regularly, do not be inflated with pride, but if you think highly of yourself because of it, then you had better eat meat. It is better for a man to eat meat than to be inflated with pride and to glorify himself."[8]

The fasting mostly teaches me I can't have everything I want when I want it. The antiphon for the Canticle of Zechariah each Sunday in Lent seems understated: *And when he had fasted for forty days and forty nights, he was hungry.*

I bet he was, I would think irreverently, but with an edge of understanding. And then I'd throw another five dollars into my "fast food envelope"—the idea being to stuff it full instead of me. The *Imitation* was a nightly chore, but taken in such small pieces—and Abbot Antony is so drenched in its values that reading it was like listening to him—it could be done.

What was nearly impossible, however, was the ordinary discipline, the things like exercising, early rising, and three pages of written *lectio* that I'd already been doing. I didn't really "add to our customary servitude" as Benedict suggests we do in this chapter, but made substitutions—for "credit" as Lenten Opera.

I hoped for a deep spirit of penance in my Lenten observance this year, but my weaknesses and sins brought me dissolution instead. If I just showed up where I'd promised myself I'd be, it would have been a beginning of Lenten discipline. But I couldn't manage even that.

Still, Isaiah reminds me that the Lord has chosen me "in the furnace of affliction" (48:10). So afflicted, so aware of my sins in a way that success would not have given me, I too *look toward the holy feast of Easter with the joy of spiritual desire.*

I am also looking forward to what's being served for breakfast here on Easter morning.

~

By the time we're ready to begin the Liturgy of Good Friday, at 2:30 P.M., the sun is nearly blotted from the sky. (Didn't I *begin* the day with Isaiah, "and behold, the darkness shall cover the earth . . . "?) The mist is starting to look like rain. No more prayer walks today I think—and then off to the Passion.

There are people *all over* the abbey church. It swarms with piety, people walking along and meditating on the Stations of the Cross, which, in this very modern church, is a series of stylized suggestions of line carvings placed in embedded tiles on the walls, like a checker game, with praying rosaries in every nook and cranny. If you don't watch where you walk, you'll go flying over people whose meditative devotion has them flat out or bowed down in some walkway.

I start to get cranky. Crowds do that anyway to me, and such religious behavior—*excess* is what I want to say, although that is judgmental—

unnerves me. Working-class Episcopalians in New England in the old church were a highly restrained lot. These people are deeply into emotive Catholicism.

Outside, the sky erupts into rain and storminess. Inside, Father Cornelius, Abbot Henry, and Brother John Climachus are chanting the Passion According to St. John. The chant is a particularly tuneless and lengthy bit of work. All the emotionalism of the congregation simmers way down. Brother Dominic falls asleep in the choir.

Memory. Mr. Neild was the rector at our small-town, low-Episcopal Church. ("Low" meant that our rites leaned to the plainness of the Protestants rather than the gaudier colors of Catholicism. The Episcopal Church of my childhood was quite roomy, and culture and tradition varied greatly depending on the average salary of the congregation. Low church was working class. High church with the incense and genuflecting belonged to the East Side of Providence churches.) Mr. Neild preached a Good Friday service attended by maybe thirty or so of the faithful. With no music, no flowers, the stained glass darkened, and the simple cross draped in black, this was generally regarded as a service "too depressing to bother with"— especially before Easter.

We settled in for a few words about the awfulness, and Mr. Neild leaned forward and said, "Ladies, how would you like to watch your son die?"

There was a breathless, horrific silence, broken only by Mr. Neild's next question. "And how would you like to stand there watching while everybody around you is laughing at him?"

I certainly didn't need reading—or chanting, or "bells and smells" as the Franciscans said—to stay still then. That was more than thirty years ago, and it cuts through liturgical numbness even now. I *got* Good Friday that year. I bet twenty-nine other people did too.

I silently erupt into major crankiness of my own as these guys around me chant, preach, venerate, and lament for the next hour. Why can't I go be Episcopalian again? This stuff is rubbish. All of it. Why can't I at least skip Vigils at 5:30 tomorrow morning? I hate Vigils. Why do I have to sit in front of tone-deaf people who love to sing and next to people who crowd me off my kneeler? Doesn't anybody up at the altar know what they're *doing*? Does any of this mean anything to anybody? Can I go home yet?

I don't know why these eruptions happen. I only know that since becoming a Benedictine, I am technically bound to fidelity, and that keeps me from jumping ship every time I go off in my mind. The year before I met Abbot Antony, I had bounced between Catholic and Episcopalian *twice*—probably responding to my dear Catholic-turned-Episcopalian father's death—joined four churches, dropped three of them, returned to the Secular Franciscans and been dismissed by them—probably a month before I would have dismissed *them*.

Just do it, I tell myself wearily when I am loosed from the service. This retreat—*my* retreat, "self-directed" as they call it—is a fantasy time for me, to be alone, to write, to study, to read, and to pray. I am not terribly gifted on the prayer end—no patience, too much coffee, probably too much arrogance, and not enough faith—so coming together five times a day incorporates the prayer life around me. Just do it. I'd blame the fasting for irritability, but I seem to have been born slamming doors shut behind me and then wondering where everybody went.

Fasting Prayer (just made up): Bless this bread we are about to eat. May it nourish our body and free us to focus on our hunger for the Living Bread of Heaven, in Christ Jesus, Amen.

In the room next to mine, the elderly nun who walks with a cane begins to sing plaintive hymns. I no longer feel crabby at all. In the distance, a tentative flute trills. I open my door to locate it. Apparently the cloister area has a flute player. It seems the perfect prelude to Compline. The singing stops and there is a moment that glows with peace.

Then the nun's cell phone rings.

My own desk phone rings moments later. "How *are* you?" Abbot Antony says. "Where have you been? I have a book to lend you. I think you'd like it."

"I've been in my room. And at the prayers." Oh, please give me credit for going to all that praying!

"What about meals? I came to find you at meals."

"I'm not eating."

"What about tomorrow?"

"Not until Easter."

Silence. "Oh. Well, be careful. Make sure you have enough to drink. I'll come over with this book."

"Do you know where I'm staying?"

Silence again. Then, "Yes, Room 26. The same number as I dialed for your extension."

He came after me last year on Holy Saturday, looking like a flapping, stilted crow in the weather with his surgically replaced hips. Last year he had a Caryll Houselander book he knew I would "love" and I was pretty sure I would hate. He was right that time, but I didn't bring a lot to read with me on that retreat either, which might have affected my interest. This year it is *Christ, Our Brother* by Karl Adam.

There are fierce signs in the main library saying that those on retreat can use the books, but not check them out. "Please do not put a monk in an awkward position by asking him to check out a book for you," says one particular sign posted several places in the library, and also in our retreat rooms next to a list of the books we can read in the library (but not check out). Abbot Antony doesn't wait to be put into an awkward position: he checks them out in his name and hands me his when he's done reading!

"I read this after I was ordained," he says when he arrives. "It was sixty years ago. Maybe longer. I was thinking about it the other day and went to see if our library had it. Which we *did*. And so I have read it *twice*. I devoured it." It's uncharacteristic of him to show so much fervor. I am pretty sure I will hate it. I never learn anything. But I am also hungry enough to "devour" anything.

∼

Compline. It is *pouring* out. And cold, like last year's dismal retreat that I barely stuck out. I am fine now, which must be grace, as it certainly isn't my even disposition.

Compline Prayer (just made up): I am a poor pilgrim who does not know how to pray—unless this happy determination to stay alone in my cell and write somehow counts as living prayer. It cannot. Too presumptuous. Too pleasing in my sight. End prayer.

I change my seat at the abbey church from center to right. There is a ribbon of ocean viewable from my seat.

It is finished.

April 22, 2000: Holy Saturday of the Lord's Rest

Some rest. Up at 5:00 again for Vigils. Five Lamentations of Jeremiah sung this morning, and heavy overcast skies, and you think, *It's going to be one of those days.*

Holy Saturday held a certain magic for me as a kid. "Taint Day" I called it: "taint" Good Friday and "taint" Easter yet. As a kid with a good imagination superimposed on a literal understanding of the world—plus a *Bible Stories for Young Readers* that I delved into so often the pictures are still engrained in my brain—I thought a lot about Holy Saturday:

> *What's he doing? Is he arguing with the Devil? Is he getting ready to come back? Is he figuring out whom to visit first? Is he remembering everything that happened yesterday? Is the Devil trying to keep him there?*

In the low Episcopal Church, the cross had been covered with black gauze since Friday, and the church itself was bare and deserted. It seemed to me, as a child, that this Saturday was the one day of the year when God was gone from us, we had done it ourselves, and we'd better be pretty careful to tiptoe through those hours until the Easter lilies came out in the pots on Sunday morning and the ladies of the church came out with the new yellow hats and white shoes—not allowed until Easter Sunday—and we in the choir were allowed to wear our heavily starched white robes.

Even as a kid, without knowing the theology or the language, I had some dim awareness that today was an extraordinary day, that the forces of life, led by Jesus, were doing battle with the forces of death, and that my salvation hung in the balance.

It isn't that stark anymore. The changes in church liturgy in both Catholic and Episcopal Churches of the late 1960s brought about a focus on the Easter Vigil, which begins at 9:30 tonight and lasts forever. (I was confirmed somewhere in the middle of the Easter Vigil ten years ago exactly, and even then, I thought we would never get out of there. Felix and his relatives—all making a rare church appearance—agreed that this one service would last them at least another ten years.)

The Easter Vigil strikes me as a way to cope with our anxiety over the emptiness of Holy Saturday. There's a battle going on for our redemption, and right now we'd like to fast forward to the ending as quickly as possible.

Chapters 50, 51, and 67: Traveling, Near and Far

Travel puts a particular strain on the monk's regulated life. The Office is to be said wherever the monk is, and if the monk is expected back the same day, he will not eat until he returns. On a longer trip, the community will pray for the absent brethren. Upon his return, the monk is *not* to talk about what he saw or heard.

To me, these chapters are key ones for ordinary oblates like me, since in a very literal sense, we "travel" from the monastery *all* the time, coming here only to visit.

Not that this is a bad thing on our part. Just as Benedict is concerned that traveling brothers bring their adventures back with them, we oblates need to remember that our "adventures" in Benedictine life are just that—the stories of travelers. This is not our home, and no matter how much we fancy the notion, we are not called to be consecrated monks, but ordinary citizens for Christ in the world.

> Abbot Arsenius lived in a cell thirty-two miles away from his nearest neighbor, and he seldom went out of it. The things he needed were brought there by disciples. But when the desert of Scete where he lived became peopled with hermits, he went away from there weeping and saying, "Worldly men have ruined Rome and monks have ruined Scete."[9]

The link between the monastery and the world is prayer. I especially like the phrase Brother Benet Tvedten uses in his commentary on these chapters when he writes, "Prayer is an obligation and an occupation."[10] I keep thinking my occupation is that niche that carries a paycheck every month—"lobbyist," "speechwriter." Brother Benet reminds me here of my occupation according to St. Paul: "ambassador of Christ" (2 Corinthians 5:20). As Joseph Holzner lays it out in his life of Paul, which I am reading here on retreat this weekend, "A Christian has this duty: to give to God what is God's, to seek the kingdom of God, and to do his duty with regard to the state."[11]

I spent a lot of time—and money—on books, trying to develop the perfect prayer life and never finding one. The Catholic Church has a rich and diverse tradition of prayer that, as a fresh-eyed convert, I dove into: the rosary, the novenas, the Marian prayers, the devotions to the saints, the exposition of the Sacrament, contemplative prayer, praising prayer, centering prayer—all of it. Every time I went on a Franciscan retreat, they assured me there was no one perfect prayer life and offered me new tools to inspect and try. It was quite dizzying, and I became even more a gyratory in my prayer life than in searching for God in the first place.

Finally I took the easy way out—I did what Abbot Antony suggested to all his oblates and tried the Divine Office. The monks use a large, four-volume *Liturgy of the Hours*, but as Abbot Antony helpfully noted, those books are left in the monks' choir stall and not dragged around. I got the *Shorter Christian Prayer* version. Although it is more than six hundred pages, it is small enough to put in a pocketbook. Mine "lives" in San Diego, but has seen duty in Sacramento, Boston, Washington, D.C., Hawaii, Asia, and Europe. It is my orientation to daybreak no matter where I am, and the Evening Prayer is my lullaby. It has the four-week psalter, which doesn't include all 150 psalms.

But the psalms included are all the great ones. And it is their familiarity over time, said slowly in heartache, distractedly in life's rush, quickly in joy, that create a rhythm underlying all of life, a beginning of perseverance that matters. It builds as St. Paul lays out a ladder: *knowing that tribulation worketh patience; and patience, experience; and experience, hope: and hope maketh not ashamed . . .* (Romans 5:3–5).

I probably would not have gotten into the Divine Office except the abbot suggested it was the one best thing for an oblate novice to do, and I wanted to be the best oblate novice. He spent an hour one day after lunch fingering the baby-fine Bible paper of my small book, while murmuring about "the richness" of the four-volume edition. I was untempted. This was plenty to master, and besides, hadn't he told me only two months ago that reading the Rule was the one best thing for an oblate novice to do, and wasn't I doing that daily already?

It is not a perfect prayer life. By that I mean it does not come out to greet all my moods, but rather accepts them and treats them consistently. Benedict says to not neglect the Divine Office, no matter where I am, that I should *say the Hours as best [I] can, to fulfill their duty as servants of God* (chapter 50).

My little rust-colored book travels to Sacramento and Washington, D.C., regularly. Like Naomi of the Old Testament, I could say to it: "Intreat me not to leave thee, or to return from following after thee:

for whither thou goest, I will go" (Ruth 1:16). It is the Divine Office, the morning and evening "bookends" of my days, my link to my monastery, my link to God.

⁓

Wafting from the cloister area is the sound of a harp carefully being plucked. Brother Bernard played it at our Epiphany party right after I became an oblate novice. It was left behind by a monastic candidate who chose to leave. Brother Bernard is novice master for the monks, and also cantor, so it seems fitting for him to take up this instrument of Psalm 150's glory: "Praise him with psaltery and harp."

Most of the monks seem to have both obligation and occupation at the monastery. Brother Maurius is the master of ceremony for Mass and also the secretary to both abbots. Brother Matthew is altar server and also business manager. Brother John Climachus sings choir and is retreat master. I don't know what the priest-monks do, although I would assume their occupations involve priestly roles. Even Abbot Antony, who is retired from his occupation ("old abbot") still has his obligation to the community's work of prayer as oblate master.

⁓

A trip around the prayer walk to stretch. The sky looks pregnant, ready to deliver rain, but under its laborious weight, the prayer walk is full of people praying. I do admire those good people and their prayers. I write this somewhat defensively because I was full of bad thoughts about them all day yesterday. My own stride is long on "walk" and short on "prayer." Let's face it; I'm stretching my legs and looking for a good rock. I have a distinctive walk that Felix can pick out of a crowd by its motion alone before he actually sees my face.

"You walk like you know exactly where you're going," he says, "even when I *know* you're lost."

This is true. I suspect I walk like I'm parting the Red Sea and I've got to get it done before they'll let me have ice cream for dessert. The sweet part is that I'm so lost that I have no idea I'm even lost at all. It's the destination that keeps moving on me. I know where I'm going. I recover a handsome reddish rock for my collection and a hot chocolate for my trouble and return to my cell.

Writing about prayer here and seeing those good souls walking tl prayer walk with their beads, their crosses, their prayer books and chaplets, or sitting on the stone benches in contemplation and feeling guilty for some ugly comparative prayer practice thoughts yesterday, all lead me to think about the subject more. I am pretty sure Catholicism was attractive to me because it was a sacramentally based church, not emotionally driven like the fundamentalists, or spirit-driven like the charismatics, or logos-driven like the Bible-based churches, or socially driven like the New Age Protestant sorts. But having said that, I wonder what I mean by it. Yesterday's liturgies (Vigils, Lauds, Sext, Liturgy of Good Friday) totaled three-and-a-half hours (I kept track). Today because of Easter Vigil, it will be more like four-and-a-half hours. Quite honestly, I get liturgically fatigued pretty quickly. This is the person who can't sit through a weekly one-hour Mass.

Obviously not everybody feels the way I do. I arrive for Vigils fifteen minutes early. Abbot Antony is already there in his place. Last year after rocking and rolling through an Easter Vigil until 11:30 P.M. and then refreshments until midnight and then moving the clocks forward to 1:00 A.M. for Daylight Savings Time, Abbot Antony was first to arrive for Lauds the next morning.

"The liturgy is what we live by," he told me when I was getting ready to dive into Easter breakfast last year.

What, then, do I live by?

My angel-oblate classmate Hildegard is here this weekend, deep in prayer and clasped hands and solitary walks and sits. *What can she be praying about?* I wonder crossly.

Milan, the oblate from Viet Nam, arrives in time for Vigils and stays through Compline—fifteen hours a day. She carries a Bible, prayer books, beads, and devotions. I see her in various part of the retreat center's public space all day doing something from her spiritual busy bag.

It's easy to say, *I have no gift for this*, and keep moving briskly along. But, without anything so grand as a "call," what is it, then, that I live by?

I review my "company" of saints for answers. When I was working with Sister Pat, my Franciscan spiritual advisor, and I was in such despair at not being liked for who I was, I asked her, "And will the company of saints be enough for me?"

Over the two years of difficulties that followed, I filled my "company" couch slowly, and with three saints, all told. St. Paul, a giant for Christ, but small in stature, who spoke to me the hours before my father's death, was first on the couch, and his company was one of self-discipline (*It is for discipline that you have to endure . . .* [Hebrews 12:7]). St. Therésè de Lisieux, the Little Flower they call her, came next for her ability to believe throughout her disbelief.("Perfection consists in being what God wants us to be," she wrote, and God obviously wanted her to be his Little Flower.

And then Abbot Antony gave me Blessed Joanna Mary, a nobody, belittled by her own for her piety. All of those in my company of saints are small in some way, "be-littled." Sister Pat had said to me, "I've been thinking of you and your trials. I've been thinking you need to understand littleness." When all the doors slam shut on the search again and again, and you finally think that God himself has said, "thanks, but no thanks" to your meager offer of self,

What, then, do I live by?

Isaiah says it, dear, cranky, scattered Isaiah: "And the parched ground shall become a pool" (35:7).

This desert clay ground, parched, becomes brick hard most of the year. When the rains finally come, they cannot penetrate the ground or nourish deep roots. Instead, the rain hits the top of the ground and glances off, forming a pool.

Desert plants develop roots above ground or very near the surface that flourish when the rains finally come. I take comfort in watching this because I am a small spirit, no Little Flower, but maybe a Desert Flower, who does not know the Lord deeply, the way my fellow retreatants do. My roots are shallow, all surface, much dug up and replanted. But I can still drink the Word of God, the Rule of Benedict, the prayer of Divine Office as they pool alongside my hardened surface.

My prayer, what I live by, maybe is smallness, a little way to Christ in a land that emphasizes bigness. "For we stretch not ourselves beyond our measure . . ." (2 Corinthians 10:14).

~

Another turn around the prayer garden after lunch (bread for me). Still no sun, but warmer. We tend to get our "weather" (meaning the bad stuff; the good is taken for granted, wordless) either from the

Arctic Express (cold rain from the north) or the Pineapple Express (warm rain from the islands). The look has not changed, meaning rain, but the directional feel has, from Arctic to Pineapple.

Okay, I have a slightly different directional feel now myself, and it changes what I see. The rock I choose—how could I have missed it before?—is perfectly small, deeply purple, a magnificent little rock that I must have.

God has made us wonderfully small.

Chapter 52: The Oratory

The Oratory is as its name signifies (a place for prayer), says Benedict. *Nothing else is to be done or discussed there.* The place of prayer is reserved for that alone. After people are done with their prayers, they should leave respectfully so as not to disturb others.

I am half to the good on this chapter.

A place for prayer was apparently important for my parents to impart to their children. When my sister was about five and I about eight, my father actually built us a small altar for our shared bedroom. It was all wood, with a small surface bearing two candles, a plain cross coming up out of the back, and a kneeler on each side, one for my sister, one for me. I remember Ellen having the easier, shorter prayer to do because she was younger, and then I had mine to say (possibly the Apostles' Creed), then both of us, the Lord's Prayer.

I forgot all about that altar until I began going on Franciscan retreats. They had a wonderful spirit about creating prayer space, even in a big nondescript room full of retreatants: a friar's well-thumbed Bible open to a much-loved reading on a book stand, a small vase of flowers, and a candle, and suddenly you were in a place where you could pray.

When I became an oblate novice and began saying the Divine Office, I created an "oratory" next to my desk in the library. I brought the child's chair left behind by the previous owner of my house—an elderly woman, so there is no explaining this chair—and put a candle on it, plus the Office. That was all, but I sent my newly widowed mother a needlework cloth that Christmas and asked her to stitch it for my oratory, which she did.

Although my first Benedictine retreat here last Easter Holy Days was unpleasant for a variety of reasons, I brought home a rock with me. I desperately wanted a picture of me with my abbot, but I didn't want to bother Abbot Antony with a frivolous picture request during his Holy Week prayer. "Bless you for that," he said three weeks later when I came back to return the book he'd loaned me, camera and explanation also in hand. The little framed picture of us—me holding the book he lent me—joined the oratory, along with the wooden image of St. Benedict that was on the "free, take one" section of pamphlets in the main library of the abbey. Lastly, a cross with the Benedict medal embedded in its center is perched precariously next to Benedict. It came from Lourdes or somewhere similarly holy and was Gregory's gift from his pilgrimage when we made our oblate vows.

That's my oratory for daily prayer. When I'm traveling, I lay out the Divine Office and my prayer journal, and they become an oratory of remembrance, part of home.

> Amma Syncletica said, "There are many who live in the mountains and behave as if they were in the town, and they are wasting their time. It is possible to be a solitary in one's mind while living in a crowd, and it is possible for one who is a solitary to live in the crowd of his own thoughts."[12]

Where I am part bad, of course, is in the official, public oratory. "And don't take your knitting to church," says Brother Benet in his commentary on the rule for oblates, probably half-humorously.[13] I never brought my stitching, although I thought about it, probably because I wasn't a churchgoer in my frantic early days of stitching. I have brought diaries, and written in them, and certainly an arsenal of books, and their associated highlighters, markers, and pens. I give myself away with my choice of words: arsenal? Who, or what, am I at war with? As my capacity for prayer grows, I will have less need of such weapons. As I learn to listen, perhaps even less.

Anyway, there is not so much danger of disrespecting the oratory at the abbey. Last monk in, it seems, turns on the lights and until then, we are shrouded in gloom or glare from the ocean below. And as they file out, we are barely ready to genuflect when the stern snap of the lights going off indicates what Benedict says so clearly: *No one is to remain after the Divine Office, except for prayer.*

~

After writing of oratories I have known, I am finally relaxed enough to *desire* prayer. I want to spend a few minutes in the little chapel where I made my vows. I plan to say a decade of the rosary and read a piece of the Bible—any piece that finds me—and here's hoping, Lord, it's not Isaiah. *Or* Lamentations!

I flip my floppy-covered Bible open anywhere—the fortune-cookie approach to listening to God. In AA it seemed we were always hearing stories of somebody determined to drink again, going off to a Chinese restaurant, and deciding to leave the decision to drink or not to the fortune cookie. The cookie always said something like, "You will make a difficult choice wisely." *There it was.* And all ended well. Whereas if Isaiah was in charge of fortune-cookie writing, the story would have turned up a cookie with a fortune like 24:11: "There is a crying for wine in the streets; all joy is darkened, the mirth of the land is gone."

The Book of Obadiah falls open, all twenty-one verses of it. I mean, Obadiah? This *has* to be Abbot Antony's Divine Providence, or AA's fortune-cookie sobriety. Whoever heard of Obadiah?

Behold, I have made thee small among the heathen: thou art greatly despised. (1:2)

Though thou exalt thyself as the eagle, and though thou set thy nest among the stars, thence will I bring thee down, saith the Lord. (1:4)

This is *not funny*, God, not one bit. But I have to laugh anyway: it reads like my work woes and sins of the last year—exactly what I am trying to retreat *from*.

I decide to struggle with Abbot Antony's "devoured" book instead.

~

Vespers, my favorite hour, and the first time we have sung it this retreat. I like the chants. I like these particular psalms; I like the fact that the Hour lasts only half an hour.

The abbey church is all gussied up for Easter Vigil. Ready or not . . . redemption comes.

~

It seems a bit incredible to feel the need to arrive forty-five minutes early for a ceremony that will run two hours. It's not like this is a first-run play or a line for a rock singer's concert tickets. But even the best of times run their course. Mine, for this retreat, finished this afternoon. Since Vespers, I haven't had enough to read or reasons to stay at the retreat at all. Finally I rely on an old ally to let me finish this race: inertia. I flop into my easy chair in my cell and read *The New Yorker* for two hours and then join the rapidly filling church.

~

Large family groups—obviously thinking thirty minutes is enough time for claiming a seat—begin showing up. I give up my end row spot for a single folding chair up against a side wall. The light is better for reading anyway.

"The ceremony starts *outside*," says Brother Stephen. "We're going to turn all the lights off, so if you're afraid of the dark, you'd better join us outside." Half the church exits immediately.

The darkness produces a wonderful silence, and the red- and orange-hued stained glass behind us begins to glow in bits of Paschal candlelight. Last year the storm was so fierce, the windows rattled to the point of nearly breaking. They could not light the fires or candle outside. Tonight we get the full effect of the breaking of light into darkness, bit by bit. Abbot Antony shuffles in happily.

Last year, I'd had a miserable retreat on top of a miserable year, but when I turned to let some stranger light my candle it was my novice classmate Hildegard who lit it, standing there like an angel. This year, Hildegard is again one of the first inside the church. I move to the center and touch her arm, so, once more, she lights my candle.

I sing my guts out when it's all over and time for "Christ the Lord Is Risen Today!" I've been singing that in Easter choir since I was seven years old.

"I miss the old songs," the lady next to me says as we file out. What has *she* been singing all those years?

Ego sum via et veritas et vita.

April 23, 2000: Easter Sunday and the Octave of the Resurrection of Our Lord Jesus Christ

You've got to hand it to the monks for persistence. The party went on until midnight, and yet they have already begun filing in for Lauds when I arrive at 6:45 A.M. The metallic, toneless bells begin their celebration five minutes later. I have not heard the bells since the Triduum began.

The sun has finally returned.

Abbot Antony arrives, looking quite pleased to be here again this Easter morning, aged ninety-one. I feel more like the burned-out fire of the Easter Vigil I passed on the way into the abbey church. The Vigil definitely takes the edge off Easter morning, like last night's jelly beans at the party edged off the hunger Easter morning after a four-day fast.

I get the demons at Lauds. Maybe the short attention span that normally keeps me from spending much time in church is a good thing. My demons seem to find me in church. This morning, my demons of desertion have an animated conversation on *when can we go home, Ma?* After breakfast (even my demons are getting a little skinny by now), and before people start charging up the treacherous hill to get good seats for Easter Mass. No, can't move that quickly (even my demons are getting burned out). *While* they're at Mass, we'll sneak away. (They're getting clever now.) Maybe . . .

I give up singing and let the demons slug it out. I'm tired.

"It means, 'I am the Way, the Truth, and the Life,'" says Abbot Antony at breakfast when I ask him what *Ego sum via et veritas et vita* means. Post-Vatican II Catholics like me have no Latin to draw on. With great consideration, Abbot Antony has waited to visit the cafeteria until after I have heaped my plate. "He hath filled the hungry with good things" (Luke 1:53) can have literal implications after four days of bread alone.

Abbot Antony thanks me for the books I donated on my last visit to the oblate library, especially the new hard-cover edition of Cassian's *Conferences*, which he thinks is very fine. I don't tell him I never could get through more than twenty pages of it. He may figure that out if he opens it and sees the enthusiastic underlining with highlighter disappear shortly after the introduction.

"If it weren't for Amazon.com, I'd never find these kinds of books," I say.

"Their stock's down lately," says Abbot Antony. I am no longer surprised when he does this world-awareness stuff. It used to knock me speechless.

The demons depart, either because of the joy and goodness of the abbot or the presence of fried eggs and crispy bacon. Hildegard's first memory of the abbot is thirty years ago, she tells me after he leaves, when she came here on a retreat eight months pregnant with her third child. "And Abbot Antony came out and carried my little suitcase for me!" Her face shines when she says this, as transfigured as any human could be. The holiest of Marthas, one of nine children with a large family of her own to tend to now, she has not known many such moments of being tended *to*, I suspect. She knows all the monks and their stories, having come here as often as she could over these thirty years since. For the abbot, she has only the deepest reverence.

I tell her about my day trips here, the difficulty of finding a place to study.

"I come here a lot for the day also," she confides. "I just ask for the use of a room for a day." That's all there is to it?

After breakfast I go back to my cell and make up my bed with fresh sheets as mindfully as I can. It is still a lumpy mess, mindfulness or not. I am no Martha at all.

The small abbey church has overflowed to outside half an hour before Mass. A non-Christian might wonder what they're giving away here today. A Christian, hopefully, would know the answer. Everybody is dressed up in Easter finery. For some reason, I blank out on Easter as a "dress" day. I have worn black until now, and switched to a white sweatshirt ensemble today, which seemed fitting at the time I was packing, but probably appears disrespectful now compared to the dressed congregation.

At lunch, after a long, uninspired Easter Mass, Abbot Antony makes the rounds of the retreat cafeteria and finds Hildegard and me talking again. I need to ask him a favor. Could he unlock the oblate library for me? The porter will be off this afternoon (they all will) and one of my problems with staying until Vespers is that I will run out of reading material. Sitting in a public space with nothing to do, I'll either fall asleep or, more likely, go home.

Abbot Antony hands me a key from his key ring and starts to leave.

"What shall I do with this when I'm done?" I ask, panicked at holding his key.

"Next time I see you," he says easily, and disappears.

Well, if I've been handed the key to the kingdom, I must use it. Hildegard and I part. She is here until tomorrow; I am obviously now here through Vespers. I pack and ask a blessing on this simple room that contained me during these days, and walk the prayer walk once again. "The LORD is upright; he is my rock" (Psalm 92:15). A handsome little quartz rock lies quietly at the entrance of the walk. There can be no other.

If the Resurrection is the greatest story ever told, the afternoon of Easter is its denouement, its falling off/go quietly ending. The monks disappear and so do most of the retreatants. It is as deserted here as Christ found it a few days ago at Gethsemane.

Chapters 53 and 61: Pilgrim Monks and Guests

Benedict says that guests are welcomed as Christ, and the greatest care should be given to the poor and to pilgrims, *because in them more particularly Christ is received*. A separate kitchen and guest quarters are maintained so as not to disturb the residents. Visiting monks may stay as long as they like, and may join the community if they wish and the monks accept, providing their "home abbot" gives approval.

I would guess (without rereading these pages) that I have shown how my particular abbey receives it retreat guests. Although much is made in commentaries about Benedict's injunction to welcome guests "as Christ," I find that this abbey pays particular care to the "extra credit" part: *Great care and concern are to be shown in receiving poor people and pilgrims, because in them more particularly Christ is received.* No collection is taken during Mass here. On retreat, no donation is required, and sometimes it's hard to even get the "suggested donation amount" out of Brother John Climachus.

"Well, how much am I costing you to stay there every night?" I finally asked him in frustration last year.

Benedictine hospitality is supposedly famous, an essential part of their "brand," to quote the marketing types. The Franciscans say the same about themselves, although it is not part of Francis's Rule. My whole life in retreats has taken place within a three-mile radius of Franciscan and Benedictine hospitality. I will say that, based on my singular experience of one retreatant in two traditions, the Franciscans were more "customer-centered." They brought your luggage in and returned it to your car on your departure. They stuck fresh little wildflowers in your room in anticipation of your arrival, and lit candles and placed them along the walkway as you left. They gave you reading material, comforting food, a good room, and plenty of silence. They let you know up front, exactly, how much these things cost per night or, for the twilight retreats, by the hour.

The Benedictines are more oriented to providing hospitality for the soul. My first meeting with Abbot Antony modeled that. "Come for lunch," he had said, and when he got that agreement, he added, "Come early, for Mass." It's the real core I see to their hospitality. "Join us for Vespers and stay for supper." They do not neglect the feeding of strangers and they offer their retreat house to all, not just paid-in-advance. But they offer of their abundance, their treasure, and their treasure is their liturgy. "The liturgy is what we live by," Abbot Antony said. Pray with us. Join our community in prayer.

> A brother came and stayed with a certain solitary and when he was leaving, he said, "Forgive me, Father, for I have broken in upon your Rule." But the hermit replied saying, "My Rule is to receive you with hospitality and to let you go in peace."[14]

And perhaps the most wonderful aspect of their hospitality is that they pray for those who ask for prayers, who write out prayer requests. They pray for their oblates—whether we are there to notice or not. Being welcomed "as Christ" when I arrive is a precious gift. Being welcomed as Christ when I am not even with them is the love of the Divine.

～

The day is a glorious one—cool, breezy, sunny, and simply magnificent. It is the quiet of heaven here in the oblate library. What do demons know anyway, and why do I ever listen to them?

～

Easter Meditation (denouement). My first retreat, nearly ten years ago, took place one Lenten weekend with women in my church. We went to the Franciscan Mission, and most of the weekend was highly structured—a good way to handle a first retreat.

I was miserable about many things, but primary in my thoughts that weekend was the violent battle to quit smoking—a battle that raged both physically and mentally.

During one brief time of "free meditation," I was pacing about the back of the mission when, a short distance away, I saw a magnificent wooden cross rising up out of the ground.

I walked so fast I was breathless to see what that symbol was there for, so far from the rest of the mission. When I reached it, the sign said, "XIV—Jesus Is Buried." I looked around—and there they were, all those great, life-sized crosses, arranged in a quarter-mile quadrangle, and people were walking along, saying prayers at each.

I had been Catholic less than one year. I had never heard of the Stations of the Cross. What I could see, even in the moment, was the metaphor for most of my religious life. I had come up behind the Last Station, never knowing or seeing the path I was supposed to take, the path the rest of humanity was on.

My Protestant friend didn't like the story when I told him, and refused to accept the metaphor. He'd never heard of the Stations either, and this didn't make sense to him. "Jesus is buried as the last station? What kind of story is that? It doesn't stop there."

This morning, my verse from Isaiah to study says, "Whereas thou hast been forsaken and hated, . . . I will make thee an eternal excellency, a joy of many generations" (60:15).

It is Easter now, not Good Friday, and old Isaiah has promises I didn't know he had in him. Promises of salvation through one savior's suffering, yes, but now here a glorious promise of eternal excellency for me. Christ, with whom I have never felt favored nation status, will smile on me when I am forsaken and hated. He knows of the eternal excellency for such of his children.

It cannot be a leveling match, can it? Where the first are last and the last are first and everybody pointing fingers at each other? Maybe the leveling is "All rise," and we must pray for our enemies so that we become worthy to join in their eternal excellency as well. Imagine the best party in the universe and you decline your invitation because of who else will be there. We do that all the time, depriving ourselves because of our disapproval (or fear) of others.

But today is Easter. We are redeemed, all of us, once more. Forsaken, we are saved. Hated then, we are now the joy of generations.

The abbey church's Stations, so modern, these tiles barely indicated in the walls. I count. There are fifteen Stations here, not fourteen like everywhere else. And the fifteenth Station says, "Rising in Glory."

~

Vespers. A few of us still here. The *entire* thing is sung in Latin—a first in my short liturgical career. Fittingly, I leave this retreat in silence.

MAY
And Blossom as the Rose

The wilderness and the solitary place shall be glad for them;
and the desert shall rejoice, and blossom as the rose.

Isaiah 35:1

May 19, 2000: Fourth Week of Easter

Liturgical exhaustion and a bad work schedule combined to keep me away nearly four weeks. It is just as well to deprive myself of a beloved bit of peace and even of holiness to discover how anxiously I have awaited its return. Even paradise grows stale; even sin has its purpose.

The weather today has improved on perfection. It is mild without even heat or chill to spice its edges. The sun caresses. The breeze carries twittering bird calls. Exotic, spiky day lilies of rust and orange compete with the last of the silky Easter lilies. (I am sure the white lilies have their own name. In New England, they were called Easter lilies because that's the only time we ever saw them—and then only in foil-covered pots, never growing out of the ground.)

As I left the office yesterday, and this gorgeous weather touched my face with the tender insistence of a lover, the woman next to me sighed, "Don't you just *love* May? We finally get good weather."

Even paradise loses perspective.

It is good to be back at the abbey, although the place seems nearly deserted. Porter Brother Paschal, who cannot find the oblate library key says, "That must mean it's open." But it isn't, and Brother Dominic takes pity on me and lets me in. The rich people talk about second homes in the desert, and even Felix yearns for that impossibility for us someday. I have a second home, here in this spiritual oasis, and someday I will get to stay.

The Gospel read at Mass is my gorgeous comfort: "In my father's house are many mansions: if it were not so, I would have told you" (John 14:2). Seconds later in the reading, the mystery from Easter: "I am the way, the truth, and the life" (14:6). *Ego sum via et veritas et vita* is still above the altar in gold and red. These abbey days I feel like the life of the Gospel is starting to stick to the ribs of my own life. I am a bit surprised, since I like to resist everything.

They are serving flavored yogurt, fresh fruit, sandwich fixings, and soup in the retreat cafeteria today. It all looks good. I have brought bread, for my day of fasting. I had been so gladly done with it Easter morning, and now this week in his letter to oblates, Abbot Antony wrote, "Could not some of those good works in our Lenten Opera continue in some measure for the rest of the year? This should not be too difficult. Remember that our Savior first showed the apostles his wounded hands and feet, both to identify himself and to make them remember. So don't put your Lenten Opera away. Let them also remind you of his hands and feet! This will challenge you to keep to your oblate way of life."

I am still trying to figure out exactly what my "oblate way of life" is, but in the meantime, I return to Friday fasting. I have not refused any of Abbot Antony's suggestions so far except to get the big Divine Office and to read St. Augustine's *Confessions*. There are limits.

Everybody in the cafeteria seems to have a buddy. Brother Barnabas comes in with an old oblate friend, and Brother Dominic sits with a group he knows. I am not in the "in group" here any more than I am in the "in group" at work or any other activity I do. The reminder, coupled with reading Thomas Merton's stern praise of solitude and eating bread for lunch, combines to give me that old, familiar feeling: major crankiness.

"*There* you are," says Abbot Antony suddenly. I have a flash of how tiring it must be for him to keep his spiritual wild child in view, and how you have to be willing to be with people to be part of the "in group."

"Maybe I'll see you later," he says and heads off to the monks' eating area on the other side. I go to get coffee. The prayer work lady, eating with the hired hands, sees me and recognizes me—even though I am not in uniform today—and she says hello.

Chapter 54: Letters and Presents

As Benedict has condemned the vice of private ownership, so here he continues by not permitting the exchange of letters or gifts. Not even from his parents may a monk accept these unless the abbot says it is okay. Not bound to poverty and probably bound too much to the "vice of private ownership" (discussed in the next chapter), I would safely figure this short chapter has little to do with an ordinary oblate like me. Directly, it does not.

Indirectly, perhaps, it is another story. In the first year of my affiliation with the abbey, I think I made a total of five bookmarks for the various brothers (and both abbots) whose paths crossed mine. With one exception, these gifts disappeared down the abbey rabbit hole. Father Stanislaus, mentioned earlier, sent a note and later told me the bookmark was on display in the library. It was not. The other gifts were met with total silence.

You don't give gifts waiting for a thank-you, but the silence troubled me anyway. Had I done something wrong, somehow broken a taboo? My mailbox used to be filled with Franciscan thank-you's. (*What's wrong with you guys?*) Are they taking this part of the Rule seriously or something?

Maybe so. The interesting thing about this Benedictine silence is that it leaves you on the other side to go through any range of emotions and attitudes. What it forced me to see—quite reluctantly—was the focus of the gift-giving. My giving was based on my needs, not the recipients'. They were simply the targets of my actions. You learn in performance, and certainly in speechwriting, that the "act" exists *between* performer and audience, rather than being directed from stage to balcony. So with giving. I cannot truly give without considering the needs of the recipient. We are either partners, linked in listening, or I am doing my solo act again.

> Abba Zeno never wanted gifts from anyone, and those who brought him something came away hurt that he would not accept. Others came to him wishing to receive a token from such a great old man, and since he had nothing to give them, they went away hurt as well. Abba Zeno decided that when someone brought him something he would accept it and

give it to anyone who asked him for something. So he did this and was at peace and satisfied everyone.[1]

The same is true with letters. As a child, I loved my hobby of international pen pals because I loved to send and receive letters. As an adult I have discovered that letter-writing is nearly as one-way a communication as keeping a diary. Nobody writes letters or even thank-you notes anymore. E-mail and dreadful, tinkly electronic "cards" substitute for writing or calling.

I continue to write a letter a month to Abbot Antony. The need is so strong on my end to share my "oblate way of life" in all its imperfections, uncertainties, and glories with him. He receives dozens of letters, cannot begin to answer them all.

"Keep writing," he says when he sees me. "I love to read them even if I can't answer." My arrogance and need is so great that I pretend he needs my letters too, rather than think he is simply being kind to this strange, show-off spiritual pen pal of his. ("See my great insight!" "Listen to how smart I got with this Bible verse!" "Wanna hear my clever story?" "Wanna read the book review I sent to Amazon.com?" "See my latest editorial on transportation." *Listen to me.*)

My abbot, my father, gives so much by allowing me to "give" him my letters.

～

The usual brisk strut around the prayer walk. I do not feel so prayerful today. Not at *all* like during the retreat when I was so surrounded by the prayerful folks that it nearly rubbed off on me.

The walk itself seems shabby in late Easter. Wildflowers and weeds—probably the same thing botanically, with one desirable to my eye and one not—are sprouting up out of tire tracks in the middle of the dirt path. The monoliths have been swept clean of the Stations again, and the Stations have a barren, neglected air as a result.

But the cactus, in full flower, reminds me of Isaiah. "And the desert shall rejoice, and blossom as the rose" (35:1). There has to be something good to say about a prayer walk, no matter how untidy, if it can remind you of Isaiah, and bring you home to the fact that you live in a desert even if it's the Pacific Ocean lying mistily beyond you. Plus you get a rock for safekeeping.

Chapter 55: Clothing and Shoes

Clothing and footwear is distributed to the monks based on the climate needs, and two outfits will be provided to each monk. Again, Benedict emphasizes: no private ownership of clothes, shoes, even writing materials. *The abbot is to provide all things necessary.*

St. Benedict at his most practical. For if this Rule can cover such mundane issues, are not his monks then free to focus on the work of God?

"What color will you wear in heaven?" I asked Abbot Antony early on. I didn't know Benedict's Rule detailed even clothing and shoes, but I would think heaven was off limits—even in Benedict's Rule. "You must be awfully sick of black after all these years. Maybe red?"

"White will do just fine," he said serenely.

When I moved from the generic job of assistant to the president at my university into the more focused efforts in lobbying, Felix asked, "So what does this new position mean?"

"It means new clothes," I answered promptly. "*Lots* of new clothes." He was relieved, finding the way I dress in academia as a general rule a little too unprofessional for his taste. Within a year, I owned fourteen "lobbyist suits," flat-faced watches in gold and silver, worn depending on the match with suit color, two color-coordinated blouses per suit, and a total of seventeen silk scarves—plus scarf pins and rings in gold and silver to match whichever watch I was wearing. Plus shoes. Many, many pairs of shoes.

If there is a secular "rule" we live by in this century and country, it is the rule of the consumer culture, and I have certainly been one of its most ardent participants. I am pretty sure my spiritual life can be purchased, since everything else seems to be, and religious bookstores drive me mad with lust.

With clothing, I have gone through phases ranging from indifference to moderate interest, but little more than that. As I have studied the Rule this year, a few interesting things have happened with my attitude about clothing. Sister Joan Chittister, in her commentary on the Rule, reminds us that if this chapter says anything to the modern world at all, "it is certainly that we need to be who we are."[2]

Like the prayer work lady, I began to be who I am here at the abbey in the way I dress: heavy cotton tee shirts and pants, shorts in summer, sandals that come off as soon as I find a place to write. Who I am has less to do with dress-up suits and lobbying (my paid work) than dress-down comfort and study (my *opus dei*, or God's work). The prayer work lady and I have more in common than I might have wanted to believe.

It hit me that clothes are our "costume" at the University Ball in March. While my fellow oblates were on retreat at the monastery, I had a mandatory charitable event that had me none too happy—until told we could either come black tie formal (yawn) or dressed as our favorite decade.

I'd never worn a costume as an adult, at least not knowingly—but the lobbyist suits were beginning to be suspect. I *had* to go as a Roaring Twenties flapper, just *had* to. "Where else can I smoke a fake cigarette all night, let my bra strap hang down, have attitude, and call it a costume?" I asked Felix. He promptly announced that if I was going as a flapper, he was going as a "drunk."

It was a fine flapper costume I rented, black and glittering with a feather boa and a big plume coming out of my headband. My short straight hair—the anathema of "big hair" California hair stylists—was perfect. My attitude finally fit too. My poses struck all the right notes. My propensity for unsubtle makeup (black eyeshadow, red lipstick) was exactly right. Every picture taken of me that night came out sparkling perfect.

"You were *on*," said a coworker, harkening back to my performer past. "Sometimes you need a costume to hide behind."

And sometimes you need a costume to come out from hiding. The lobbyist works for my boss. The flapper performs for God, is everything he made me to be, even if it's a little too flashy-trashy for the neighborhood I inhabit.

I returned the flapper costumer promptly, but the genie who got let out of the bottle that night has refused to go back in. She doesn't need that particular costume to perform for God now—any plain cotton tee shirt and pants will do. The body has been freed so the spirit can soar.[3]

> Abba Theodore of Pherme's clothes were such that one of the Fathers covered the Abba's shoulders with a cape. The old man put out his hand and snatched the cape off. The Father asked, "Abba, why did you do that?" Abba Theodore said, "Are we still the slaves of men? We did what was necessary, the rest is superfluous. He who wishes to be edified, let him be edified; he who wishes to be shocked, let him be shocked; as for me, I meet people as they find me."[4]

And Abba Isaac used to say that Abba Pambo believes the monk's garment should be such that he could throw it out of his cell for three days and no one would take it.[5]

And that really is all Benedict could ever want for a rule about clothes.

~

A marvelous, sleepy silence of a perfect springtime afternoon, punctuated only by the distant whine of the prayer work lady's vacuum cleaner. Here in the oblate library that Abbot Antony prepared for us, overlooking the tiny inner courtyard now bathed in late afternoon light that Hildegard has meditated upon so often, I feel as comforted as a well-loved child. Which, of course, I am . . .

~

Vespers. The silence is so complete in late Easter you can smell the wax of the Vigil candle after it's lit. Healed and restored and in just a few hours. Time to sing my favorite Hour—if they do it in English this time.

May 29, 2000: Sixth Monday after Easter

It is Memorial Day, and therefore an odd day to be here at the monastery.

"Is it okay to come?" I asked Brother John Climachus by phone on Friday. I hate to call any of them and bother them, but I was concerned about what would be available to a day-tripper. "I know the monks aren't big on celebrating Memorial Day, but . . ." But I don't know what. Surely the lay people who work at the monastery are all off today, and maybe there are no retreatants or open cafeteria, or place where the oblate library key can be found.

"Oh, please come," says Brother John Climachus in his carefully enunciated, high-pitched voice that reminds me of a junior angel-in-training. "You are *more* than welcome to come on Monday."

They are words that make me feel like Isaiah's rose suddenly blooming out of the desert. I have been happy ever since, knowing I can spend the day here, Memorial Day. This project and my being here as a day visitor felt so rocky at the beginning. I don't know if it was the monks in their cloistered ways or my own prickly sense of not belonging and not being wanted that made it so awkward—perhaps both. And then there were the dangers of being forced here by the Franciscans and having read too much Kathleen Norris, both leading me into expectations rather than realities of *this* monastery, *this* awkward oblate.

"Well, it is nice to see *you* here," says that kindly voice, roughened with great age. Abbot Antony must patrol the oblate library regularly, as I am quite early today thanks to a shared car situation, and in the oblate library with my coffee cup well before Mass at 11:00 A.M.

It is quiet today, and the monastery is shrouded in "May Gray." In Lake San Marcos where I live, the sun is out, and the temperature is moving into summer range. Here, just ten miles west and 30 minutes south, the fog bank lays its heavy hand over both sun and temperature. They are related entities in San Diego. You get both or none. When I moved to San Diego in June of 1987, I was surprised and disappointed by those deeply overcast skies and cool, drizzly days. Not the PR of southern California I expected. The gray would rest over the thin coastal strip where I lived and worked as a temporary secretary. By 2:00 or 3:00, there might be hazy sunshine. Or there might not. By 4:00, it would be subsumed back into the fog bank. "Offshore flow" was what the meteorologist called it. "June Gloom" was the nativespeak.

This year it came with Easter and has been dubbed as "May Gray." It enhances the quiet and adds to the solitude of a secular American holiday spent at a monastery. Not a waving flag or hot dog anywhere to be seen.

Ego sum via et veritas et vita. The words remain above the altar. Brother Robert ushers himself in, using his motorized wheelchair. The whispered prayers of fellow oblates, the chanted psalms of monks. I do not feel like the "temp" who came to California in 1987 or even like the gyratory of my world before or since then. I have borrowed the Benedictine ideal of stability from the monks here, and they have been generous in providing from the treasury of it.

Father Jerome reads the Gospel today. I have never spoken to him, but have watched his progress from wheelchair to walker to cane with great interest and maybe even a little concern. He looks like my childhood minister Mr. Neild, who, in turn, looked a little bit like my dad.

When he gets up and makes his slow way to the pulpit, I am thrilled that he once again gets to participate as a priest at Mass. His voice is strong and clear, not like his hobbling body at all.

I don't know any of them. As the retreat master, Brother John Climachus has interacted with me. As oblate master, so has Abbot Antony. Once in a while, I feel a jealousy that Hildegard knows the monks and their stories so well, that Nancy and Michelle help Abbot Antony with oblate meetings and mailings, and that Leah works in the library with Father Cornelius. Like everywhere, there are insiders and outsiders, and like always, I get the outside seat. It surprises me to experience this much joy for Father Jerome's small recoveries. I am growing attached, I think. I am starting to listen, even when there are no words being said.

Chapter 56: The Abbot's Table

The shortest chapter of the Rule (three sentences) says that the abbot must always take his meals with guests of the monastery.

I didn't know the monks ate in a separate area from guests when I accepted Abbot Antony's first invitation to dine. I arrived all excited, wondering what they were reading, and wondering how I would converse with the abbot if they were all listening to the reader. I ended up in the retreat cafeteria, which is where I have taken all my meals. And I still have no idea where the *real* abbot's table is, since I have seen Abbot Henry come to the guest area only twice: once when the three of us in my tiny class made our novitiate vows, and once, a year later, when we stayed for supper after our oblation and Vespers. Both times he stopped by to congratulate us, and then said the identical thing: "I need to go sit with the others and make sure the younger monks are behaving. That's in the Rule, you know."

Abbot Antony is another story and will sit with his coffee cup full and his soup bowl half empty for any number of guests at the abbey. When I brought my mother, visiting from Rhode Island, to meet him and eat lunch, the abbot produced ice cream from the freezer, which was as magical to me at that moment as watching Brother Maurius make salt shakers disappear. Abbot Antony may have the word "retired" on his abbatial business card, but he will never retire from Benedictine hospitality.

> Once some of the elders came to Scete, and Abbot John the Dwarf was with them. And when they were dining, one of the priests, a very great old man, got up to give each one a little cup of water to drink, and no one would take it from him except John the Dwarf. The others were surprised and afterwards they asked him, "How is it that you, the least of us, have presumed to accept the services of this great old man?" He replied, "Well, when I get up to give people a drink of water, I am happy if they all take it, and for that reason on this occasion, I took the drink, that he might be rewarded, and not feel sad because nobody accepted the cup from him." And at this all admired his discretion.[6]

Once, having promised to meet me for lunch after Mass, the abbot forgot. I waited a bit and then left, a bit embarrassed. At 9:00 P.M.—when I would think old monks who get up really early should be asleep—the phone rang. It was Abbot Antony, upset because he now remembered what he had forgotten at noon.

"Maybe I was the angel you were supposed to meet unawares," I teased him from the Mass's reading that day. ("Be not forgetful to entertain strangers: for thereby some have entertained angels unaware" [Hebrews 13:2].) "Isn't it late for you to be up?"

"But now I can't sleep!" he wailed. And feeling like no angel for my teasing, I agreed to show up the next day.

I feel bad about taking my abbot away from the habits of his table. I know they read aloud during meals, and it must be disturbing to miss whole chunks of a book because you are entertaining tart, would-be angels, unaware.

In southern California, you have the same opportunity as the monks to live this piece of Benedictine hospitality regularly—whether you want to or not. When we bought a house after a year of making do in a beach "cabana," people at work said, "Wait until you see how many friends and relatives you have. A house in San Diego brings them out of the woodwork."

It sure did. For the six months following close of escrow, we were feeding, entertaining, driving around, and cleaning up after an onslaught of guests who never seemed to catch on that we also had our own work and chores to manage, our own lives to live. Knowing my inherent crankiness, I can be sure I was not gracious about all the company. It slowed down after everybody had done a few visits each, but we're still subject to being an essential part of somebody else's plans for a vacation getaway. As the monks do with their lives of cloister, inundated by the likes of me.

But what Benedict knows that I am still learning is that we're all guests and travelers on this great journey to the New Jerusalem. And that it can be good spiritual manners to set aside our journey for a while to host others along their way.

~

Both Mass and lunch in the cafeteria afterward are mobbed. I have no sense of the numbers or schedule of fellow pilgrims on the journey. I should be glad to see so many on the same path, since my normal workday life is very secular and anti-religious. I can get cranky at anything, but try to enjoy the mob today for whatever reason brings us here on the last Monday before Ascension.

The prayer walk is absolutely ratty with weeds—not very nice to walk along at all. I try not to think about the origins of animal droppings in several parts of the path. The fog bank is trying very hard to lift, and succeeds in some places, but the ocean is very indistinct, a soft-blurry blue like the way everything looks when I take out my contact lenses.

Interesting rocks are hard to come by these days. The rocks seem to be the only part of the prayer walk cleaned up lately. I find a murky white one that looks full of blood below its hard, dull surface. It is as good a metaphor of my heart as anything, so I bring it back with me.

Hildegard is in the oblate library when I come in for the afternoon work. "Is it the fourth Monday you come?" she asks. "I saw you at Mass and realized . . . "

"It's whatever day I can manage," I tell her. "I'll stay out of your space and you won't bother me either." I pull up the other chair so she can have the view of the little garden she so loves and I can have the view of the tile art of *Sanctus Benedictus*. It is no use.

"I have been here an hour and must take a walk," Hildegard says and rushes out. I run into her later when I go for a coffee refill. "I am preoccupied with . . . " she says, touching a pin on her chest. I have no idea what she is talking about. She is assuming I know something that I either do not or forgot or did not understand at the time. She rushes off again. I would be hurt, but the privacy is awfully nice too.

Chapter 57: Artisans and Craftsmen

The artists and craftsmen in the monastery, like everyone else, will labor in humility under obedience to the abbot, says Benedict. In the sale of their wares, the monks will be honest in their dealings and sell below the going price, to avoid *the evils of avarice*, as Benedict says.

All I have ever wanted to be could be contained in the word "artist." When I was a young musician studying in college, one of my first textbooks was a dictionary of musical terms. I found "artist" defined in there in lengthy, neo-spiritual terms and fell in love with art as the reason for living. Even today when I "should" desire sainthood or something equally pious, the artist still wins out every time.

For me, art is passion, art is prayer brought out in created things. Art is the work of the heart. I don't think Benedict would argue with any of that, only with the sin that makes the artist "special" and therefore different (better) than others. I subscribe to that too, of course. And for most of my twenties and thirties, I also subscribed to the potential at least of making money "off" my artistic gifts.

"Write the trashy novel," Felix would urge.

"I'd be prostituting my talent," I would answer loftily.

"Prostitute it just once, just a little," he would say. "Make millions and then you can write anything you want."

For a while, I tried to write "what sells" but finally gave it up because it was boring me. For sixteen years I kept a diary instead, where the practice of art became a very private thing indeed. At some point it was time to move past the audience-less art form. My life was falling apart and I could no longer record its sameness. Writing a life was substituting for living a life, and I broke away to begin anew.

What I learned in those silent years of writing to myself was how to write. What I learned with no audience was to think past self-expression into something else. Perhaps, like the monks, I learned in solitude what I needed in society. I began to write speeches, essays, and editorials for work. I announced to my new university president that I was the presidential speechwriter—and began to learn how to write presidential-sounding speeches. I began this study project for my fellow oblates.

I don't have to worry about becoming Ananias and Sapphira, as Benedictine worries in this chapter. Ananias and Sapphira were among the earliest followers of the apostles, who, carried away with Peter's long sermon about Jesus' life, death, and Resurrection, sold what they had and gave the money to the apostles, "and distribution was made unto every man according as he had need" (Acts 4:35). Unfortunately, they didn't give *all* the proceeds to Peter, only pretended to do so. Called on their secret, they both dropped dead. The bits of money my writing has brought in I have given away. If I made a great deal, I would give that away and thus be forced to return to my job the next day. I am not a humble artist. It's my work that keeps me humble.

> When people came to buy from Abbot Agatho the things he had made with the work of his hands, he sold to them in peace. His price for a sieve was a hundred pence, and for a basket two hundred and fifty. When they came to buy he told them the price and took what they gave him in silence, not even counting the coins. For he said, "What is the use of me arguing with them and leading them perhaps into sin by perjuring themselves and then perhaps, if I have some extra money, giving it to the brethren? God does not want alms of this kind from me, and it does not please Him if, in order to make my offering, I lead someone into sin." One of the brethren said to him, "And how are you ever going to get a supply of bread for your cell?" To which he answered, "What need have I in my cell for the bread of men?"[7]

I don't know if I'm really an artist at all. I thought it would feel fancier (more "artistic") than sitting in this modest oblate library, drinking the monks' coffee, trying to stay awake in an afternoon's silence, trying to make sense of the Rule I have chosen to live by and grumble about. It is my prayer, for a person not mentally disciplined enough to pray any other way.

But this writing is the work of my heart, and if carrying about a cheap spiral notebook gives me permission to listen to a monastery's drone on a late spring afternoon, then it is a good thing for me indeed.

~

Maybe the sun was "sort of" out for the twenty minutes or so I walked the prayer walk. Maybe it wasn't. That was it for the entire day. Now at Vespers, it is chill and overcast, not summery at all.

JUNE
I Am the Door

*I am the door: by me if any man
enter in, he shall be saved.*

John 10:9

June 9, 2000: St. Ephrem

"Packing your busy bag for monk camp?" Felix asks as I industriously
load up my traveling tote bag with the necessities for an eight-hour
shift at the St. Augustine's Abbey.

Indeed, I do have a bit of the pre-camp excitement in me today. The
week at work has been intense, focused, full, and not particularly
prayerful beyond the regular, "Please, God, get me *through* this day!"

Well, he did, and if I am not yet balanced in the daily way that the
Benedictines encourage, I have these two days a month of monastery
vacation (versus "vocation") that I cling to in order to right my list-
ing life.

The weather is magnificent today, even by San Diego standards,
which are quite picky. When Felix went to put out the trash at 7:00
A.M. he said it reminded him of an early summer morning in northern
New England, when the air had the crispness of a fresh apple and the
stillness of an untouched mountain lake. "And you'd forget the morning air because it warmed up so soon afterwards," he continues, in a
bit of a nostalgic moment for a world where the breezes murmured
against big full fir trees rather than crinkled against dry, flat palms.

It is rare to witness the diamond-hard blueness of a summer sky
with the tart temperatures of early spring. We get one or the other,

rarely both. I scamper up the treacherous road to the monastery like a liberated chipmunk. Weather in San Diego—we get what we're given, and we are usually given generously. If that isn't a metaphor for a life lived in Christ, I don't know what is.

But even alleluias grow ragged with repetition. The last days of Easter pour out into the big burn of Pentecost. I, for one, am ready to resume the time of Ordinary.

Chapter 58: Admission of New Brothers

I'm glad this isn't the first chapter. *Do not grant newcomers to the monastic life an easy entry*, it begins. *If someone comes and keeps knocking at the door, and if at the end of four or five days he has shown himself patient in bearing his harsh treatment and difficulty of entry, and has persisted in his request, then he should be allowed to enter.* This chapter lays out the procedure for acceptance into monastic life. It involves persistence on the inquirer's part and persistence on the part of those already in the monastery, testing the newcomer's resolve at various points over a year's time. The ceremony for his acceptance into the order is given, as is the injunction to give away all he possesses before entering the monastery for good.

As my mother's Episcopal priest put it, "No wonder you fit into the Benedictines. You were brought up Episcopalian. It's a great, warm, welcoming tradition—if you persist."

Hmmm. Don't Episcopal churches have a motto that says, "The Episcopal Church Welcomes You" under the coat of arms and name of church (and times of services for welcoming you)? St. Augustine's Abbey doesn't even do that.

I read a short article about the abbey in a weekend section of the newspapers. I was "into" retreats of the Franciscan variety at the time, and the description of plastic sterility at the Benedictines didn't sound welcoming. Every time somebody doing a retreat at the Franciscan retreat center complained about traffic noises or whatever, the retreat brothers would say, "We're not cloistered. If you need that experience, go see the Benedictines up the hill from here." It sounded like a punishment, like being sent to your room without dessert. It sounded forbidding and remote. We would all cling to the Franciscan and say, "Really, everything here is *just fine*."

When my father was dying, I took a mental health day and found the abbey—with constant directions from a monk via my cell phone as I kept getting lost. For all the friendliness of the direction-giving monk, there was not a soul around when I finally got there. The place did seem cold and forbidding. The porter was in his office, but I was afraid of him. And I didn't know what I would ask him anyway. *Where is everybody?* It didn't seem a polite question to ask. There were a few retreatants leaving, and a black-robed monk was helping them carry luggage.

The church was open and empty, very modern and uninviting. The monastery library listed the monthly oblate meeting and asked the visitor not to take any books. There was a section for the oblate books. No one anywhere. I looked around the windswept hilltop, said a prayer for my father in the empty church, and made my way down the hill. It was February, Lent, silent and unwelcoming.

Two months later, my father was dead. I tried to find solace with the Secular Franciscans, but in their own way they were shutting me out as effectively as my first experience of the Benedictines. Once or twice over the difficult summer, I went back up that hill. Once I got shooed away by a lady sweeping the walkway who said, "You can't come in here. This is where the monks are."

Could have fooled me. Other than a glimpse of that one carrying luggage the first time, I never saw a monk until I called in September and asked for the oblate master.

> A brother told Abba Poemen, "I want to go to the monastery and dwell there." The old man said to him, "If you want to go to the monastery, you must be careful about every encounter and everything you do, or you will not be able to do the work of the monastery; for you will not have the right even to drink a single cup there."[1]

"Run, don't walk, up the hill to the Benedictines," they told me. *Keep knocking on the door*, says Benedict. And Abbot Antony opened it. I met with him. I went to one oblate meeting. I thought it was boring. I called him afterwards—the need to connect was so terrible—and said, "Can I see you for lunch tomorrow, and can I become a novice with the next group?"

"Yes and yes," he said firmly. And weeks later, I went up the hill alone on the afternoon of the Feast of Christ the King—the end of the liturgical year with Mass readings full of end times. For perhaps the first time in my gyratory life of spiritual exile, somebody showed up as promised, as Abbot Antony slid into the little chapel to help us begin our new journey. With Gregory and Hildegard, I received the medal of Benedict, blessed by Abbot Antony and later sewn into a bookmark for my Office prayer book.

Vade Retro Satana!
Nunquam Suade Mihi Vana!
Sunt Mala Quae Libas.
Ipse Venena Bibas!

Begone Satan!
Tempt me not with your vanities.
What you offer me is evil.
Drink the poisoned cup yourself!
—Prayer on Medal of St. Benedict

I received a copy of the Rule and the suggestion to study it. Apparently, I signed an enrollment notification and received a copy of it, but I don't remember that, only how the sunset at Vespers was orange and pink gaudiness while I stumbled through the chants.

Hildegard hoped to convince the abbot to let us "graduate" with the large June class that had gone before us. "He's . . . you know . . . " she would say with nervous gestures to our ancient abbot. She was afraid he'd be dead in a year.

But the abbot runs things by the book, as if we were being received to the orders themselves, not "just" oblates. Having banged on the door long enough, I was admitted and reviewed by *a senior chosen for his skill in winning souls*, as it says in this chapter. I was given that first copy of the Rule "on account" from the bookstore and I read it through. At two months, I became a novice. At six months, I got a letter saying, "How's it going?" At the last checkpoint, four months before final vows (and right on Benedict's schedule), we got a reminder that our time was approaching, and how were we doing with our promises?

Well, *I* was considering a run for elected office, and was quite taken in other directions. I drove up the hill to Mass at the monastery, and

Abbot Antony came out to see me afterwards.

"I'm thinking of running for office," I said. "I don't know what to do."

"Did you get my letter?" he asked. "Did you read it?"

Oh dear, he's losing it, I thought. It took me a minute to figure out what he was speaking about. "Yes, I just got it."

"And did you read it?" He seemed rather insistent.

Dear Persevering Novice Oblate [that letter had said]:

Your novitiate has more than passed the halfway mark and I sincerely hope and pray that you have at least begun to incorporate into your everyday life the ideals which our Holy Father Benedict encourages us to strive for. This is the time when I ask you to stand before God and St. Benedict and ask yourself questions concerning your fidelity in observing the Oblates' ideals and to renew your determination to promise your fidelity in observing the Oblates' practices.

I tried to remember what he'd said about stability and fidelity to vows. And realized that *he* wasn't "losing it" at all. *I* was. Did I want to be a gyratory, or did I want to make an oblation of myself to God, as I'd set out to do months before?

I came into the fold four months later. The wild gyrations had stopped cold. *Did you get my letter? Did you read it?*

I had, and was received into this community *no longer free . . . to shake from his neck the yoke of the rule, which, in the course of so prolonged a period of reflection he was free either to reject or accept.*

But I was free in ways I had never imagined possible before.

Abbot Antony explains to inquirers that Benedict did not create a Second Order or Third Order like later groups, notably the Franciscans, did. You either are or are not a Benedictine. Given that, and the unusual call to stability—I am an oblate of my monastery, not an oblate of the Order of St. Benedict—I suppose it serves everyone best to see a little persistence up front.

~

Father Cornelius, the librarian, celebrates Mass. He is eighty-six and never does a sermon, so I'm always grateful when I see him as celebrant. Even though he's a baby compared to Abbot Antony, he isn't "retired" yet, by Benedictine standards of the word, and was even one of the "lamenters" of Jeremiah over the Holy Days. He acquitted himself quite well, too.

I'm prepared for a quiet lunch, and hopeful of getting one since I forgot to call Brother John Climachus and tell him I wanted to come today. Abbot Antony arrives with guests. The guests were supposed to be bringing a "prospect" oblate from another monastery who moved to San Diego and is interested in becoming an oblate here. But the prospect apparently ate something disagreeable in an Old Town restaurant last night and ended up not coming. "Mind if we join you?" asks Abbot Antony, as if it were my hospitality being shared. He sits down before I can answer. It is a multi-layered conversation, as I feel obligated to talk about the oblate program, but I really want to hear stories. When the visitors talk about speaking Polish growing up, I ask the abbot if he speaks German.

He brightens up. "Oh yes! We are a Swiss motherhouse and German-speaking. I can't speak it well now—it's been too many years—but seventy years ago, of course. In fact, our table reading was always done in German at Indiana. You should have heard some of the Irish boys reading in German. Quite unusual pronunciations."

The visitors talk of the cold they experienced in a Benedictine abbey in England during one of their many travels.

"Did you know the cold in Indiana when you guys were getting up at 3:00 A.M.?" I ask the abbot.

"Oh, yes! Peter used to wrap his legs in newspaper before he went out, it was so cold."

There is so much I want to hear from my abbot—silly stuff, memories of a life. He is well trained to listen to *us*, and someday he will be gone, and those little stories with him.

The visitors explain how their friend in Tucson, Joe, lived here ages ago. Sick, feverish, driving around, he found himself up this hill, which must have been quite the delirium twenty years ago as this place must have been *extremely* isolated. The monks took him in and fed him, gave him a bed, and took care of him until he was better. In Tucson, twenty years later at a parish revival, he speaks of these Benedictine "angels," and begins to cry.

Hmmph. No knocking on the door for four or five days *then*, I think.

The abbot is going to take them for a moment to the oblate office to lend them a video for their friend before they leave. "You have an oblate office?" I ask. I am invited to see it also. It is in the same door I was shooed away from by the woman with the broom two plus years ago. These visitors are getting quite a different first impression—and I'm getting to tag along.

"Are you coming to the August oblate retreat?" Abbot Antony asks me as we walk along.

"Absolutely."

"Are you staying for supper tonight?" he asks, as I prepare to head off to the prayer walk.

"Vespers," I say. "I'm staying through Vespers."

"Oh, please stay for supper."

I would never forgive myself if I didn't and then he died in his sleep tonight or something.

Since Benedict and his sister, Scholastica, lived in communities just five miles apart, they met once a year to talk and pray together. At what turned out to be their last meeting, Scholastica begged her brother to stay longer, but he refused since his own rule forbid monks to spend the night outside the monastery.

Scholastica asked God to intercede. A fierce storm suddenly broke out, forcing Benedict to stay. "God forgive you, Sister!" he cried. "What have you done?"

"I asked a favor of you and you refused it," she replied. "I asked it of God, and he has granted it."

I would rather not put Abbot Antony—or me—to such a test.

⁓

It's hard to find a decent rock on the prayer walk again. Where could they all have gone? I only have about fifteen, so it can't be me. I finally secure an orange rock the size of my hand with flat, smooth sides, very pleasing. The path is now badly overgrown with stiff, purple weeds. The presence of animal turds along various parts of the path is troublesome. Too small for the crows, and I don't want to think about what else is out here where I'm walking with open-toed sandals.

Chapter 59: Sons of Noblemen or of Poor Men Offered to God's Service

Benedict describes how the ruling classes may offer a son to the monastery with particular emphasis on rules for giving property to the monastery without rights of inheritance to the child. The poor follow the same instructions of offering the child, without dowry.

The commentaries are not much help to ordinary oblates here. This is probably because they are not written by ordinary oblates about what the Rule means to ordinary lives, but by Benedictines trying to explain what Benedict meant for monks. I've read one that emphasizes how nobody can offer up their children now like then, and about the lack of distinction Benedict makes between rich and poor.

But I was offered to God as an infant in baptism long before I made myself into an oblation and signed that paper at the altar of the little prayer chapel. The week before we made our final vows, Gregory was fretful about needing more to "do" as an oblate than as a novice. What would this final step entail in terms of work assignments other than prayer?

"You are fulfilling the vows made at baptism," said Abbot Antony, almost testily. "That's your life's work."

It didn't sound very interesting. I would have been interested in some exotic assignments as well, maybe uniforms and secret rituals.

Jesus offers a "word" in the Gospel of John when he says, "I am the door: by me if any man enter in, he shall be saved" (10:9). That's not very exotic at all. My way or no way, it sounds like. *I am the way . . . Ego sum via . . .* No way but through Christ.

I was made an offering to Christ at a month old. My mother, practically an infant herself at twenty years old, flew with a ten-day-old, unbaptized baby from El Paso, Texas, to Providence, Rhode Island (when flights like that took ten hours), and I was baptized two weeks later in the Episcopal Church. "If the plane was in danger of going down, I would have baptized you myself," she explained to me when I was preparing for confirmation as an adolescent. I was pretty impressed by the gravity inherent in that determination. *We were giving you to God no matter what.*

And what was promised in my behalf? My godmothers and godfather, in the words of the old 1929 Episcopalian Book of Common Prayer used then, renounced "the devil and all his works, the vain pomp and glory of the world, with all covetous desires of the same, and the sinful desires of the flesh."

They did? And I wasn't consulted?

They declared on my behalf that I would believe "all the Articles of the Christian Faith as contained in the Apostles' Creed."

And then Mr. Neild, the rector baptizing his first (or second, there is some dispute here) baby at St. Luke's Episcopal Church, looked at my sponsors and said, "Wilt thou be baptized in this Faith?"

And these three people, two of whom remained strangers to me forever, said, "That is my desire." And, "by God's help," they agreed to "obediently keep God's holy will and commandments and walk in the same all the days of thy life."

And having boldly signed up all the days of *my* life, they passed me on to baptism, to a life in Christ.

Tell me they don't sign up the children anymore!

Once in the door, there is a way of life in Christ. My confirmation vows, meant to renew those promises undertaken in my behalf, did not "take." Confirmed as an unlovely, early adolescent in the Episcopal Church, and many years later as the end product of a confused Catholic "conversion," I said "I do" because it said to in the script and to question that would have led to some embarrassing scenes.

Unlike most unthinking confirmands, however, I was granted another chance to confirm what those people promised on my behalf forty-seven years ago. After the abbot nursed us through our year of novitiate, he stood before the tiny altar of the prayer chapel that once served him as the abbey church and said, "By now, you should know, from this year of experience as an oblate novice, under what conditions you are about to make your Final Oblation as an Oblate of St. Benedict."

The initial oblation was made at my baptism, but I got to do the final offering myself. I still have to renounce the devil, the vain pomp of the world, and the sinful desires of the flesh. At least now I know what they look and feel like. At least now I know what I'm renouncing. This time, my patron was not the friends of my grandparents, as my baptism sponsors were, but Blessed Joanna Mary Bonomo, serving as "godmother"/namesake.

There may be other ways, other words, to salvation for others. These were the ones that offered me and moved me past the door to the land of the New Jerusalem.

〜

I leave the oblate library for a break to pray in the chapel. Signs all over the retreat center have emerged since I disappeared to study, closing off public space next week when I planned to be back.

I find Brother John Climachus. "Can I use the oblate library? Or should I make other plans? I don't care about the food or the cafeteria. I just need to know if there's a place for people like me to write."

The oblate library is okay for "people like me," he decides. The abbey is far less a locked door to me than it was at the beginning of this study, this Jubilee Year.

"I went to the oblate library and you weren't there," says Abbot Antony as I turn around. He wants to tell me about St. Ephrem, whose day we are celebrating. Every year he pulls out of his file a poem by Ephrem to read in honor of his day. Translated by one of the "old ones" at St. Meinrad's in Indiana, Abbot Antony has carried it with him ever since his days there.

"I thought you would like to read it," he says. "I think you like things like this. Read it slowly."

Overcaffeinated—for otherwise I would sleep the entire quiet afternoon away—I try to taste the poem slowly in the prayer chapel while a nun tries to meditate on the tiny Stations of the Cross posted along the walls—and also stay out of my way. The chapel is very small. The translation is awkward, which actually helps the early aestheticism discussed. This "Song on the Ascetic Life" sings of fasting, thirsting, vigils, and prayers. If we are bound to the New Jerusalem, we are joined in the abbot's beloved Divine Providence—a funny "place" for a kid who grew up in Pawtucket, right next door to the city of Providence, Rhode Island. Dear Abbot, your poem of a saint who lived in the 300s A.D. talks of oblation and baptism just as I am doing 1,700 years later.

> Mind (and wit) were altar;
> Will, the minist'ring priest;
> For a spotless lamb, I
> Sacrificed my person—
> Thus made I the Off'ring.
>
> Endless on watch I was
> That no oil come near me;
> For I'd been anointed
> Long ago in baptism
> With the Spirit's unction.[2]

"When will I see you again?" he asks at supper.

"I'm coming back next Friday."

"Oh?" His eyes widen. "There's a big retreat here next week."

"That's okay. I can't eat here, but Brother John Climachus says I can use the oblate library."

"Good. I'll bring you a banana." He glides away. "I am so glad you like the poem. You really need to use the big Divine Office, the one the Pope uses. It has poems."

June 16, 2000: Eleventh Week of Ordinary Time

June Gloom. When I moved to San Diego from New England thirteen years ago this month, the weather I found here shocked me. I would make the rounds of interviewing for some dismal job at miserable pay and the person offering me the job would say earnestly, "It's the weather. People would pay *us* to come here to work."

"Yeah? How much?" I would ask. The day would eventually break, overcast and muddy, and stay that way until late afternoon, when a heavily filtered sun might grace us for an hour or two before sliding off into a murky sunset. I didn't know June Gloom or on-shore flow or any of that. I just knew this was *not* what I expected of summer in San Diego. The Chamber of Commerce had lied to the world.

Familiarity is everything. June Gloom comes every year and separates the high liturgical season of suffering and redemption from the great mass of Ordinary Time. Like June Gloom, we are in a month of specialty weeks designed to wean us off the high of Easter: Feast of the Holy Trinity, Feast of Corpus Christi, Sacred Heart of Jesus Sunday—all the break we need to settle down from Easter and continue on our journey home.

I am halfway through this Jubilee Year called by Pope John Paul, halfway through a year of Fridays at the monastery studying the Rule. I feel like all the "best part" and richness of the experience are probably done and that the rest of the year here will be a dutiful crossing off of days the way I once did with a little calendar I made of months left until retirement, when I was having a bad time at work. Maybe I'm victim of June Gloominess or post-Easter letdown, despite the specialty feasts. I remind myself of the day some ten or twelve years ago when I was working on my summer garden and the day was as quiet with perfection as anything I had ever experienced. And with all my heart I prayed to the nameless deities I used between religions. *Let the clock stop now*. And had my prayer been answered, I would have lived in that moment I thought was Eden forever, but would never have stumbled into the agonies of Lent that were still ahead of me, or the glories of Easter that would be mine to claim as well.

Onward Christian Soldiers was always my favorite childhood hymn. Go forward, or you will never arrive at the New Jerusalem.

The signs announcing the Big Retreat! Do Not Enter! that appeared last week are gone this week when I arrive, and there are only a few cars in the retreat center lot. Mysterious ways, this abbey . . . But the retreat center's living area is blocked off and somebody is preaching or teaching to all the brothers assembled there. Unfortunately, the coffee is on the other side of the brothers and the blockade.

The bookstore is open. The Big Office Abbot Antony mentioned, the one with the poetry in it, he said, the one the Pope uses, is available at a truly big price—$185. I can't afford the poetry.

A set of younger monks on retreat (not from here) come outside from the talk, smoke cigarettes, and make merry grumbling about everyone else's lack of holiness or wisdom. It is a tough life on either side of the Rule. They talk exactly like I think.

Mass. There are rows of folding chairs supplementing the choir stalls to accommodate the hoards of visiting monks while we have plenty of room in the congregation—exactly the opposite of Easter Mass. As the bells begin their toneless call, Brother Robert whirls in via motorized chair. He, at least, seems guaranteed his regular seat. The procession this morning is truly a marvel of monks.

For people like me, unaware of the inner life of the monastery, Mass serves as the daily newsletter. Last week we prayed for Brother Matthew who was in the hospital for tests. He reappeared by Vespers. This week we pray for the Benedictine conference, so I make a good guess that this is what is displacing me—and even the monks who live here to some degree.

Lunch. I sure am grateful for self-sufficiency today. Fasting, I have carried bread with me. At the last moment, I added a plastic bottle of water that—with "Do Not Enter" signs between me and the coffee, and a marvel of monks in between as well—I am especially grateful to have. The sun is out. The bells for lunch toll. Joy of joy, I even have a copy of the *Angelus* stuck in my workbook, which I undoubtedly liberated from the retreat cafeteria, and I pray it while the bells toll, knowing the monks inside are doing the same.

It has a different feeling to it, maybe not communal, but not solitary either.

The prayer walk is windswept today, and still seemingly free of any decent rocks for the someday rock garden. The ocean has turned to a cobalt blue, sharply etched against the light blue sky. The mysterious animal droppings are still on the pathway, but bleached white by the sun. No fresh ones, at least.

A new monolith has appeared since last week at Station 8 ("Jesus Speaks to the Weeping Women"): a small cross laid into the ground, made out of medium-sized rocks with springs of wild raspberry-colored flowers propped into the cracks. Next to that is a large circle of quite large rocks (*where are they finding them?*), carefully placed, and carefully edged by smaller rocks. It is a very elaborate, very loving effort. Station 13 ("Jesus Is Taken Down from the Cross) catches my breath—the wild purple-colored flowers have been arranged to fashion a living, wild cross around the thirteenth monument. It is gaudily beautiful; the wildflowers on the ground surrounding it look a little thin for giving so much to this effort.

I am always fascinated at how strong the need is to build these altars that I call monoliths. Is it out of respect or the need to mark our path the way the bleached animal droppings do, or what? I, of course, have no such need, I think—and then go off to find a small dark rock (barely larger than a pebble) to remind me of Obadiah, to remember that I am small in the schemes and hearts of others. I have no need to build monoliths because I seem determined to carry home the prayer walk itself, one rock at a time!

Chapters 60 and 62: Priests and the Monastery

These chapters deal with priests: admitting them as members of the community, and monks who have been chosen from within the community for ordination as priests. In both situations, Benedict emphasizes that the priests are still subject to the discipline of the Rule and obedience to the abbot.

The uneasiness with which Benedict deals with priests who wish to be admitted to a monastery and with ordaining priests from among the monks clearly reflects the tensions of the time. Monasticism was primarily a lay order, and the desert fathers are full of stories of monks running away from the "honor" of ordination to priest or bishop about to be bestowed on them, and Benedict himself did the same. "Just because he is a priest, he may not therefore forget the obedience and discipline of the Rule," says Benedict—sounding a bit peevish at it.

> The elders and monks in the desert of Scete came together and agreed that Father Isaac should be ordained a priest to serve the Church there. But Abbot Isaac, hearing this, fled to Egypt and hid himself in the bushes, deeming himself unworthy of priesthood. A large number of monks set off to catch him. They stopped near Abbot Isaac's hiding place to rest and turned loose the ass that carried their baggage. Now while the ass was feeding, he came to where Abbot Isaac was hiding. At daybreak, the monks were seeking the ass and found where the old man had hidden himself. They were about to tie him up and take him away, but the old man did not allow them, saying, "Now I can no longer oppose you since it is perhaps the will of God that I, though unworthy, should receive priestly orders."[3]

Like most people of any religious persuasion, I grew up familiar with the clerical, ordained ministries as well as (in the last thirty years at least) a growing group of lay ministries. I knew the family priest and feared the bishop when he came to "test" and confirm us.

My family was thoroughly socialized into parish life. I remember one New Year's Day when my father got my help (for five dollars) to stuff pledge reminders into envelopes. He was the church treasurer for years, although, as a CPA, he often wished he'd be asked to build a stage or cook for the pancake breakfast—anything but what he was doing for a living. My mother was an altar guild member, cookbook coordinator, and later, a bell-ringer. When my father died, she took over his late, last ministry as a Eucharistic minister.

I stuffed envelopes, delivered cookbooks, sang in the children's choir, soloed in the adult choir, and substituted for the organist on vacation before I went to college. I spent (it seems in retrospect) an inordinate amount of my growing up in church-related activities, although church itself was a once-a-week phenomenon.

As an adult trying to get back into mainstream churchgoing, I tried what I knew. I went to Eucharistic ministry classes. I sang in a folk choir. I played percussion for a youth group. I trained as a lector, and learned how to speak all my "t's" and "ed's" to the back of the church. I made sure I was present at *some* church, no matter where I was in the world or what my schedule was, once a week.

It never did "take" for me the way it did so well for my parents. They were so suited to socialize in Christ, and I lived in fear of it— and considered myself a bad Christian for my inability. It's the Martha/Mary thing all over again. Mary may be praised for the "best part," but she doesn't have any friends, and will never go to the ham-and-bean supper.

I didn't know about monastics until I found that little photocopied flyer about Secular Franciscans at a retreat at the Mission. The response to the very *words* "Secular Franciscan" was powerful: *There's a place for people like me.* Without knowing, I *knew*, suddenly, that there was another way besides parish lay ministry and meetings to respond to God in my life. I'd had that experience of words hitting such a deep chord in me only once before, when somebody was taking me to my first AA meeting, and trying to determine how "bad" a drunk I was.

"So do you ever have blackouts?" he asked cheerfully.

So, that's what they're called, I thought. How could I know a blackout if I was having them? By their very definition, they have left you out of the picture and become a black hole of mystery. But the word *blackout* suddenly gave definition to the edges around the black holes of mystery. So too the sudden sense of non-clerical religious life. *That's what they're called.*

It doesn't have to be either/or. Even Benedict accommodates the priestly with the lay monastic. For Benedict, it's not where you come from as much as where you plan to stay—emotionally, as well as physically.

～

I settle on writing in the retreat center's big open area, where I ate jelly beans after Holy Saturday's vigil, and where I once tried to write on a Friday, feeling miserably unwanted and finally fleeing early. How long ago could that have been? All I could remember today during Mass was the Gospel story:

> Then came she and worshipped him, saying, Lord, help me. But
> he answered, and said, It is not meet to take the children's bread,

and to cast it to dogs. And she said, Truth, Lord: yet the dogs eat of the crumbs which fall from their masters' table. Then Jesus answered and said unto her, O woman, great is thy faith: be it unto thee even as thou wilt. (Matthew 15:25–28)

How badly I have wanted to be part—of the Catholic Church, of parish life, of Secular Franciscan life, and now of this Benedictine way. Even being on the edge is fine, I think. You don't *always* have to play the leading role in your own life story.

And it just isn't as isolated today as it felt then. Father Vincent stops by and I ask him about his transition to prior and whether it's going okay. Except for the few brothers who would happily string him up by his thumbs, things are good, he says.

"You sound like us," I say. "No different from regular folks."

"But there *is* a difference," he says. "We live in such close proximity. You can get away—to places like here."

The retreatant monks on smoke break go back to the conference, and the gurgling of the angel fountains for sale at the bookstore compete pleasantly with the chants and prayers behind me.

The bookstore lady comes over. "What's your name?"

"Carol."

"No, that's not it."

"Really, it is. Carol."

"No, I mean, Abbot Antony was walking around here, and he asked if I knew where one of the oblates was, but a special kind of oblate, something he said in Latin, *bono* oblate? Could that be?"

"My last name is Bonomo. It's Latin for *good man*."

"That's what he said: *Bonomo* oblate. He was running around here with a banana for you."

I leave early, but I feel like I have found a welcome here, even in my departures and my absences.

JULY
Search and Ye Shall Find

"Ask, and it shall be given you;
seek, and ye shall find;
knock, and it shall be opened unto you."
Matthew 7:7

July 7, 2000: Thirteenth Week of Ordinary Time

Even by San Diego standards, the weather is jaw-dropping, drop-dead gorgeous. No matter. I am cranky without relief today, snarling at other drivers on the freeway driving to the abbey, wanting to be any-where else *but* here, this life.

And it isn't even big stuff, never is, that really sets me off. Two years ago, it was big stuff during this time of Ordinary—my father was dead. I wasn't comfortable in the Catholic Church, and I couldn't talk myself back into an Episcopal Church that had changed so much in my absence. It wasn't working between me and the Secular Franciscans, and I didn't know if I would ever find a spiritual pillow on which to place my weary head.

Those were times of real agony. Today I am not really feeling grief, but peevish frustration—having looked forward to this retreat day for a while, is it going to be one of *those* days again. Am I going to end up going home right after Mass, still snarling at the drivers along the road too well traveled?

The legislative meeting was a snore, and for this I got up forty-five minutes *earlier*, on a *vacation* day, to be the only vote in the chamber *against* removing state legislative term limits. As the desert fathers would have said, "What is that to me?"

I've been trying to get my mink coat into storage since May, but the only place that does storage is only open Monday through Friday when I am working. Apparently my maid is supposed to drop off my mink, but I didn't have any reason to be downtown either, and we are now into July. I carefully packed the coat last night and brought it with me to this morning's early chamber legislative meeting. Alas, even maids don't get up early? The fur storage people don't open until ten o'clock, and I ended up dragging my poor mink coat back home before heading to the abbey, filling my car with much cursing.

And then there's the matter of the Divine Office, the "big" one recommended by Abbot Antony. I checked it out at the abbey bookstore last visit. For some reason, I had a price tag of $60 in my mind, but I wanted to check on it. The $185 reality was quite stunning. Recommended by my beloved abbot or not, $185 sure was a lot of money for a lot of prayers I would probably never use. When I got home, I went online to Amazon.com, and there it was. Shipping and handling included, I would *save* $60. I promptly ordered it and then settled back to wait the three to five weeks of backorder time. (The Divine Office, parts I–IV, as prayed by the Pope, is a little too obscure for even Amazon.com to keep in stock. On the other hand, there *were* a couple of reader reviews posted, so I'm not the only one after this thing.) Last week, I wrote to the abbot and mentioned how tired I'm becoming of my regular "spiritual lite" reading, how I was ready to move on to more substantive fare, how I hoped the Big Office would lead me to some good readings, and how I'd saved a bundle by buying it at Amazon.com.

Two hours after I mailed my letter to him, Amazon.com e-mailed me to note that the Office could not be obtained and my order was being cancelled.

Humbled, I brought a check with me to the monastery to buy their overpriced Office and be done with it. The bookstore—along with the *entire* retreat center and cafeteria—is closed for the *entire* month of July.

Okay, so it's one of *those* visits. The Divine Providence that Abbot Antony loves is obviously saying "no" and pretty unsubtly, lest I miss the point.

I go into the abbey church for Mass in one of my lesser Christian moods, in no mood for anything but reflections on life's basic unfairness.

Abbot Antony's communion cup hand is all bandaged up. He didn't sound very good when I called yesterday to confirm my head count for the St. Benedict Feast Day celebration. I hate how calling his extension goes right into his cell where he could be praying, reading, napping, or just about anything.

"He fell again," says Nancy after Mass. Indeed he is black and blue along the side of his face when he comes out to greet us, and he cheerfully pulls up his black robe sleeves to show us his additional wounds. The ladies cluck and assure him that he'll live longer than any of us.

"Oh, I wouldn't want that," he says. "But I do hope you're all going where I'm going," he adds. "We'll all be together." He turns to me. "What are you reading?"

"Don't go there," I hiss. I tell him about Amazon.com and his eyes grow big and alert. "I just told the bookstore they're being undersold by Amazon.com," he says. "Maybe you should tell Amazon.com where *they* can get the Big Office!"

"The bookstore is closed too!" I practically howl.

"I'll get you the books," he offers. The others begin talking, and I'm wondering if this day might actually get better. "Ask and it shall be given you," says Jesus (Matthew 7:7). *Speak up.* "Abbot, is it possible to work in the oblate library this afternoon?"

"Oh yes, certainly." The iconographer, Margaret, he just introduced me to, has a key, and she offers to unlock it on the way out. "Save you a few steps," she says kindly, to Abbot Antony.

With everything closed up, it is a good thing I'm fasting. I didn't know the entire retreat center was closed, the big open area and everything, although I should have. When I called Brother John Climachus to tell him I was coming, his tape machine had the message that the retreat center was closed for the entire month. I thought that meant the sleeping areas, not *everything*. But I was going to fast, and so I packed water as well, just in case. I take my bread and bottle of water to the prayer walk and find a little bench to sit on. The sound of the bells is a bit distant, but still clearly audible. I pull out the card I keep as a marker for one of my commentaries: *The Angel of the Lord declared unto Mary.* I "hear" Abbot Antony's dried out vocal chords lovingly say those words in my head. *And she conceived of the Holy Spirit*, I respond mentally. In the company of the abbot's great spirit, we say the *Angelus*, and then I break bread, outsider still, but clinging to the outside of *this* community, *here* above the ocean, the place where the great spiritual desert crashes into the enormous sea of God's mercy.

When I was barely a teenager, I belonged to Rainbow Girls, a "daughter" group founded by the Freemasons, full of mysterious ritual, white gowns, and the opportunity to socialize with non-Catholics. This was big stuff in the early 1960s of small-town New England.

The worst office you could get was the one called "Outer Observer." The Outer Observer got to march around the hall like everybody else in a white gown, but when you went to your official station, hers was a folding chair outside the meeting room. Hers was the solemn responsibility to keep watch against intruders, who might bear our secrets away. We didn't know quite what those secrets were, but we were pretty sure we had them. Parts of our ceremonies called for whispering. There was also an Inner Observer, but I don't remember her role unless it was to remind us we left somebody outside who had to be pulled inside when we voted—out of sight, out of mind and all that.

Ironically, since Rainbow Girls were considered somewhat anti-Catholic when I was growing up, the Outer Observer role reminds me for all the world of St. Zosimus. St. Z was placed in Santa Lucia monastery in Sicily by his parents when he was seven and he spent the next thirty years watching over the relic of St. Lucy and tending the door. When the abbot died and the monks couldn't agree on a successor, the bishop of Syracuse was called in. He looked them over and asked if anyone was missing. Somebody remembered St. Z, still watching the relic and tending the door. As soon as the bishop saw him, he said, "Behold him whom the Lord hath chosen."

I am no saint outside these doors tending faithfully to humble tasks, but on days like this it helps to remember that there *is* a reason (Divine Providence) even for outsiderness.

The prayer walk is flooded over in two spots. Some pipes in the sprinkler system are apparently broken, and I have to tippy-toe around the path in spots. I find a deep reddish rock, broken cleanly on two sides by tractors or other equipment. It is a good rock for remembering the broken, annoying days.

When I return to the retreat center, all the doors are locked everywhere, and I can't get near the oblate library to even see if it is unlocked. How could the iconographer manage when the whole area is locked away?

Isn't this where I came in?—like my first experiences of the monastery? I drive home almost cheerful in my resignation, and supervise the landscaping project going on at home instead. "What color roses do you want?" says the site foreman. "You've got fifteen bushes coming."

"Fourteen red or pink," I answer. "One white." The white roses will someday be for the abbot.

Chapter 63: Rank in the Monastery

The unions would have loved Benedict. *The brothers will rank in order, depending upon the date of their entrance, the merit of their lives, or the order of the abbot,* says Benedict. While unions tend to scream mightily against merit ranking, it is not Benedict's first preference either. *With the exception of those promoted or demoted by the abbot, everyone shall take his place by the date of his entrance to the monastery,* Benedict continues a few sentences later.

The commentaries make good sense out of this way of ordering a community, where respect flows all ways (*juniors will honor their seniors, and the seniors love their juniors*), and seniority is not based on who you were *before* but how long you have been in formation on the road to the New Jerusalem.

Still, who wants to be new? Who wants to start again at the beginning, when that "beginning" has humility stamped all over it? Not me. I want to build on where I've been, get college credit for those life experiences as the ads in the back of magazines promote. Returning to the Secular Franciscans, I heard that harsh reality: *You'll have to start over again.* But hadn't I learned that on the road home, from my father's death, with a notebook and a stuffed Beanie Baby tiger named Francis next to me for company and 3,200 miles alone between life and death?

In a word, *no*.

I'd never been in a union or the military or any ranked system until I walked into Alcoholics Anonymous. You're ranked there, not on your date of entry, but on your sobriety date.

I liked my initial sobriety date: February 12, Abraham Lincoln's birthday, as I pointed out to my social worker. "Well, he *did* emancipate the slaves," Ron murmured in response. I wavered around for two months, alcohol- and AA-free, before bingeing off for a few days, unsuccessfully trying to get roaring drunk. Having failed the roaring drunk part, but doing quite nicely in the crazies department, I let myself get checked in to the university's infirmary for a few days' D&D (detox and denial) and plenty of Valium and sleeping pills, thanks to the admitting psychiatrist.

"Get off the pills too," said Ron.

"These are *medically* prescribed, Buster. See where it says, 'Dr.' on the prescription in front of his name? Can you do that?"

"I'll match my success rate against theirs any day," he said. "Get off the pills. Oh, yeah, and find a Higher Power too. You're going to need one."

"Do I have to change my sobriety date? I *like* February 12."

"That's up to you," Ron shrugged, stole the chocolate cake off my plate, and departed to leave me to my doped-up demons. It was a very long night.

The next day I gave the attending nurse all my pills—including the ones I came with, prescribed by a different doctor and saved for "emergencies." I said a Hail Mary, although I wasn't Catholic and didn't know what the rosary actually was. I just thought I needed a woman Higher Power, and Mary probably had kind eyes, like the attending nurse I was handing my pills to. She was from Rhode Island, like me, and she said, "You'll do it; you'll make it. Rhode Islanders are tough."

The worst was the date. I left the infirmary on Friday, and on Sunday, I showed up alone at the big open AA meeting in town.

"My name's Carol. I want to join."

"Great!" said the gorgeous young woman at the back table who was, I later learned, the group secretary. She wrote down on a member list, "Carol," and paused. "Sobriety date?"

"Friday. What was Friday's date?"

I swear she paled. I was busy trying to look like a tough Rhode Islander, not a raw drunk.

"April 13," she said.

"Friday the thirteenth? Great. It'll be my lucky date." By then the old-timers were circling me. *Just out*, they must have been thinking. *Barely stopped shaking, no sponsor, nobody with her—a real live one.*

Being new sucked. Being new and acting so together didn't exactly help. I was unapproachable and unafraid through my second anniversary of sobriety—at which point, I finally began to look and act like the newcomer brat I'd been all along.

Newcomers are great teachers to the old-timers. They always said it in AA—although we never believed them—and Benedict says it too: *In all cases order shall not be prejudiced by age, for Samuel and David, but youths, sat in judgment of the priests.*

> There was an elder who had a well-tried novice living with him and once, when he was annoyed, he drove the novice out of the cell. The novice sat down outside and waited for the elder. When the elder opened the door and found him there, he did penance before him saying, "You are my Father now because your patience and humility have overcome the weakness of my soul. Come back in; you will be the elder and Father; I will be the youth and novice; for by your good work, you have surpassed my old age."[1]

It's all in the perspective. They tell the story of the newcomer who walked into an AA meeting, shaking and stumbling, and some of the old-timers got hold of him and told their stories to sober him up.

"This program works!" said Mort. "I've been sober thirty-two years."

"It really does work," added his buddy. "Thanks to AA and people like Mort, I haven't had a drink in nearly seventeen years."

The newcomer turned his bleary eyes on the third man. "And you?"

"Oh, me. I've been sober a month."

At that, the newcomer shook his head amazed. "How'd you manage a *whole month* without a drink?"

It's the same with our humble ranks as oblates. I'm no longer the newest, but still very close to bottom in any seniority. I sure act new. Apparently I needed practice—RCIA, AA, Secular Franciscans, and now Benedictines have all "begun me" anew. I never heard of anybody the abbot talks about, never read the books or saw the films or understood the religious practices. I still can't remember the difference between Commons and Proper in the Office, and I don't care about the "stuff" I don't know. Facing Abbot Antony, the most senior member of the monastic community, I am open-handed in my ignorance. But there is a place for people like me as well as people like Abbot Antony in the Rule.

On St. Vincent Ferrer Day—April 5 when you're talking *real* Ordinary Time—Abbot Antony wrote me, "Keep on the way you are going. It is the right one. People who have thought differently than the Church have accentuated the Truth for us. You are right in the midst of it."

So even the bratty newcomer has a part to play.

July 11, 2000: The Solemnity of Our Father St. Benedict

June Gloom is no respecter of calendars and hangs heavy and cool this July morning. It is a treat to leave the office for a few hours to celebrate the birth of Western monasticism, in St. Benedict.

He has two feast days, unlike the rest of the lot. Benedict's death day should normally be the big feast day, since death recognizes date of arrival in eternity (and Benedict is such a stickler for things like rank). But his death date usually falls in Lent, when feast days are at a minimum. So we gussy up the day of his birth as a solemn feast, although I notice the abbot's language is less forceful on the pleasure of our attendance than in February. ("For those able to come for the Mass on the Feast of our Holy Father Benedict, July 11," he wrote, "you are invited to have lunch afterwards. However, it will be necessary to let me know a few days before.") I don't even remember there being a celebration in July last year when I was an oblate novice.

Nonetheless, the dates are probably not as important as what we honor. In the little book the abbot has been reading to us at oblate meetings, we are reminded of how little is known of the man Benedict, how we follow a Rule, not a personality. We know as much about the man as the innocuous painting of a bearded man holding a book that decorated the exposition and is crowned with white daisies.

The little abbey church fills up early and quite noisily. The retreat center parking lot is full, which makes no sense since the retreat center itself is still tightly closed.

Holy Benedict, we adore you, in our silence and in our noise.

Extra clanking bells for the occasion too. Father Abbot Henry emerges from the thin holiday ranks of priests and monks, from the murky gloom we call "summer," dressed in gold and red, as magnificent as a beautiful bird. Mass begins.

Hildegard is in Ireland and Germany for the summer. I haven't seen Gregory since before Lent, and his appearance today is rewarded by listening to my shrieking, "Where the *hell* have you been?" when we gather in the retreat dining area. Brother Maurius has kitchen duty. It hardly seems fair to make the monks work the retreat cafeteria on such an important feast day.

"Oh, this is such a happy day—no problem," he answers. "Today we get wine and music. No women though—too much trouble!"

Gregory has one of the Big Office books. "How did you decide to do that?" I ask. Last I knew he was on the little one like me.

"It's a funny story," he says. I think all Big Offices must come with a funny story by now. He decided to try extra readings for Lent, getting them off the Internet. If he liked it, he was going to buy the big set.

"Let me know what you decide," Abbot Antony said to him.

Gregory figured the abbot could get him a special price or something, so he came back later to say yes, I want the big set. And told the abbot a few more times that he was ready for the Big Office, and felt like he was getting put off, not knowing what was happening. One day the abbot handed him the four-volume Office and said, "Use these as long as you want."

Gregory tried to pay for them, but the abbot insisted—"Use them as long as you want." Gregory learned they belonged to an oblate who died and his books were donated to the abbey.

Well, I can do that too, I decided; label my things carefully so whoever goes through my stuff when I die will know to send them to the abbey, along with returning my oblate vows like you're supposed to.

Nancy and Gregory are both going to be at the retreat in August, which is my next time at the monastery. Nancy says it's a "highly structured" weekend, which makes my free-range, cranky soul a little nervous. Despite a long and reasonably good history of structured retreats with the Franciscans, I no longer like following somebody's idea of a good retreat—even my abbot's.

The sun finds a gap in the sky and begins to poke through. I return to work. Four hours later, I have the Big Office myself, purchased at a church supply store in Escondido, leather covered—and *still* thirty dollars cheaper than the monastery bookstore (even if it had been open to buy something). For me and to share with some nameless, maybe yet-to-be-born oblate. It will take me a month to figure out how to use it, I think. There is literally a diagram of how the offices "look," a guide for the Liturgy of the Hours for 2000, three separate booklets of prayers—solemnities and feasts, night prayer, and assorted daily prayers—*and* a red supplement of saints. There are Proper of

Seasons, Solemnities, Ordinaries, Psalter, Proper of Saints, Commons, and Office for the Dead.

But one section stuns me, as certain to be there as the abbot is certain of his eternal reward: Appendix IV. Poetry.

There's poetry in it, he promised me. And on this Solemnity of St. Benedict, I find the poetry indeed.

Chapter 64: Election of the Abbot

Once again, Benedict returns to the subject of the abbot. First he discusses choosing the abbot, using the criteria of *goodness of life and wisdom of teaching*, rather than rank within the community. Once in office, the necessary virtues are enumerated for the abbot. Moderation is especially stressed: *He must so arrange everything such that the strong have something to yearn for and the weak nothing to run from.*

Obviously the role of the abbot is central to the success of Benedict's ideas of community. Early in the Rule (chapter 2), the qualities of the abbot are discussed in enough detail that we spend seven days on it in daily reading. The abbot's role and responsibilities are mentioned in five of the seventy-three chapters of the Rule directly, and eight more include discussions of his responsibilities—18 percent of the Rule. Chapter 64, on how the abbot is chosen from the monastic ranks, takes two days to read.

I wish we gave the same care to choosing our spiritual directors in the non-monastic world ordinary oblates live in. We trust these people with the care and nourishment of our souls, but how do we choose them? And why?

Although I lived through seven years of psychiatric caretaking of one sort or another, one year of group therapy, three years of social-work monitoring, and four years of AA meetings—some of these concurrently—I never heard the expression "spiritual counseling" until I went to confession for the first time. Being told to find a spiritual counselor as part of the "absolution" process was traumatic, particularly as it came *after* conversion class (RCIA) and my entry into the Catholic Church. (*What have I gotten into here?*) On the back of the parish bulletin, where the ads for cars, insurance, and funeral crypts were, was an ad for spiritual counseling. I'd heard Father Howard at Mass a few times and was favorably impressed, so I called.

"I'm very good and very expensive," he said. "What's your problem?"

Damned if I knew. The "problem" seemed to be the confessional, so I stopped confessing. That helped until I started going on Franciscan retreats at the Mission. The friars were always roping us into some sort of confession game. "Twelve of you have come to me asking me to hear confession," Father Rusty would announce. "The rest of you undoubtedly want to do the same thing now that you know what the first twelve asked for. Now there's twenty of you and only one of me, so what we're going to do is. . . . " And we'd take a rock from a basket and when we were ready to let go of our all sins, we'd bring the rock to the altar, and I always got the biggest rock I could find to drag to the altar. Or we'd write out our sins and burn them on a pyre or something.

After a while when I started going to weeklong retreats, I'd sign up for spiritual counseling each day and try to figure out what was or wasn't a sin, and was the road to hell really paved with good intentions as my mother always said? "How do I find a spiritual director?" I asked Father Rusty after I'd heard him and Sister Mary Lou talk about theirs at great length.

"Oh, Carol, I'm just really busy . . . "

"I'm not asking *you*. I'm asking you how to *find* one."

"Well, ask around . . . "

"That's what I'm doing!"

I wrote to Sister Mary Lou while I was on a plane to Washington, D.C. Did she take people for spiritual counseling, know of anybody . . . ? She wrote back recommending a Franciscan nun who had just come to the area, Sister Pat. I held on to Sister Pat's business card for a while.

In one fell swoop, *all* the Mission's retreat staff was relocated elsewhere, and we were saying goodbye to Brother Zuniga, Father Rusty, and Sister Mary Lou. Once the escape hatch—my literal "retreat" was removed—my boss abruptly left, and an interim arrived who, after a few difficult meetings, said, "Have you considered counseling?"

"*What?*"

"Counseling. Getting help. Your anger's going to eat you alive."

Somehow I heard his concern in the hard words. I called Sister Pat, and we agreed to meet once a month. I still couldn't name the problem, but there was obviously *something* going on. I cried uncontrollably that summer. The retreat staff was gone. My best friend and coworker suddenly decided that early retirement looked good and exited.

"They're all leaving," I cried to Sister Pat. "And I'm staying. It's usually the other way around. What's happening?"

And then my mother cancelled the annual trip she and my father made each Thanksgiving to San Diego. "He isn't feeling well," she said. "They can't figure out what's wrong. All he has is a cough. He sleeps all the time."

No, God, not that. Don't go there. He's only sixty-five years old, for crying out loud. Don't leave me, Daddy. Not now.

We went there, and Sister Pat walked with me the whole way. While some family and friends either denied what was happening or actively struggled with the rapidly moving symptoms, I waited, eyes wide open, heart breaking into jagged ugly pieces, eyes streaming tears. I could have drowned if all those tears stayed inside, but they poured out of me—every loss, every disillusionment, every abandonment, every "otherness" and outsidedness, every "no" of my life, every hurt, all of it breaking down. "RAGE, GOD!" I wrote in black and gray in my collage diary—"And you, Our Father, who art in heaven, there on the sad height, washed up, curse, bless with fierce tears. It doesn't matter which, now . . . "

"Littleness," said Sister Pat. "This is littleness." And she prayed with me and for me, and finally sent me empty-handed back to Rhode Island so my father could die with his last message all done with enormous eyes in a wasted face: *Take care of your mother*.

After he died, and I drove home, the Secular Franciscans let me know my needs weren't theirs, and Sister Pat was moving on. I didn't want the Benedictines, and they weren't anything like Kathleen Norris wrote, and they didn't even *sing* nice, for crying out loud, but the new oblate said, "They do spiritual counseling, and it's free."

Spiritually broke, I thought it sounded like a deal. As a spiritual director, Abbot Antony is not a "companioning" sort. Instead, he shows "discretion and moderation" as Benedict asks when guiding spiritual brats like me, tempers his suggestions *so that what the strong may wish and the weak not flee may be the state of affairs*.

Abba Moses asked Brother Zacharias, "Tell me what I ought to do." Brother Zacharias said, "Are you asking me, Father?"

The old man said, "Believe me, Zacharias, my son, I have seen the Holy Spirit descending on you and since then, I am constrained to ask you." Then Brother Zacharias drew his hood off his head, put it under his feet and trampled on it saying, "The man who does not let himself be treated thus cannot become a monk."[2]

I have not fled yet. "What I like with Abbot Antony," said Father Vincent to me once, "is that he makes it simple."

Simple and sturdy, persevering in all things. He may have chosen me as much as I chose him, but as this chapter of the Rule ends, quoting Matthew, may it be to Abbot Antony also: *Amen, I say to you, over all his goods will he place him* (Matthew 24:47).

AUGUST
Bring Forth Fruit

They shall still bring forth fruit in old age;
They shall be fat and flourishing . . .

Psalm 92:14

August 4, 2000: Seventeenth Week of Ordinary Time

I am so glad to be here for the oblate retreat that I arrive at 9:25 A.M. on Friday. There was never any notice of when we were to arrive, or when the retreat would officially begin. We were probably expected to filter in around Vespers (5:00 P.M. in regular time) or dinner. I was up by 5:45 A.M., and packed by 8:00. My poor pet cockatiel was packed into his cage with a three-day supply of food and water before he barely chomped his breakfast.

Despite today's anxiety to begin, the retreat really began its preparation a week ago when Felix flew to China for a few weeks. In the silence that followed, I listened during Mass to Old Testament readings of the miraculous feedings by Elisha ("He said again, Give the people, that they may eat . . . So he set it before them, and they did eat" [2 Kings 4:43–44]), and New Testament readings of miraculous feedings by Jesus ("And Jesus took the loaves; and when he had given thanks, he distributed to the disciples" [John 6:11])—and then began a seven-day fast as a way to bring me into the retreat.

It all sounded very spiritual and holy at the time—I was painting my St. Carol portrait with big strokes—but it was probably nothing more than the same anxiety to "start" that brought me here at 9:25 A.M. when the Friday retreatants were still enjoying a few last hours here.

153

"May the love of Francis 'of Assisi continue to lead you where you must go," wrote Sister Pat on the inside cover of a Franciscan omnibus of writings she gave me days before I left for Rhode Island to watch my father die.

It is two years later, and this is the only Franciscan book remaining in my collection. It had belonged to an elderly Franciscan nun of Sister Pat's motherhouse, and while it sometimes pained me to see it, I just couldn't toss it out. Another beginning for this oblate retreat— I could return the book at least part way to the Franciscans.

The Mission is between my house and the abbey. It is one of the twenty-one missions in California, and in my mind, one of the most beautiful. The first time I drove there in 1991, the ten-mile drive seemed to take forever, and in the pouring, dark rain of late afternoon, there suddenly loomed up this magnificent white mission, like a dove landed on the desert floor. It was love at first sight, and I found as many times as possible to spend hours there, many retreats, Mass on Sundays when I could get there, anything to be at my desert dove.

But the cemetery has always been my favorite part of the Mission. In the 1930s, its gates were used in a Hollywood film about Zorro, but within those gates is an oasis from the desert—leafy trees and green grass stubbed with memorials, some of them the oldest in these parts. The children's section could be the saddest part of this oasis, but here—partly because of the intertwined Spanish and Indian cultures— it is the place filled with teddy bears and Barbie Dolls and Tonka trucks, still playful, still alive with memories among those markers. The children never grow old and move away in this place. The old, crumbling stone markers contain an equal number of Anglo and Mexican names. The nameless are part of the large monument for all the Indians buried here.

The columbarium niches for cremated remains are formed into beautiful dark marble walls along two sides, with panels named after Franciscan saints. Felix and I will rest in "Anthony of Padua" for all eternity. The joke, as I explained it to Felix, was choosing a nice Italian saint as the namesake for interment. Felix, who is most decidedly Italian, assured me there was no such thing as a "nice Italian saint." The joke was on me anyway. St. Anthony of Padua, I discovered after I bought our niches, is Portuguese.

This cemetery and I have some stories together. At my first long visit—a weeklong silent retreat—I structured three of my days as

"Past," "Present," and "Future." On "Past" day, I went through the Mission museum on a self-directed tour and took all the time I wanted looking over the old history, where Mexico, Spain, and the United States came together violently and then separated. On "Present" day, I explored every inch of the Mission's retreat center, its library, chapel, and the Stations of the Cross walkaround. On "Future" day, I visited the cemetery, as excited as a kid on a field trip.

Two years later at what turned out to be my last Franciscan retreat, I was doing a midlife workshop with Father Rusty and Sister Mary Lou, and decided to go back to the cemetery for a visit. What better field trip during a retreat when you are reckoning your past and admitting your inevitable future than to visit your own tombstone?

I went past the Zorro gates and to the niche wall, to St. Anthony of Padua, and found our marker. This time, unlike all the other times, I made my eyes move *past* the first name (Felix) to the other one. I began to cry so hard, I had to keep walking past, but then I came back and ran my fingers slowly along the name: BONOMO. One finger traced out C-A-R-O-L and then the birthday and the dash that was waiting for its completion.

Everything that was ever important to me . . . I heard that as clear as a bell in my head, crystal clear and mournful. (My ego trained as a prima donna when I trained as a singer in college.)

Oh, the cemetery and I had memories together long before I knew that Benedict said to *keep death before one daily*. And we are not done yet.

Now I am returning here to bring back the last bit of my Franciscan life to the retreat center library before driving up the hill to the rest of my life as a Benedictine. It continues to amaze me, this place, with its beauty and orderliness. The soul of the Franciscan is an orderly one, with a clear administrative talent I envy. I suspect I fell in love with Francis himself through the beauty and marked serenity of this Mission—and that the love of Francis led me to where I must go.

∼

Up the hill to the wild ones, with the weeds and disorder and cheerfully ragged retreat center. Brother John Climachus, fresh back from visiting family and backpacking on his holiday, knows me by name now and is glad to see me, but I can't have my room yet. It is still occupied.

"But it's a great room, worth the wait." he says cheerfully. He should be in sales.

"Which one is it?" I ask suspiciously. I already know my room for next year's Easter retreat, ordered up during this past Easter, and it's the worst room in the joint. He describes the newer, remodeled section, "closest to the prayer chapel," facing the courtyard.

I graciously agree to wait.

I take my first prayer walk and, suitably, choose a rock from near its entry that is big enough in my hand to keep me from making a fist. As I begin to walk, my eye catches a fresh grave along the row of crosses under the abbey church and windows. It's too new for the marker to be marked and leaves me feeling as wary as the reported rattler did on the walk.

It is very warm and humid even here, so close to the ocean. Inland, where my little house is, the temperature will clear 100 degrees easily today. These are late September dog days, not early August weather, and the roses aren't the only things suffering. But warm as it is—the monastery lacks air conditioning in summer as well as heat in the winter—I am so glad to be here.

∽

There is a lovely image of a saint in front of the altar, candles, and the Blessed Sacrament. For the first time, I know who it is—St. John Vianney, patron of parish priests. I've been reading the Big Office, and, although I cannot fathom the *how* of the Office of Readings, I read a portion of his catechetical instructions just last night. His words on prayer are both simple and refreshing, especially to those of us who cannot yet figure the Office of Readings in proper—or common—order yet!

> Prayer also makes time pass very quickly and with such great delight that one does not notice its length. Listen: Once when I was a purveyor in Bresse and most of my companions were ill, I had to make a long journey. I prayed to the good God, and, believe me, the time did not seem long.[1]

Based on his endorsement, I packed only one book to read and left my needlepoint at home.

Father Jerome is now well enough to do the sermon. This is a marker of good progress for him. When I first saw him, he was part of the Wheelchair Alley. He can walk now, although slowly and carefully. I am waiting through the sermon for the monastery "news bulletin," the intercessions—even though I am beginning to understand about that fresh grave. When the bells began their dull clanking call to Mass, there was no counterpoint of Brother Robert's motorized wheelchair. May he rest in peace, here on this hill.

Abbot Antony finds me at my corner table in the cafeteria.

"I'm sorry about Brother Robert," I say.

"Oh don't be!" he responds enthusiastically, as thought he's heard a good joke. "That's why we're here. He's so happy. He was ready." The abbot seems a little envious of Brother Robert's new-found happiness. After he died, Brother Robert's monastic family had been looking at photos of him when he was young, in the army. "You would not have recognized him," Abbot Antony says.

"He seemed like a bit of a character," I say, drawing this from reading something he wrote in the abbey newsletter, with a title of "Abbot Martin Marty Meets the Indians."

"Oh, he *was*. I heard his novitiate vows and his final vows, and brought him out here from Indiana. He came with Father Cornelius in the second group." And now he has seen him off to heaven, joyfully.

"What are you reading?" he asks suddenly.

Now, *how* can that question catch me off guard? But it does. I actually went to the trouble of going to the Carlsbad Library a week ago and got something called *Monks and Civilization* by Jean Decarreaux, and have even read four chapters of its tiny print and copious footnotes, so as to have a good answer to this question. Hearing the question, however, I freeze up and say, "I'm reading something . . . not very good. You know, we really need an oblate reading list so this doesn't happen to people and we know what's good reading for us."

When trapped, blame the abbot.

He is doing something like that, he says. How's the life of Paul? Is it a good life?

It takes me a moment to realize he is referring to the book I read over Easter. Maybe.

Father Jerome is in our dining room. So are at least fifteen other anxious oblates and also thirty-two volunteers from Brother Benno's Kitchen. The place is mobbed. I congratulate Father Jerome on his physical improvement, that steady march he has made from wheel-chair to pulpit this year. "I'm glad for everybody's prayers," he says.

"We have to pray for you," I say. "There are more oblates than monks."

Another walk around the prayer walk, waiting for my room to be ready. First stop is to Brother Robert's fresh grave, to say a decade of the rosary for him. His is my first death here, and I remember how Abbot Antony once marveled, "There were no deaths here for twenty-five years, and then they began . . . " The last death before Brother Robert was in 1993.

~

My room is *not* "closest to the prayer chapel," but next to closest. The breeze finally pulls itself off the ocean with great effort, but it doesn't penetrate my southerly facing room. This was a good thing during Easter when it was cold, but is not so great now, especially as the afternoon sun crosses over. We have a schedule for this retreat: the monastic *horarium* of Vigils (5:30 A.M.), Lauds (7:00 A.M.), Mass (11:00 A.M.), Vespers (5:00 P.M.), and Compline (8:00 P.M.), and then the Grand Silence. Plus four "conferences"—I think those are lectures?—and the Sacrament of Penance.

Who has time to read?

~

Daisies growing everywhere.

~

"Can I borrow the key to the oblate library?" I ask the bookstore lady. "The books in the monastic library are too hard for me."

"Glad I'm not the only one," she says as she lets me into the oblate library. "I can't figure out the Divine Office either, and Abbot Antony keeps telling me: just follow the directions."

But, self-conscious of my non-edifying reading habits, I try to choose a few decent books. The oblate library is a mess of check-out cards dating to 1998, unfiled, of books declared in the catalogue and nowhere to be found, of boxes of junky books, donated perhaps, stacked against a wall so you cannot get at the library books. I'm glad I am not trying to study here right now.

~

We stagger through Vespers. All the organists are away or on vacation, and at one point, the chant sags until it breaks down completely. In the vestibule are suitcases for the latest arrivals to the retreat. I like the image of arriving here and going straight to prayer, but it probably has more to do with the fact that both guest master and porter are in here praying too, and nobody can get a key to a room until we're done with Vespers.

~

Conferences, according to the notes in the back of one of my Rule of St. Benedict translations, contain "sound spiritual advice on various general and particular questions."

Conference 1: Father Jerome, in ski hat and white, cowled work shirt.

He talks about today's Gospel and how "no prophet is without honor except in his own house." People say, "You're nothing special; where do you think you come from?" They are overwhelmed because they have no faith. But we *are called* to live a life of faith.

The values of the world are no longer important, says Father Jerome. St. Benedict has given us a way—one of the oldest ways to live in faith. The Rule is about faith. It has not been forced on us. We took it up as oblates. Pray for grace to be faithful to our call. August 1 was his golden jubilee as a monk, says Father Jerome. But August 6 will be Abbot Antony's seventieth jubilee—something none of us knew. "So there's no tooting my horn; Abbot Antony's got the whole band," he says cheerfully.

He suggests we write our story quietly, prayerfully during this retreat. Drop in the milestones. As we write our story, we see the hand of God. What is the next step? Stay in silence. Listen. Why has God called us here? "Today, if you hear the voice of the Lord, harden not your hearts," as we say at the opening of the Divine Office.

Listen to the small and ordinary of our life, he says. This is Benedictine spirituality. There is a grace waiting for you this weekend, he assures us, his face rosy with confidence. You will have another grace to be thankful for when you leave Sunday.

~

Compline. Brother Bernard startles the dusky silence with his hand-wrung fertilizer machine along the grass outside the church. The sky has filled with dirty clouds, and the wind has stopped. When Father Jerome asked us to begin by centering ourselves in prayer and listening for God, the breeze began rustling through the palm trees outside.

Inside the abbey church, the light is dim. The candles around St. John Vianney glow softly around his image. Silence grows and spreads like the clouds.

August 5, 2000: Dedication of the Basilica of St. Mary in Rome

Prayer before Lauds (made up): I would like to think I'm open to you and listening for answers. I am probably not. I reject answers I get (give me another one), make up my own "hand" and call it your hand, or you have to be shouting to be heard over my own din. This is the material you get to work with. I'm sorry about that. As far as an agenda for this retreat, as Father Jerome mentioned we all have, I suspect mine was to run away from home for a few days. And even that's not working because I have to call Felix's mom every day and get really unhappy about that. I'm sorry for all of it, but I'll ask anyway: so what is the next step?

~

I skip 5:30 A.M. Vigils, something I would have liked to do during Easter, but lacked a good excuse in my mind. Last night's bathroom noises were consistent until after 10:00 P.M., sporadic all night long, and resumed in earnest by shower-takers from 5:00 until 6:30, when everybody was either praying or catching up on *their* sleep.

There is a ghostly mist when I stepped outside at 6:45 A.M., a good silence.

It takes much longer for the morning gloom to clear here, perched above the ocean, than at my home, twelve miles inland. It is a metaphor that I find amusing.

Conference 2: Abbot Henry.

Move from the structured monastery here and the Rule,
interior monastery, the one we can carry with us, Abbot Her
gests. He offers us three areas that will help incubate an inner
monastery.

Hospitality: Every guest is welcomed as Christ. Accept the other
person. Christ may be sending a person for a particular reason. Be
aware of God's constant presence. We either fear or forget God in our
life. Our hospitality is a kind of prayer, he stresses. The prime quality
of the person who is hospitable is *humility*.

Humility comes from "humus," Abbot Henry continues, the soil, the
lowly. Humility comes from us; we are one among many. The guest
allows us to remember to do that. What is our cross? he asks.
Control? Accumulation? Once we let go of things, we can let go of
our will. The more we are aware of Christ's presence, the more we
can align with his will. Then we recognize the transitoriness of life.
The more we put stock into what is fading away, the more disappointed we will be.

Anxiety and tension are spelled L-I-F-E, he continues in his smooth,
unchanging (unyielding) voice. "Peace" is the ability to deal with anxiety and tension with underlying joy.

The monastic accepts the guests and accepts the Lord. Where do
we oblates find this acceptance? In *silence*.

Silence is the third area, maybe the most basic building block to the
inner monastery, says Abbot Henry. Silence is the desert where you
find God in prayer. Imagine having a place in your home where you
can go in silence and be with the Lord. We find solace in distraction;
we are afraid of our imagination and memory. But silence is where our
imagination and memory can serve our prayer. Silence makes us aware
of God's everlasting presence.

We all leave the conference jabbering non-stop over Abbot Henry's
superior wisdom.

A free hour! The bookstore opens. Everybody rushes there or to
the monastic library to sign the card for Abbot Antony's seventieth
jubilee and to offer up a spiritual bouquet. I am still trying to figure
out what a spiritual bouquet is, so I look around the monastic library

instead. There on the bulletin board is a neatly typed three-page list entitled, "A Partial Bibliography for Benedictine Oblates."

!!

⁓

The oblate with the baby sits in the row in front of me during the liturgy. The baby is either in a sling hung about his mother's body or perched on the edge of the pew in front of her. He seems to like the chants and makes little goo's. At Lauds, bored, he played with his toes. Better than beads, I thought, and Lauds bores me too. At Mass, hungry, he was breastfed. In public—church no less!—this is an activity that can make a tidy, childless, cranky sort like me crazy as a general rule.

But it is the Dedication of the Basilica of St. Mary in Rome—"Saint Mary Major"—today, and the gospel reading of the Annunciation radiates mothers and birth. Plus my cranky button is broken since I got up this morning. I don't know why.

⁓

Fried chicken smells waft from the retreat kitchen at noon. This morning the air was full of pancakes and syrup. After seven days' fasting, you notice the smells and forget that the food behind them isn't very good. I'm sure sin would have the same impact—if I ever gave it a seven-day break.

Chapter 65: Provost of the Monastery

Rather than choosing a prior (second in command after the abbot), Benedict prefers deans, and urges extreme care in choosing priors to avoid factions and power struggles. If a prior is still necessary, the abbot should choose his own prior, rather than putting it to community vote.

I've been stalling in my study of the Rule because I haven't seen much for the ordinary oblate in this chapter. At St. Augustine's Abbey, Father Vincent is the prior. Even Benedict doesn't seem too crazy about the role, beginning the chapter with, *Often the appointment of a provost gives rise to grave scandals in the monastery*. The first three paragraphs elaborate on why having a provost is a crummy idea, there's one (short) paragraph on appointing one if you have to, and finally two more paragraphs of admonitions for the provost, now appointed.

The commentaries warn about assistants trying to subvert "real" power as though we were discussing military coups or dictatorships or something.

As I struggled to find the relevance, I began to wonder less about Benedict's focus on who should choose the provost and more about serving under these people.

If you must put somebody above others, have the abbot do the appointing, says Benedict. Fine, but what is it like to live under a rule as an ordinary oblate and also under any appointed "seconds" like saints, or abbots, or parish priests?

The abbot, according to Benedict, is Christ's representative (chapter 2). The provost is the abbot's representative to the community. In my own small life as an ordinary oblate, Christ is who I am ultimately responsible to (or should be). Abbot Antony is my "provost," appointed to mind the Lord and tend to the needs of his sometimes wayward flock of oblate-sheep.

Father Stanislaus was oblate master before my time, and there is the core of longer-established oblates who lived under his guidance and teaching. Abbot Antony took us on in his "retirement" in his late eighties, and began to snare us in astonishing numbers. There are now more than two hundred oblates of St. Augustine's Abbey, some of whom drive eight hours from Las Vegas to attend the monthly meetings and then drive all the way back.

Abbot Antony is not a stern or difficult oblate master/provost, but he's not exactly a pussycat pushover of kindly indifference either. You attend a meeting or two and suddenly your novitiate vows are scheduled. If you don't panic and run as many do, you face permanent vows a year later. "I'm not ready" or "I'm not worthy" seem to fall on suddenly deaf ears, but in fact, Abbot Antony listens better than anyone I have ever met. It's just that those arguments are meaningless when you are vowing a lifetime of preparation to meet Christ face to face. Who is ever ready or worthy to begin? Who will ever complete such an assignment and move on to another while they still live?

At one of the oblate meetings, Abbot Antony offered us a daily test as oblates: "Here is a test of whether you really love God," he began, and we suddenly sat up, alert. "Have you done or avoided or given up a single thing today solely because you believed that God wanted you to?"

I quickly lost interest—not my kind of facts-and-figures sort of test. I thought it was something Abbot Antony made up, but he was reading from reflections on Pascal.

Abbot Antony, as oblate master, is truly Christ's provost here to reflect values and actions in accord with God's plans for us. For somebody who wanted a grand plan—preferably one with immortality in or around it—could I not even manage this small test?

Such arrogance, I cannot imagine anything that God "solely" would want that is not part of my advanced spiritual practices already.

Then I remember my reading choices. Abbot Antony would say that what I read is fine for entertainment, but am I not looking to be edified? Both, I want to say, but Abbot Antony separates reading for edification and reading for entertainment, as I have not.

It may be very hard for me to discern what to do, avoid, or give up *solely* because God wants me to. It is not nearly as hard for his emissary—in this case, Abbot Antony—to discern.

"The servant is not better greater than his lord," says Jesus in the Gospel of John (15:20). So the Lord is my master, I say grandly, and Abbot Antony is his provost, placed between us as intercessor, interpreter, and spiritual "cop." While this may be true, it does not take into account that I place myself at the top of the hierarchy all too often. My wants, my needs, my petty desires all seem to reign supreme. My reading choices.

> Abba Motius said, "Wherever you live, follow the same manner of life as everyone else, and if you see devout men who you trust doing something, do the same, and you will be at peace. For this is humility: to see yourself to be the same as the rest."[2]

St. Benedict knows the humanness of the ordinary. He permits provosts to administer and regulate and discipline the community. Benedict, Blessed Joanna Mary, Abbot Antony, and all the other intermediaries the Lord places in the gap between him and me are not really to police, but to protect and guide me on the road to the New Jerusalem.

I was pretty sure when Father Jerome spoke of agenda here that mine was to escape. Could it actually be that I will munity (and myself in the process)?

I do not recognize myself without a cranky button. I find today that even the difficult things—checking in on my elderly mother-in-law by phone, for example—is better accomplished if I think I am doing it for God (my "provost") than for Felix, who is in China on business and therefore a handy target for resentments.

~

Conference 3: Father Aloysius (former prior).

We know a lot, but we forget, begins Father Aloysius in his rolling *basso profundo* voice. We need to re-collect, re-member. We forget who we are before God. We forget where we were before God. We forget to be grateful for not being where we were.

Sinner is who we were, he booms out. A spiritual life is a life open to the Holy Spirit. Sin tends to toughen us, callous over our consciousness. Become a new name in God: *saint*. It is what God calls us to—and God gives us what we need to claim this name.

We have lost a sense of sin. The Sacrament of Reconciliation doesn't just take away sin. Sin tends to toughen us. The Sacrament of Reconciliation allows us to remove the calluses of sin.

We don't really relish spiritual experience, Father Aloysius suggests. Prayer becomes rote. Mass becomes boring, a "hardening of hearts," as the psalms say. The hardened heart is "hard of hearing." Calluses are ear wax.

Confession is not a matter of "feeling bad"—this is a Protestant way of reconciliation. We make an act of contrition. We go to God in the company of the saints, not alone. It is the company we want to be in. It is *context*. During the Penitential Rite at Mass, Jesus becomes present and we are in that company and say Our Father. We ask God's forgiveness in the Mass.

But there is more, he goes on, an additional sacrament. Besides the forgiven community, we make our individual confession.

To start again, to re-collect, is one of the great gifts of Catholicism. You will want it more, he finishes.

~

It is not quite the full oration of oblates as we had for this morning's conference. Abbot Henry tends to pack them in because he's the abbot, and he has such an even-handed way of speaking even about tough truths. Father Aloysius is quite stern in his delivery.

Our numbers reduce even more as we are lined up for the Sacrament of Penance. ("Behind Door #1, we have Father Prior Vincent. And behind Door #2, Father Ignatius. Lady and Gentlemen Oblates, take your pick.") I assumed oblates would dote on this stuff—they are *very* devoted to Catholic practices—but I've been half sick since I saw this on our schedule. Part of the ongoing curse of a bad conversion class is that we didn't cover penance, confession, or even sin. I read the difference between venial and mortal sin in a book once, but I have trouble remembering which is which, and keep hoping I won't mix up the words and give some poor priest a heart attack some day.

But my confessional life was bad beyond conversion class failures. The first time I ever went to confession, the priest yelled at me for not knowing what to do. The second time I went, to a different priest, I made an appointment to see him and told him in advance I was new. He stood me up for the meeting, and worse, a wedding was being held, and the church was filling up with wedding guests eyeing me critically—I was rather obviously *not* dressed for a wedding—and saying, "Can I help you find someone?"

(Right. *The priest who stood me up at the confessional*.)

After that, my experience of the Sacrament of Reconciliation—which sounded better than "confession," but still wasn't getting done no matter what it was being called—took place with Father Rusty's confessional games, all big rocks dragged up to the altar in communal confessionals. It's been a while. In addition to being full of sin, I have no confidence, and I want to go home. "You should say an Act of Contrition for the RCIA deacon who did this to you," says the oblate mommy standing next to Nancy rocking the baby and listening to *me* be the hysterical one.

"I don't know what an Act of Contrition is!"

"They won't laugh. They're very good," says Nancy. "You need to have a regular confessor here like I do. Father Prior is very good"—her confessor. "Father Ignatius is too. Maybe best for you. Go stand in his line." The oblate mommy has just gone in there.

We are one raggedly line, long because it is single file, in front Father Prior's door.

"I'll take whoever's up when it's my turn," I say, Divine Providence and all.

"*Get in the front of Father Ignatius's door!*"

I get. The door opens.

"Nancy made me come to you because I don't know how this is done."

"Okay. Usually you start out by saying, 'Bless me, Father, for I have sinned . . . ' and then say how long it has been since your last confession."

"The way is narrow and hard," he says after my amateur recital of sins. "We wish it were wide and easy. God measures how much we loved, and love can be found in perseverance. Persevere."

He asks if I am ready for an Act of Contrition and gets *my* Don't Know How to Do Anything act.

"Okay, you can find prayers to use in the bookstore, but in the meantime, I'll say one and you pray along with me . . . "

In short order, I am outside, forgiven, facing an anxious, still-in-line Nancy. "It was okay," I tell her. "Thanks."

I go into the bookstore and find a ridiculous book, *An Easy Way to Become a Saint*, because it spells out confessions, includes Acts of Contrition, and only costs five dollars. Plus now I feel guilty for all my spiritual-lite reading—too venial to confess but enough to feel guilty over—so I buy Francis de Sales's *Introduction to the Devout Life*.

"Wasn't it yummy?" says oblate mommy dreamily, choosing her own book purchases. It takes me a moment to know she is talking about confession with Father Ignatius, not food.

It is no use. My sins have barely been forgiven and I'm in the monastic library when Abbot Antony stomps in with a book in his hand. I wave to get his attention, but I already have it. "Aren't you in room 26?" he asks. "I've been looking all over for you."

I show him the bibliography of oblate reading that I am vigorously copying out, in true medieval Benedictine tradition since there are no copy machines available to the public. "I put that up," he says virtuously.

"Well, *I* didn't know it existed," I snarl, as graciously post-sin as possible. I show him the de Sales book.

"Very nice," he says without looking at it. He is here to show me *his* book (*The Lord*, by Romano Guardini). "You must taste it," he says, as if the Word were communion of another species. "It is the third time I have read it."

I surrender. I put away the bibliography, and he glides off after recommending a chapter for taste-testing.

"Did the abbot find you?" asks the bookstore lady as I am returning to room 26. "He was looking all over for you."

"He had a book for me," I say sadly.

"He doesn't give up," she laughs.

No, he doesn't. He embodies perseverance.

Nancy sees the book under my arm as she leaves the confessional area. "You'll love that," she says enthusiastically. "It's great."

"The abbot gave it to me to read," I say mournfully.

"Yes, I saw him going all around here looking for you."

Where could I ever hide? It is like trying to hide from the eyes of God.

～

By Vespers, it is completely overcast. We sing (badly) the beginning of the Transfiguration. The monks march around a lot and sing offstage.

By post-break prayer walk, it is a bit chilly, a swift change from yesterday's airless aridity.

～

This retreat is so different from the Easter one. It's warmer, of course (even tonight), and more ordinary (even for Transfiguration). Before Compline, the outgoing kitchen server and incoming kitchen server stand before the altar for a blessing, and I am suddenly inside Benedict's Rule for real. *Right after Sunday Lauds, both incoming and outgoing servers shall fall on their knees and ask for the prayers of all . . . and shall receive a blessing . . .* (chapter 35).

August 6, 2000: Feast of the Transfiguration

The Transfiguration is the summer lightening of the coming Resurrection.[3]

Therefore, since each of us possesses God in his heart and is being transformed into his divine image, we also should cry out with joy. It is good for us to be here—here where all things shine with divine radiance, where there is joy and gladness and exultation; where there is nothing in our hearts but peace, serenity, and stillness; where God is seen.[4]

This feast day (a mysterious one, full of bumbling, unfamiliar chants) we sing of the Lord's face "shining like the sun." Antiphon 1 of Morning Prayer says, "Today the Lord Jesus Christ shone with splendor on the mountain, his face like the sun and his clothes white as snow."

It seems like such an odd celebration, this deep white glory that is months past Easter, even more months before Christmas—like summer lightning, which we sometimes get in the mountains here.

Deeply overcast today, refreshingly ordinary weather, if you are not living in San Diego—here it is noticeably *not* "ordinary" at all. I am sorry to see the retreat wind down but not sorry to see breakfast arrive. It has been, in its own quiet way, *my* summer lightning, before the flat days ahead.

✴

It occurs to me that rather than be so thrilled that the abbot chases me around with books in his hand—oh, special me, favored oblate—I should be humbled. Spending an entire weekend with oblates, I see the kinds of books they read and apparently absorb. I am quite the lazy, undisciplined one, and my poor abbot is just trying to get me to the level of the rest of my class.

This is a discernment I would rather not have been gifted with.

✴

Conference 4: Abbot Henry.

We don't put enough credence in the psalms, Abbot Henry begins. The Spirit inspires them. Jesus memorized them. There is a Presence within us. To turn there gives us our real strength. Our strength must come from the Lord.

Life as a monastic is a life of adventure. "Wildness is not wilderness if there's someone with you," said John Muir. We pray in common, which catapults us into private prayer, which enhances our common prayer—and our life in God.

Jesus allowed the Transfiguration to take place to assure his disciples of who he was. A retreat is our transfiguration, where we see Christ in a different light. It helps us through valleys, as the Transfiguration did Jesus' disciplines. And there will be valleys. Chapter 31 of the Rule of Benedict tells of the qualification of a cellerer, qualities we should all have: wisdom, which is not necessarily knowledge, mature in conduct, temperate. Brother Benno says, "Humans are the only animal who don't stop in the middle."

Respect things, the gifts of this world. Abbot Antony still (in his ninety-second year) will stand when reading if he doesn't have to sit, and will read by the window so as to preserve the light.

Be observant of those things we are charged to care for.

This chapter tells us that our disposition is to be one of service to one another. Then you are fulfilling what is within you, the adventure before you.

~

Oblation Renewal. Abbot Antony has decided that all oblate retreats will end with a renewal of our oblation.

I renew my oblation and offer myself to Almighty God through the Blessed Virgin Mary and our Holy Father Benedict, as an Oblate of the St. Augustine's Abbey, and promise again to dedicate myself to the service of God and mankind according to the Rule of St. Benedict insofar as my state in life permits.[5]

How nice, I think, since this retreat began with letting go of my Franciscan "stuff"—literally, maybe figuratively as well. But that is my last coherent thought, and I can barely breathe the words for choking on the surprise gift of tears. Maybe I am beginning to catch the meaning of offering myself to God—eighteen months later.

~

"Who died?" asks one of the new ones, who keeps her copy of the Rule (undoubtedly "liberated" from the bookstore by Abbot Antony as mine was) in an air-lock baggie—for freshness?

Abbot Henry expands on Brother Robert's last weeks. His legs had completely failed and in the last days he had a small heart attack as well. They moved him to the infirmary where others could stay and keep an eye on him. The second night Brother Robert stayed in the infirmary, Brother Stephen could hear Thomas snoring. Mid-snore—silence. Brother Stephen got up and went in to see if Brother Robert needed anything or was trying to move about. In fact, somewhere in the middle of a snore, crippled Brother Robert gained enormous mobility on the road to Jerusalem.

"May you be so blessed as to come to God mid-snore," says Abbot Henry.

Abbot Henry tells us of a funeral custom the abbey had under Abbot Antony. When Abbot Antony and family were in Florida, they would sit on the beach at sunset and when the sun finally sank over the Gulf, they would all applaud, for the sun had finally made it home. When Abbot Antony did the cemetery services, he would lead everybody in applause—for a person finally arriving home.

⁓

At Mass, during our intercession "newsletter," we learn that Abbot Antony made his vows seventy years ago today; Father Cornelius sixty-eight years ago today; Father Aloysius, fifty-eight years ago today. The Great Transfiguration has been shared around. The vacationing bishop who presides over Mass today reminds us that this constitutes about two hundred years in the service to God.

Everybody in the congregation applauds.

⁓

Lunch. Abbot Antony revels in hospitality, "working the room" (the retreat cafeteria) better than any lobbyist.

"Did you read any of the book?" he asks me.

"I'm up to page 129. It's wonderful. Guardini has a deep scholarship, but a light touch. I thought it would be too hard for me."

He is pleased. "I hoped you would like it!"

"Well, you've got to bring me up to the level of the rest of the oblates," I say. "They're quite advanced."

"So are *you*!" he says generously, eyes wide. "I know that you are looking for reading that is fruitful, not just entertaining. I thought this would appeal to you."

I want to finish it, but it's checked out to Abbot Antony. In fact, he tells me, he checked out both copies because lending it to me interfered with his own third reading. "I don't want to get you into trouble," I say. "Maybe this week, all the good will over your jubilee and all . . . "

"Only God knows," says Abbot Antony, "and he will be pleased."

August 7, 2000: Sixtus II, Pope and Martyr

The abbot, with modesty becoming an old Benedictine, did not want to celebrate his seventieth jubilee on a Sunday when big crowds file into the small abbey church. The fact that it was also the Transfiguration probably assisted his humility even more to ask that his renewal of vows take place the next day instead.

Which is why it is Monday morning, and I'm dressed in a white suit out of respect, having already done breakfast with a local politician, and now return to this quiet abbey. It feels odd, especially with me in my lobbyist garb, so soon after being here as a retreatant.

There was a hideously unsubtle, Kool-Aid green posterboard "card" to sign for the abbot in the monastic library over the weekend, along with several "spiritual gifts tally sheets" to make into a spiritual bouquet to be given to the abbot, along with a real bouquet of white roses. We were to consider, prayerfully, what our spiritual offering would be, and these would then be totaled up and presented anonymously. All was to be kept secret from the abbot.

How? He prowls the halls and that very library where the Kool-Aid card was with books in hand, seeking out un-edified oblates. The Kool-Aid green is strong enough to send signals to its mother ship on Mars.

I cannot find an official definition for a "spiritual bouquet" by looking in any Catholic encyclopedia or dictionary, not even by peeking through my *How to Be a Saint* book, just purchased. As I look at the sign-up sheets, I am not the only one confused. "Please write down the numbers of rosaries you wish to offer up for Abbot Antony . . . " ". . . with the number of Masses and communions . . . "

"the number of liturgy of hours . . . " "the number of visits to the Blessed Sacrament . . ."

I can kind of figure out what these are, although they seem to give us an awful lot of personal spiritual power, "willing" these acts to benefit someone else, like a bequest in a last will and testament. But, "Write down the number of Holy Hours you wish to offer up for Abbot Antony . . . " How is that different from the Liturgy of the Hours? Which have their own sign-up sheets? And, "number of *lectio divina* . . . "? Well, I don't understand anymore. And the number of acts and hours offered per person are staggering in their quantity, although I have no doubt as to the quality. The usual number is seventy, which certainly honors the abbot's seventy years as a Benedictine—but seventy Masses? Seventy visits to the Blessed Sacrament? Has anybody tallied how long this might *take* them?

Then the "Spiritual Gifts Tally Sheet: Other" catches my eye, where people have written in:

• ten acts of patience
• seventy acts of patience
• forty hours of devotion
• ten confessions
• eight cooking and cleaning hours
• choir

and a partridge in a pear tree?

Clearly I'm missing yet another beat of the rhythm of popular Catholic culture. And yet the intentions, which is what Abbot Antony will see, are the best.

I decide that since *lectio* in its oldest sense meant memorizing psalms, I will memorize Psalm 95, which opens us to the Divine Office each day. (*Come, let us sing to the Lord* . . .) When the abbot showed me how to say the little Daily Office, he noted that other psalms could be substituted for Psalm 95, but just as quickly dismissed that idea saying, "This [95] is the oldest tradition. It dates back to the Rule itself at least."

There are twenty-five stanzas. Memorizing them over twenty-five days will remind me for a long time to come of the father who taught me to pray this Office. If that reminder is a prayer for Abbot Antony, how much nicer for everyone.

Finally, I tackle the Kool-Aid monstrosity. The heartfelt words scrawled on it are intensely moving. I do not have that kind of heart, but I can give the abbot back what he gave me the week of my oblation. Along the top, under the "Congratulations, Abbot Antony, on 70 blessed years," I write, possessed by the spirit of Walter Hilton:

> Keep your way without halting, and remember your goal is Jerusalem; that is what you want and nothing else . . .

~

The old abbot gets to choose the readings for his Mass. His choice of Gospel seems especially poignant:

> And the multitude sat about him, and they said unto him, Behold thy mother and thy brethren without seek for thee. And he answered them saying, Who is my mother or my brethren? And he looked round about on them which sat about him, and said, Behold my mother and my brethren! For whosoever shall do the will of God, the same is my brother, and my sister, and mother. (Mark 3:32–35)

As Father Aloysius gives the homily-tribute, he speaks of a man who knows the Benedictine saints and ancient abbots as friends. (Certainly this was true when Abbot Antony made the formal introduction to me of Blessed Joanna Mary Bonomo.) And then Father Aloysius indulges himself in reading in Latin a hymn Abbot Antony clearly knows and loves. As Father Aloysius speaks in Latin, the abbot's face shines like the sun as he sits in his radiant white robes.

"Those that be planted in the house of the LORD shall flourish in the courts of our God," Father Aloysius concludes with Psalm 92, reading from the Office translation. "They shall still bring forth fruit in old age" (13–14).

The old abbot seems *made* out of the words he has absorbed through his entire life. He marches forward to Abbot Henry, stumpy with his replaced hip, and reads his renewal in a clear, quiet voice. It breaks your heart to hear this saintly striver vow to really begin what he is just learning in the Lord, like the old desert story.

> At the hour of Abbot Pambo's departure from this life, he said to the holy ones around him, "From the time that I came

into this place of solitude and built my cell, and dwelth in it,
I do not call to mind that I have eaten bread save what my
hands have toiled for, nor repented of any word that I spoke
until this hour. And so I go to the Lord, as one that hath not
yet made a beginning of serving God."[6]

His voice trembles at his intention and then he goes on. He renews
the vows of his youth in the wisdom of his old age. When he is done,
we applaud.

I leave lighthearted with gratitude for this extraordinary witness of
faith and perseverance. All serendipity, or as Abbot Antony would
say, Divine Providence, to choose this summer retreat when everybody, including me, wanted the winter one, to stumble so into this
affirming moment, unannounced to all the oblates, but there for us
to witness.

I feel so blessed.

August 21, 2000: Twenty-First Sunday of Ordinary Time

Dear Abbot Antony:

The last time of quiet I had was the oblate retreat nearly a month
ago. It feels so good to sit at my little desk this afternoon and listen to
the fountain in the front and the wind chimes in the back of the house
and spend this hour "visiting" with you by letter. My mother arrived
for her annual visit *minutes* before Felix returned from China. I tried
to remember to practice hospitality during these last several weeks. I
was not very successful.

Your seventieth jubilee celebration continues in my life. I was not
familiar with spiritual bouquets, but I wanted to take part anyway, so
I "pledged" twenty-five days of *lectio*, since its practice has been one of
your suggestions, and certainly has become one of God's many gifts to
me. I chose to reflect with Psalm 95, one phrase per day. Since it's the
invitatory that opens us to the Divine Office each day (like "Listen"
unfolds the Rule), I wanted to take time with it. I memorize a line a
day, and then mentally recite as much as I've learned while I exercise
on the treadmill at the gym each night. There is something in the
repetitive physical exertion and my stumbling memorization that
becomes as close as I will ever get to "praying without ceasing."
Eventually the words and my feet fall into rhythm, *being* and *doing*, not

"thinking." I am sure that St. Benedict would be pleased to see this current-day manifestation of living his Rule!

The jubilee was a beautiful, living reminder of perseverance and fidelity. It was inspirational to me to be there. Although I do not live in your kind of community, as a childless woman I have needed to find communities such as the oblates where I can "find my way together" as it were. The readings you chose for Mass were very powerful, especially the Gospel of Mark, where Jesus says, "For whosoever do the will of God, the same is my brother, my sister, my mother."

Perhaps I was more receptive to listening because we had just left the oblate retreat. I was so anxious about the retreat because it was "structured" with conferences. I get anxious about weird things. I was afraid I'd be bored or bothered when I wanted to be alone or—who knows. The conferences were very helpful.

When we renewed our oblate vows, I hope God heard what was in my heart because he sure couldn't hear the words. I cried the entire way through. I remember our oblation on the Feast of Christ the King, when Hildegard could barely speak for her emotion. I am one of those people who move quickly, but whose understanding follows more slowly. I might have the beginning, nearly a year later, of understanding what those words I was saying meant.

Of course, the next day I watched you say some similar words as if you were just starting to understand their meaning, and I realized that the road to the New Jerusalem will be a long one, and that the Word will not be fully comprehended until we meet him on that road.

I am sorry I will not be at the September oblate meeting. My stepdaughter is getting married next weekend. She has asked me to be the Eucharistic minister for the wedding, and I am very honored by that. Felix and I will then spend a few weeks vacationing at Cape Cod. I barely return home before I head back to Washington, D.C., to meet with our congressman.

While I will enjoy all of this, I would have enjoyed beginning the study of the Rule with our oblates. As you know, I have spent this Jubilee Year studying and writing and thinking about the Rule and its application to the life of an ordinary oblate, like a university lobbyist. In my study I am up to chapter 66 and how (in my view) we all need to serve as porters to the "inner monastery" that Abbot Henry talked about in his first conference. It allows us to meet the risen Christ in fragments every day as we ask for a blessing in the people who come to us.

I hope to return to the monastery for the day of the Feast of Michael, Gabriel, and Raphael. That was the first time I went to the abbey and talked to someone (you!). Now I like to return there for this feast each year. I love to hear the Gospel of John when Jesus knew Nathanael under the fig tree before he was called.

I think the Lord knew me and my need before I called you and placed me under your spiritual guidance for a little while, just like Nathanael.

Pax,
Carol (Joanna Mary)

SEPTEMBER
Under the Fig Tree

September 29, 2000:
Feast of Michael, Gabriel, Raphael, Archangels

As I drive up the hill this morning, I am surprised at how intensely glad I am to be here after all these weeks. I love the abbey and what it represents to me: the surprise is that, for all these weeks away, I did not miss it at all. Earlier this year, these visits were my salvation and sanity. Now, it is not so much that life "intrudes," but simply is.

But the intensity is real. This absence of eight weeks is the longest in quite some time. I am not sure if the place has changed or if it is I who have changed.

Maybe both.

You can taste the silence today. The threatening clouds of morning gloom are rapidly retreating, and even the sky and air have a renewed freshness after summer's heat.

But maybe that's me I'm talking about again. I am breathing the metaphors of the monastery today. They are *me*. Over these times here and now times apart, the monastery has become me, the way the Rule and the Word and the Office have become Abbot Antony. It does not work the other way around. We are not going to put our imprint on the world but to become imprinted, infused by Christ.

as if that interior monastery Abbot Henry spoke of became a
y when I wasn't looking. I had been back East in the land of Cape
for weeks, where the ocean is on the "other side." "It is a wild,
rank place and there is no flattery in it," as Thoreau said. It is a great
land of memories and the most incredible light, a light that the artists
never grow tired of. As we walked along our "other" ocean, one day
Felix scavenged a special ribbed rock, a quahog shell, and a tiny clam
shell. "For your rock garden," he explained.

I was going to explain to him that my (future) rock garden was to be
made from all those prayer-walk rocks I'd gathered this Jubilee Year—
and it is. But do the prayer-walk rocks have an exclusivity contract? I
wondered. Are they the only ones that "count"? I brought his special
rock and shells home, and they joined my shelf of collected rocks.

Many years ago, Felix and I walked that same bit of rocky shoreline
in North Truro, and my eye caught sight of an absolutely perfect minia-
ture conch shell. I picked it up and admired it, put it in my pocket and
continued along, pleased. Then I saw another one. And another one.
And another . . . The beach was covered with this exact sort of shell.

Sadly I pulled the first one out of my pocket and looked at it again
and said out loud, "So what makes this little shell special then?"

The answer came to me so violently I nearly crushed the shell with
its impact: *Because I chose it.*

And here, among my prayer-walk rock reminders, are Felix's rock
and carefully chosen shells. They are mixing together, my carefully
constructed, separated lives. There are no rules for a rock garden, only
one Rule I am trying to understand and live to the best of my abilities.

The Cape was such an experience, like being granted the opportunity to visit a place greatly loved once more. I had anticipated the visit,
loved its moments, and cried when it was over, and then it receded
into the past.

This place, however, I realize today, my third celebration of the
Feast of Michael, Gabriel, Raphael, Archangels, has never left me, my
way station to the New Jerusalem.

And the literal road up to the monastery, as of today, is newly paved.

Before Mass starts, there is time for a stroll around the prayer walk.
In January, I began memorizing a psalm (Psalm 150) during those
walks. I have three in my memory now (150, 23, and 95), and one-third
of the morning gospel canticle. There are many ways to measure

progress. Brother Robert's grave is still heaped high but not nearly like before, and is now marked with the plain wooden cross, identical to the other seven markers There are many ways . . .

There seem to be *many* suitable rocks today. Where did they come from? I find a large red one, like a Cape Cod sunset. So many rocks, so little time. The liturgical year will soon be moving into eschatological times. Can the calendar year and the end of this study project be far behind?

Mass is celebrated. That lovely reading where Jesus says, "Before that Phillip called thee, when I saw thou wast under the fig tree, I saw thee" (John 1:48). I am in tears of remembering as I watch my old abbot absorb those words for one more season.

Jesus is not done speaking then, as the abbot and I were not done at that first introduction. "Thou shalt see greater things than these," Jesus continues.

Oh, Abbot Antony, I have. I am only at the beginning now. It has taken a lifetime of false starts, bad roads, and dead ends before I wound my way here and faced the porter.

Chapter 66: The Porter of the Monastery

Benedict wrote a job description for the monk who serves at the front desk to the monastery, preferring an older monk, *whose age keeps him from roaming about.* The porter should ask a blessing from all who approach the monastery.

This is the chapter that opens Benedictine hospitality, the way the front-office receptionist sets our first impression of a company. Of a short three-paragraph chapter, the longest paragraph teaches us about where the porter is located, his qualifications, his responses, and the opportunity for an assistant, if necessary.

Whoever arrives at the door, even a poor man, must be welcomed properly—for who knows but that the visitor may be an angel, unawares? It is not a hospitality of going out, like I would characterize Franciscan spirituality, but of bringing in and accepting and welcoming what God gives. Chittister calls this "Benedict's theology of surprise"—like popping out of a cake![1]

Has my arrival ever been treated as a blessing? Not usually. There are rarely porters like those Benedict requires in life's journey. This study of the Rule has paid ugly witness to my false starts or hostilities in AA, RCIA, Catholicism, and Secular Franciscan Orders, as well as all the grousing about what I felt Benedictine hospitality should include. After difficulties in my early experience with Catholicism, I finally, miserably, showed up back at the Episcopal Church's door.

"I don't know what I am anymore!" I wailed at Father James.

"A lapsed Episcopalian," he said promptly. "Let's get you back." He recommended me for Cursillo, and I soon found myself welcomed into a mountain camp in Julian for a "short course in Christianity," where I would not even carry my luggage or pour my own coffee. I would learn to be served, along with all the other invitees.

It was difficult hospitality. It was hospitality without compromise, on terms set by the giver, not the receiver. My arrival was hardly treated with a blessing. I was told you were only supposed to "do Cursillo" after your husband had done one, and mine is a stout disbeliever. Your sponsor was supposed to bring you there, the Cursillo organizers explained. I had no idea what they were talking about. Father James had no idea about that rule. He'd never sponsored a person for Cursillo, nor had anyone from my specific Episcopalian church done it before. Neither the Cursillo organizers nor Father James knew how I might "mix well with this kind of spirituality."

Sure I would mix—like gasoline and a match, we "mixed." I didn't know any of the songs everybody else was singing so lustily. As a kid, I probably knew four hundred of the six hundred hymns in the original Episcopalian hymnal. In my twenty-year absence from the Episcopal Church, that beautiful body of song had been replaced by folk songs, and I was left behind, without a voice.

The discomfort was in the little things, like when we burned our sins. I forget what night we wrote our sins on a scrap of paper, and I listed impatience, intolerance, selfishness, and a few others and watched them go up in flames with everybody else's while absolution was given. It didn't work. There was no preparation: you needed your sins to be handy one-worders, and mine were too slippery for a quick fix.

There was my first healing service ever. I asked to be free of my "demon of addiction" (which was smoking at that particular moment), and cried as the prayers were said. The result was that I felt despicably low and unworthy and fraudulent when I returned to smoking after lunch.

I tried all of the program at first, the way you have to try the AA program whether you like it or hate it. But the mood here was relentless, and laggards were left behind on *this* road. I began to pull away emotionally as the experience wore on. Something called Agape—it all sounded like a foreign world to me—meant we were supposed to literally feed each other, drink from each other's cup (wine, so much for sensitivity to recovering alcoholics), and, of course, hug each other like crazy. If I didn't want to eat, and couldn't drink this *delicious* wine, surely I wanted a hug? I went outside to smoke and waited the thing out, like I was now trying to wait out the entire weekend, and I only came back at the end because I felt sorry for the woman working the Cursillo who drew my name as a prayer partner. I let her walk me to my room and then escaped before the hugs began again.

By the time I got home, driven by strangers, everything had glazed over. I listened to Felix tell me about his weekend because I couldn't come to grips with mine. "There were some nice things," I began enthusiastically. "And some really bad things I wasn't comfortable with."

"What were the bad things?" he asked instantly.

"If they had said the word *charismatic*, I would have known not to come. But they didn't. I thought it was going to be a school. I like school. It took a long time to understand what was going on, and I was trying so hard to be open." I told him about the Agape, and how panicky I got when somebody tried to make me drink wine as part of a love feast. I told him about the last morning, where we were awakened at the crack of dawn by nearly two hundred people who began pouring into our bedrooms to say good morning, kiss, hug, give flowers. I supposed this could be a powerful love fix for some. I was trapped—literally—in my bed by two hundred people who presumed, because it was their thing, that it was a wonderful gift to grab me whether I wanted it or not. The act committed on me by two hundred strangers was a violation of me. "I felt like I'd been raped," I whispered to Felix, whispering as though they could hear me. When I began to cry, they told me how wonderful it was to cry for being so loved, when in fact, I was crying because I hated the experience so much.

In the final service a few hours later, all the sponsors and families were present, except for my situation, where I was finally (almost) being left alone. There was one last surprise. We were called individually by name, knelt down in front of the priest who said something from the Bible that I no longer remember. "The response I hope for," said our Rectora; "is, 'It is I. Yes, I will go'." Or something like that. It was done alphabetically, so having watched just one person, I was called next. As I walked up, I thought, do I or don't I give the response demanded? There must have been five hundred people watching my "commissioning" without giving me the chance to understand what they were railroading me into. The words I no longer remember were calling me to active evangelism and lusty efforts to convert people to Christ. "It is I. Yes, I will," I said without quiver or hesitation. I smiled at all of them. My smile said, *I bet you thought I wouldn't do it.* I sat down and added a silent phrase to the vow I had just taken publicly: *I did this under duress.*

It was under duress. It meant less than a confession under torture. But there I was, prepared to dedicate myself to prayer, study, and action in the Cursillo way. I returned a new person with a new way of life. Until Felix said too quickly, "What were the bad things?" I tried a few good ones, but then whispered, "I did what I had to in order to get out of there." With that, the secret violation was open, along with the shame I felt for my enthusiastic promises at the end, the particular shame of saying yes to God in front of those people, when the answer needed to be *no, not yet, or not this way*—but where there was no option for honesty.

> "What good work is there that I could do?" Abba Nisterus the Great was asked. He answered, "Are not all actions equal? Scripture says that Abraham was hospitable and God was with him. David was humble and God was with him. Elias loved interior peace and God was with him. So do whatever you see your soul desires according to God, and guard your heart."[2]

No wonder I was so primed for an interior hospitality that welcomes me where it finds me—under the fig tree like Nathanael or whoever—and blesses me. We all need to serve as porters for others to the inner monastery. Abbot Antony knows what others may not—

that being the porter at a monastery (officially or not) allows him to meet the risen Christ in fragments through others every day. *That* is a "theology of surprise."

I feel like I have said all this already, in my letter to the abbot. The inner monastery is beginning to supplement the "real" one.

OCTOBER
Entertained Angels Unawares

Be not forgetful to entertain strangers:
for thereby some have entertained angels unawares.
Hebrews 13:1

October 13, 2000: Twenty-Seventh Week of Ordinary Time

The drive up the hill feels melancholy today. That sounds funny to me even as I think it. Where I come from, fall is an unmistakable announcement of a changed landscape. It is the cidery smell of apples still not picked, undercut by the sad pungency of a skunk dead on the country road. It is the soft swish of colored leaves giving up their season and the counterpoint honking of the Canadian geese heading south for the winter—a sound that used to fill me with despair: *What do they know about the winter ahead that I don't know?* It is the sight of the orangey harvest moon hung low over the trees, and quickly shortening days.

In New England, fall was all those smells and sounds and sights. Here it is fall because we shut the skylight window this weekend, the one that we opened right after Easter. It is fall because the roses are bursting out in one last great heave before we cut them back at Christmas. It is fall because the poinsettias are coming into bloom.

"Pay attention to the foliage," an earnest, concerned counselor told me early on when I moved here. I was in her program ostensibly to quit smoking, but I was really blubbering about my loss of home, of New England, of all that was familiar to my life. I could no longer recognize even my misery.

"It's the foliage that tells you the seasons," she said.

And it has, all these years since, from poinsettias to margaritas, to lilies, to roses, each in their full-throated season. Fall is full of melancholy because the roses are breathing their last.

But Abbot Antony taught me liturgical time. His first letter to me—I still have it—is dated Feast of St. Matthew (September 21). I don't know any more than that about when it was written, and I don't need to know any more than that. In this world I have been born to by baptism, consecrated into by confirmation, introduced into by Abbot Antony, and mentored in by Blessed Joanna Mary, it is the melancholy of end time. The liturgical year is packing up its tents in visions of the end of the world.

All the way up here, I think about work, do serious cell phone calling. Once here, all that seems to drift away. The quiet of this particular Friday morning feels like a gift that sinks deep into bones wracked with noise.

~

The oblate meeting on Sunday was quite the opposite, all joyous noise and gathering. Abbot Antony made a point of saying hello to everyone, welcoming each with his own anticipation that no angel will arrive unawares.

"Where have you been all my life?" he asked, coming over to take my hand. The times between visits have felt further apart than at the beginning of this study project (which contributes to the sense of melancholy). But it also has begun to feel like the monastery and its life is no longer a thing apart, to be visited and left, but that it has slipped into my pocket, like a rock on the prayer walk, and returned home with me.

I returned the book he lent me so long ago at the oblate summer retreat.

"And did you like it?" he asked.

"Oh very much. I wasn't sure I could read it. It took a long time. But it was worth it."

"Good. It was a test. I didn't think you would finish it. I have read it three times. I will find others for you to read."

The oblate meetings for this year are devoted to studying the Rule.

Our next regular meeting will be September 10. Please bring the Holy Rule. In this and succeeding meetings we will be examining the ways in which our Holy Father Benedict's Holy Rule should be influencing our life.

As we dove into the Prologue with him (*Listen . . .*), Abbot Antony cheerfully suggested we take a peek at the last chapter. "It will show you what you're getting into," he said. "Don't worry; it won't ruin the story." He began to read it for us: *Are you hastening toward your heavenly home? Then with Christ's help, keep this little rule that we have written for beginners. After that, you can set out for the loftier summits of the teaching and virtues we mentioned above. . . .* Are there any questions?"

True virtue: silence. Part Benedictine, part terror.

The Rule is about life lived in *community*, Abbot Antony stressed. This is followed by the distressed, guilty silence of loners and misfits like me, sitting way in the back, avoiding eye contact, book at the ready in case the meeting gets dull. "We must know ourselves and each other better, so we can love each other better," Abbot Antony continued. Still no eye contact. We are a tough group to love. "I will start with a story about myself," he said—and the room relaxed, since most of us love our abbot.

Silly me, thinking I know him, but I didn't even know he had two sisters and four brothers, or that his mother died when he was thirteen and his father was a steamboat captain who spent most of his time on the river.

But glimpses of the person I know surfaced as he told of an intruder to the family home while he was visiting from the seminary one New Year's Eve. Abbot Antony got out his father's pistol and was prepared to handle the intruder. "But if I killed him, I was afraid I wouldn't be ordained, so I gave the gun to my oldest brother and said, 'You shoot him.' But we scared him away with all our movements."

One or two oblates spoke then, with gentle musings on the Blessed Sacrament and this morning's sermon. I was feeling smug and superior to talking in generalities—having abandoned it only a few years ago—and began to mentally rehearse something suitable to share about me that included identity.

And then it happened.

"My name is Jim, and I'm an oblate," said a gentleman I'd never noticed before. He was parroting the beginning of an AA testimony.

"Hi, Jim!" said a bunch of in-the-knows. I was stunned, suddenly feeling *very* not-different-at-all.

Jim told about a life of alcoholic hell after the murder of his daughter ten years ago. He told of finding his way to church and the numerous rejections there, of a Secular Franciscan experience without spirituality, of finding the Benedictines, but not being able to enter, of calling the abbot, "whom I consider now my spiritual father."

It is amazing when this happens, this living in community that Abbot Antony suggests is at the heart of the Rule. When I was in graduate school, writing my thesis, my subject was the rhetoric of Alcoholics Anonymous and how stories make communities and these communities of stories can heal drunks. One story came to mind as I listened to Jim. Although I read it six years ago, it now feels like a modern day desert story, and the desert amma is Malinda P.

> I kept waiting for someone who was my age, with my lifestyle, who had my politics, to tell my story. . . . I kept listening, kept doing what was suggested, kept talking, kept looking for that person who was going to tell my story. One day this guy with a jelly roll haircut and a pack of Marlboros rolled up his sleeve sat down at the table and told my story. I couldn't believe it. Here was somebody that was completely unlike me, I thought, but . . . I identified so strongly with his story. That changed my life, kept me sober, and from then on, I realized that it was possible for anyone to tell my story, regardless of how we might differ in outward circumstances or appearances.[1]

That's it. Benedict tries to give us guidance for living in community. Abbot Antony is right that this knowing—what AA called *identification*—is key to loving each other. Even Abbot Antony, whom I regard as a saint, is one of seven siblings who lost his mother young and held a pistol in his hand to shoot an intruder. Jim has suffered a daughter's brutal death and the indifference of organized religion. Jim and I have come under Abbot Antony's careful instruction, even as Abbot Antony has been formed by God's intermediaries long since deceased. A community of believers and doubters, but a community nonetheless.

"And here is where I plan to stay," Jim finished.

Amen, I want to answer. *Yes, me, too.*

Chapter 68: The Work of the Impossible

This short, one-paragraph chapter states simply that if you're assigned something you cannot do, you should "with complete gentleness and obedience" accept the assignment anyway. If you see it is too much for you, explain that to your superior. If the superior still holds to the original order, then, *Trusting in God's help, [you] must in love obey.*

Early adulthood for me was just as confused as adolescence, but I had more freedom and a bigger allowance for acting out. "EST" (Erhardt Seminar Training) was the rage of the late seventies, and you were either getting "it," or not getting "it."

I took out a loan to get self-actualized in the seminars being offered in Boston. I can only wonder what the loan officer thought when she saw *that* on my "reason for loan." I got "it" in the only dramatic, self-serving way I knew, and went on to flirt with post-EST training and seminars for those who might perceive a greater call to group psychology guerrilla tactics for a fee.

At one such training session, I listened in horror as a modest, unassuming young man explained the drills to leadership.

"They told us we had all afternoon to recruit five people to sign up for the next seminar." In 1978, the basic seminar rate was about $800 plus hotel and transportation costs. In 1978, that was a lot of money.

"I didn't know how I could possibly talk five people into that kind of commitment in about three hours," he continued. I told them that. They said, 'Don't think about it; just do it.' So I walked to the zoo and watched the animals a while. Then I got up off the bench and started talking to a few people . . . "

If that's the kind of "training" you got to get "it," count me out, I decided, and walked away from the "human potential movement" as they called it then. It was probably a good move for me and my pocketbook, but ironic when I see Benedict's Rule today.

The commentaries tend to stress the "who" that establishes the impossibility of the task at hand. "The reality is that we are often incapable of assessing our own limits," writes Chittister.[2] "The function of leadership is to call us beyond ourselves, to stretch us to our limits. . . . " Another commentary cheerfully suggests "often enough we are amazed that miracles occur when we consent to do something that at first seemed burdensome or impossible to do."[3]

"It's not about doing miracles," Abbot Antony says instantly when he stops in the cafeteria for his ten o'clock coffee and finds out what I'm studying. "It's about grace."

I am inclined to agree with him, not just because he's my beloved abbot, but out of an examination of my own life, with grace and without. I tend to turn my life into a great "to-do" list, and my quest then becomes nothing grander than checking things off as "done." And then what? Do I get to go home? It's my Puritan Protestant heritage, I think, where *doing* is the reason for *being*. The impossible enters into the picture because its assignment is being written off as "mission impossible" before it is begun. I've done it to myself. I had visions of crossing the finish line of the Boston Marathon before I could jog a mile. When the shin splits left me limping, I knew the marathon was impossible—and gave up the mile jog.

That's not about stretching your self limits; that's about putting the destination before the journey.

> A brother questioned Abba John the Dwarf: "What ought I to do? A brother often comes to fetch me for work, and since I am ill and weak, I get tired out working; what should I do to keep the commandment?" The old man said, "If you are strong enough to go out and come in, go to work; but if you cannot do it, sit down in your cell and weep for your sins and when they find you filled with compunction, they will not compel you to go out."[4]

"What have I to do with thee?" Jesus asked his mother (rather testily, I always thought). "Mine hour is not yet come" (John 2:4). Honestly, what are the world's needs to do with me, if I am not able to accomplish their solution?

In the gospel story where Jesus gets testy with his mother, the miracle *is* the result—water into wine. But we can get sidetracked by the miraculous part of the story. When Jesus responds to his mother and the small need her request represents, his hour *is* at hand, just like that, as he listens to others and trusts in God rather than himself.

God makes us ready for what we alone cannot do ("grace"). But it is others who press the grace button "on" with their needs and actions. We need to rely on God. We need others to help us come to rely on

God—like a human pyramid, where we stand on the shoulde
others or are pushed to the top. We need Jim of the oblate me..
where suddenly it is our story now we are hearing.

In St. Gregory's biography of St. Benedict,[5] St. Benedict calls
Brother Maurus to save a boy fallen in the lake. Brother Maurus
rushes out to obey his abba, running across the lake's surface and
returning with the child. While Benedict ascribes the miracle to obedience, Maurus claims it due to the command itself. He could not be
responsible through his obedience for the miracle, he said, because he
had not even known he had performed it.

I understand this not-knowing in a way. Was I called to be a
Benedictine oblate? Had my time come to become this particular
thing? Or did I just keep doing the little things my abbot asked, and
found myself professed as an oblate?

It is not to miracles, but to an ordinary life that God calls us. And
sometimes we make our life a series of the impossible until someone
reaches out and our hour becomes at hand.

Mass. It is quiet and plain today, even with the large Filipino con-
tingent finishing their retreat. Ordinary Time—no feasts, no fancy
work, just ordinary life, the monks', mine, of coming before God, celebrating the ordinary of it all.

Father Jerome is back in a motorized wheelchair, taking up the
space once held in the back of the choir by Brother Robert. Father
Jerome was strong enough to be the celebrant last time I was here, but
not doing so well today.

At lunch, Brother Maurius is on duty. I like how he finishes the *Angelus*
with the meal prayer: *Bless us, O Lord, and these your gifts, which we are about
to receive from your bounty, through Christ our Lord. Amen. Bon appétit!*

"It is chowder. From New England," Brother Maurius says
patiently as the Filipinos pass by the suspicious red soup. I try it: thick,
red, spicy, full of clams and corn. It is a good soup—but *not* New
England clam chowder. None of the retreatants try it.

The Filipino group moves out. "See you next year!" one gentleman
shouts to Brother Maurius. As the gentleman drags his luggage out
the door, I hear him finish under his breath—"I hope . . . "

I suddenly remember how my father and I took our leave of one another. It was Christmas, and the diagnosis was barely weeks old, but already I could see this might be our last time together. He was frightened—horribly so—and would suddenly break out in tears. The rule was: he doesn't want to talk about it. And indeed, "it" was death, the end point, and he was still in his first mile of illness and treatment.

I followed the rule and talked around and over what I saw in those terrified eyes. I think he was grateful for a "normal" visit from his daughter, no matter how strained and abnormal it really was.

My last night's visit there, I retired to the guest room and beyond my closed door, I heard my father's difficult steps to his room. A tiny rap on my door. "Have a safe trip."

"You too, Daddy." I don't know if he heard me. He was already moving past, in so many ways, and I never caught up with him again except to sputter the words St. Paul had given us in the night before he died.

But I faced every day of his dying, whether in rage, despair, or desperation. My heart stayed open and my eyes stayed full of tears, and God so gently filled me with his grace and walked beside me as he brought my father home. And the impossible grief of it all was accomplished.

~

No prayer work lady, none of the regular rhythm I knew from the first half of the year. I have not spent a weekday studying here since early July. I am out of sync somehow. Brother John Climachus nods politely when he passes, but seems not to recognize me. Abbot Antony also seems more distant, perhaps fading away to the next part of his journey. The oblate library is like a weed-choked garden, full of boxes of donated books stashed in the corner and pamphlets and books stashed wherever there is shelf space. The library book check-out cards are piling up and haven't been processed since at least April. A sad, neglected feel in the room. The clock has the wrong time again, and the window is shut with grime.

I force the window—weight lifting has its spiritual benefits—to let the breezy air and late sunshine in. I reset the clock. I ignore the clutter and stir up the dust molecules considerably as I shove a chair in of the window to write and think.

The year is running down.

~

Abbot Antony finds me in the oblate library and approves of my reading St. Frances de Sales. "It is very Benedictine," he says.

St. Francis de Sales is Franciscan. "What does that *mean*?" I ask, as suspicious as the Filipinos reviewing "New England clam chowder."

"St. Frances de Sales, he is very moderate," Abbot Antony says. "That's all the Rule is about."

So why have I made it so difficult then? Because moderation was not part of AA training. AA was all (drunk) or nothing (sober/sane). Because moderation is not my watchword. My enthusiasms run hot, then cold. The "answer" to my seeking has frequently been "no," and I have not persevered beyond that. Because I am a slow learner, and need to put things into my own words to trust them.

October 28, 2000: Thirtieth Sunday of Ordinary Time

It seems odd to be here at the monastery on an ordinary, non-oblate Sunday afternoon. But Felix is off traveling again—Korea this time—and I am a bit rootless as a result. Sunday afternoons alone, as my widowed mother will attest, take planning.

Once I went to Korea to see the exotic East where Felix has spent so much time and had so many adventures. As we walked through Nam Dae Mun, he suddenly turned to me with a stricken look on his face and said, "I feel like I'm introducing you to my mistress." It was a wonderful way of expressing this secret, hidden part of him, suddenly exposed. When he came with me to the monastery the one time, I understood what he meant, because the monastery is *my* secret heart, my oratory.

In his *Introduction to the Devout Life*, St. Francis de Sales reminds us to frequently "retire into the solitude of your heart." He notes that St. Catherine of Sienna, being "deprived by her parents of all suitable time and place wherein to pray and meditate, our Lord inspired her with the thought of making an oratory in her heart, whither she could retire mentally, and amidst external distractions enjoy internal solitude."[6] Lacking such mental fortitude, we find our secret gardens as our stations in life permit—Felix to the Orient, and I to the monastery, our oratories, our "mistresses."

The air outside shares the restlessness of autumn, all rustles, but few leaves falling for the effort. It's cool, in the half-hearted way it gets here, an edgeless sort of cool that mostly serves to remind you that summer is absent rather than that winter is approaching. There is a birdbath with no water in it outside the oblate library where Hildegard spent so much time in prayer and where I have now, this year, taken up a bit of residence.

"Why, you are *here*. I didn't realize," says Abbot Antony at my elbow at lunch, startling me from my reading. Nobody would know I was here. Earlier in the year I hated skulking around the retreat areas, "illegally," but the arrangement with Brother John Climachus no longer works either. I don't know why. Since our summer oblate retreat, when I've called to announce my intentions, Brother John Climachus's tape says no reservations are being taken and to leave a name/number if you are calling about an existing reservation for a retreat.

I stopped calling. But I've learned self-sufficiency too. I bring my own food and even bottled water in case I can't get near any coffee. I bring the *Angelus* so I can pray before meals no matter where I am physically. I bring reading materials, writing materials, study materials, could live out of my car if I had to. That way the monastery can live as it must, and I can still carry on as well.

But today the welcome mat is out, full retreat house or not. "Let me make sure the oblate library is open for you," says Abbot Antony.

"I'm going to take a walk first," I say.

"And then it will be open for your use," says Abbot Antony. "You may feel free to go through the three boxes of books that were donated to us." I don't catch the name of the individual, although it is clearly one familiar to the abbot. "It will be quite a while before we are able to sort through them or catalogue them. Feel free to take them home to read."

What a lovely birthday present, I think. I turned forty-eight two days ago. When I met the abbot, I was forty-five and he was rapidly approaching ninety—"twice your age!" he marveled.

But I've been gaining on him ever since.

The monoliths along the prayer walk's Stations are elaborate, but tidy—crosses made of rocks, of twigs held down with rock piles carefully constructed. Silk roses have been arranged alongside many. I realize I would probably be doing the same thing if I were here on a retreat when I wasn't also trying to cram study the Rule. A pure white rock follows me to the car for the future rock garden.

Chapters 69 and 70: Neither Presume to Defend nor Strike Another

Regardless of familial or friendly ties, no one in the monastery is allowed to defend (protect) another *because it can be a most serious source and occasion of contention*, says Benedict, in chapter 69. Likewise, in its mirror image, no one has the authority to excommunicate or strike one of the brothers (chapter 70). Benedict quotes the rather unlikely Book of Tobit for his reasoning on prohibiting striking another: *Do to no one what you would not want done to you* (Tobit 4:16). In its mirror version, we know this as the Golden Rule—*so always treat others as you would like them to treat you* (Matthew 7:12).

Are these two chapters really so self-serving as Benedict makes them out to be? I was driving to Long Beach, a distance of a hundred miles made into hours of stop-and-go traffic by the mysteries of Los Angeles traffic patterns, thinking about these sections, pondering how they might have been incorporated into my life. I was having no success. These prohibited actions—defending, striking—are prohibited "horizontally," among brothers or sisters who are otherwise equal. Although it's rather hard to imagine that happening, at least striking another brother *could* be done—if the abbot has delegated this power. But equals among equals cannot single another out, whether for good or bad— *because it can be a most serious source and occasion of contention*.

I realized my problem in relating to these chapters came because I had never been part of a community. Now this is a serious irony speaking. I have been born Episcopal, converted Catholic, returned to the Episcopal Church, and crawled into the back of Catholicism's lame/lapsed/late section, desperately seeking anonymity there. I have been an AA member, a Secular Franciscan, and now a Benedictine oblate. And these are only the communities along the spiritual journey. I have joined and departed more civic and service clubs than I care to admit. I have been, as my father liked to put it, none too kindly, "a joiner."

But not a "stayer." Stability, that odd backbone of the Benedictine vow, has never been part of my repertoire. And without it, I can join anything and everything, but I will never *belong*.

And *belonging* is what I have been looking for.

A story came to mind, thinking about the rules of belonging espoused by Benedict, as I drove to Long Beach. An old story, never recalled until now: The first graders stood around the old, upright piano, singing lustily as Mrs. Weymouth pounded on the keyboard. It was one of those times, rare even for first graders, of being one voice, one group, one first grade class getting ready for the Christmas show. "Oh, the weather outside is frightful . . . "

Mrs. Weymouth suddenly stopped playing. The lusty baby voices trailed off at different speeds. "Who was that?" she demanded. The first graders looked to each other, wondering who was in trouble. "Who has that marvelous voice?"

First graders looked at each other again, unaware until that moment of any individuality. Finally one girl near me said, uncertainly, "Me. It's me."

Mrs. Weymouth pulled her forward. "Let's all sing again." And with one of their number set aside, the first graders began again, more tentatively. "Oh, the weather outside is frightful, and the fire is so delightful . . . "

"It isn't you," Mrs. Weymouth said abruptly, stopping mid-chord. Unceremoniously, she pushed the youngster back into the group. "It's *you*," she said to the girl next to the one who had spoken up. "Come forward. Start singing, everyone."

And pulled out and set apart, I sang. I sang solo, never again to be part of a chorus, always joining, never belonging, until the journey put Abbot Antony in my path, until I began chasing the choices he laid out for me if I truly wanted to get to the New Jerusalem.

Now, yes, I belong. It didn't happen when I said my words of novitiate, or even my oblate vows a year later. Maybe it was in the renewal of those vows, choking on tears and unable to say the words myself, having to let my oblate retreatants say them for me. Maybe then. At some point, I stepped back into the circle, where all of us were chosen by God and none of us were choosing or excluding another. This is how Benedict means us to live in community.

It has clouded over and cooled off considerably. We will, pe
get the promised rainstorm after all. (Joke I've made since mov
San Diego: if a weatherman loves weather, why would a good or
in San Diego?) I have a headache from thinking too much, or fasting,
I'm not sure which, but despite the Sunday afternoon silence, I no
longer feel lonely or disjointed. This place has a way of filing down my
mental edges, although I am less "desperate" to get here and more
relaxed about it when I am. Is an oratory truly that when you can
approach it with detachment? I nibble the edges of the books I found
in the uncatalogued—much Thomas Merton, a biography of Benedict,
even St. Augustine's *Confessions*—which I leave on top of my take-home
pile in case the abbot comes by and examines what I'm taking home.

Perseverance, I remind myself. Very Benedictine to persevere. I
return to the *Devout Life* and wait for Vespers.

October 31, 2000: Vigil, All Saints' Day

Mass on Halloween night. It feels like a clash of the secular and
sacred. I'm relieved to enter my parish church and find at least fifty
other such souls.

"Congratulations," says Father Don, opening up his homily.
"Congratulations for wanting to be counted among the company of
the saints. You want to be saints! But as our bishop says, 'Don't rush
out and get holy cards printed with your image on them just yet.
There's still a lot of work to do.'"

So true. In this year when, ostensibly, I am studying the Rule of St.
Benedict to understand its application to ordinary oblates like me, I
find my study is taking me to unexpected, unglamorous places, like my
parish church.

"Experience the blessings of public worship," I just read in
Introduction to the Devout Life. "There is always greater benefit and
comfort to be derived from the public service of the church than from
private devotion, God having promised a special blessing on this
union of hearts and souls."[7]

Who could have told me this in the L3 section of church? Oddly,
in these last few months, I've begun acting as if I am part of the public worship in my parish. I've even moved myself to a more "mainstream" seat than the L3 section. And I very much want to be part of
tonight's service.

I think as a Protestant kid, I had All Saints' and All Souls' days rolled into one. We may have treated it as one in my church. Even up until this year, in that unthinking, unblinking way I can carry kid beliefs forward, I thought All Saints' Day was about "dead people," preferably ones I knew and missed.

My saint-a-day book—bathroom reading for the last three or four years—came as quite a jolt. "Today we honor all the saints, known and unknown, famous and not so famous," it begins.[8] Dimly, I remember hearing that if your saint doesn't have a separate day, this is the collective feast day.

There have been many things that have bothered me about poor Blessed Joanna Mary Bonomo since Abbot Antony introduced us in March of 1999. One was that she wasn't famous. Two, she wasn't even a real saint. "Blesseds" have one miracle under their belts, but need another to be certified in the pantheon. Beatified by Pius VI in 1783, Joanna Mary didn't seem likely to be up to that hurdle anymore. Three, her last name (Bonomo) is my husband's stepfather's name, hardly the "relative" Abbot Antony claimed her for me. And fourth, there was precious little to be learned about her other than the single paragraph Abbot Antony saw and copied for me.

I could find her in no martyrologies, Benedictine or other. If I were reading my page from the abbot correctly, her day would be February 22, after St. John, abbot of Lucca, and before Henry, monk of Memmenrode. And we actually celebrate the Chair of St. Peter on that day, as Christians have since the fourth century, so none of these guys will *ever* get their day of glory (on earth).

But she was all that I had, and the abbot whom I loved delighted in the introduction, and now my vows as a Benedictine oblate have her name and mine intertwined. I had to work with what I had. I made fanciful collages of strong young women and tried to evoke her presence in my life.

Last week in my birthday box from my mother, there was a two-foot high wooden statue with stand, something she'd seen and "just liked." A brown-skinned, beautifully styled peasant woman, offering a modest bowl of fruits, the statue could be anyone in her anonymity. I decided she could just as easily be Blessed Joanna Mary in *her* anonymity, and hung a crystal rosary from her offering and placed her in my tiny oratory.

"Choose as your patrons some saints in particular," says St. Frances de Sales, "to whose life and imitation you feel most drawn, and in whose intercession you feel an especial confidence. The saint whose name you bear is already assigned you from your baptism."[9]

I know even less about any saints named Carol than what I know about Blessed Joanna Mary, but the names are intertwined now. Since putting that representation in my oratory, Blessed Joanna Mary has become a daily, beautiful presence to me, a refuge in my mind during times of stress.

Here, today, it comes together for me, however briefly, and the monastic vows "bleed through" into my oblate, ordinary life. *I get to take communion with Blessed Joanna Mary tonight*, I think. And on a night we associate with ghosts and goblins, I trot off happily to partake of the communion of saints—Blessed Joanna Mary in particular—not afraid and certainly not alone.

NOVEMBER
Candle of the Lord

The spirit of man is the candle of the LORD.
Proverbs 20:27

November 3, 2000: Abbot Antony's Ninety-second birthday, also St. St. Martin de Porres

The monks seem to celebrate the saints' feast days the way we celebrate birthdays. I remember that from one of the first days I went to Mass at the abbey, and September 21—an ordinary day to me—was anything but ordinary for Brother Matthew, who was mentioned in the intercessory prayers in a special way with his apostolic namesake.

The same is probably done on January 17 during Epiphany for Abbot Antony. His namesake, St. Antony of Egypt, was also an abbot, one who strongly desired to live the simple life. But no matter how deeply he lived as a hermit, people pursued him in their need for spiritual counsel. He is the "father of monks," and lived to the age of 105, exhorting those he came in contact with to the message of Christ.

This Abbot Antony, my abbot, is merely turning ninety-two. I think we know his "regular" birthday and fuss over it because we are oblates and still date things from our worldly entry rather than our saintly departure. It's hard to come up with a birthday gift, but we do it every year because that's what we do in the world, and because we so love our old abbot. This year we collected money so he could pick videos from a catalogue for the oblate library collection.

What do you give the man who has everything and owns nothing? I wondered last week. The man who is celebrating ninety-two years on earth in anticipation of the eternity of heaven? In my arrogance, I decide to send him *his* spiritual bouquet, the one that took nearly all of August's *lectio* to write and memorize, Psalm 95, that begins each day's Divine Office.

Felix was still in China, and his computer screen was dark. I borrowed it and begin typing from my *lectio* notebook: *Come, let us sing to the Lord. . . .* Twenty-five days of *lectio* at two pages per day. I typed and typed, reliving the psalm, the abbot's face shining like Transfiguration itself, the warmth of the breeze at the monastery on quiet summer afternoons. I typed and typed, the foolish words that seeped from my sleepy morning pen for twenty-five days to give glory for Abbot Antony's jubilee in a Jubilee Year.

When it was done, just in time to send it for his birthday, I printed it up and stuck it in a cover like kids use when they are trying to dress up a weak homework assignment by using a nice presentation. I took one of my flower stencils and drew all over the cover because I like coloring things. And then I shipped it off to him, feeling for all the world like this "spiritual bouquet" had turned into a bunch of dead, dried flowers that I was returning.

"I sat down and read it immediately," Abbot Antony says when he finally tracks me down. He has been calling me at home for two days and had nice conversations with Felix, but now sounds irritable that it has taken me so long to get back to him. "I am now reading it for the third time."

"You read it all the way through in one sitting?" It is my turn to be indignant. "It took me twenty-five days to write it!"

He promises to read it slower next time. "St. Augustine's *Confessions* is also written as a spiritual memoir, like your writing," he says. "Have you read that?"

I have not. I'm embarrassed at the nerviness of sending him my quarrelsome little morning ramblings. "I thought it would be interesting to see something you know so well in a new perspective," I mumble. "Happy birthday!"

"It *is*," he agrees. "I will read it more reflectively now."

November 24, 2000: St. Andrew Dung-Lac and His Companions

It is the day after Thanksgiving, and pretty quiet on the retreatant side of the monastery, this, the last week of Ordinary Time for a while. After an early, prolonged piece of San Diego "winter" (i.e., frost delays on the golf course at Lake San Marcos), today promises a hard blue sky, mild temperatures, and a chance my hands will stay warm until early darkness at least.

As hard-bitten New Englanders who had known the nip of frost damage to fingers and toes, Felix and I spent our first winter in southern California stomping the neighborhood in shorts, tee shirts, and beach-flippies, crowing to each other, "Isn't this wonderful?"— and undoubtedly looking like tourists the entire time. By the following year, we were bundled up in front of the fireplace mumbling, "What happened?"

Acclimation, of course. Adjusting to the prevailing climate. As I sit in the deserted retreat cafeteria, sipping coffee in the hour before Mass, Brother Dominic trundles kitchen supplies in and says hello. Father Vincent and Brother Nicholas acknowledge my presence as they cut through on their various ways. We all have our work to do, even as we acknowledge the Christ present in each other. I am not disturbing them anymore. They are not disturbing me.

Acclimation.

"This is about the only place in America they don't know about pregnant chads," says a big, burly man walking around the cafeteria waiting for his meeting with Abbot Antony.

I know he is referring to the remoteness of worldly politics and the otherworldly weirdness of the recent presidential elections. But I think, *You'd be surprised what they know around here.* He begins telling me about the archabbey of St. Meinrad where he's visited, so I just listen instead.

Abbot Antony never shows up. "You can ask for him through the porter," I say, trying to be helpful. The big man finally wanders off in the opposite direction.

There are only a few chapters left in this study. I bolted through so many early on, then paced myself out a little bit after the Easter retreat. One chapter in November, two in December, preferably after the Christmas rush.

I had wanted to schedule a last overnight stay here in December, to finish the study of the Rule and just to sit in the presence of some year-end quiet at the monastery. But every time I called the guest master extension, Brother John Climachus's careful, cheerful voice repeated the same taped message: no room at the inn (I am paraphrasing here, wildly). No further bookings this year. Leave a message.

Shoot. I know the retreat center does a good business. During the Easter retreat, I made my reservation for *next* year's Easter retreat—and got the last available room. A really icky one at that, not renovated, facing the parking lot. Maybe I have no understanding of church group or religious bodies' retreat schedules. But an overnighter during the Octave of Christmas? It doesn't seem right that the place is filled.

Finally last week, I decided to just leave my name and number for the call back. I would beg for a room, any room, ask to be put on a waiting list, anything.

Someone answered the retreat master's line, a vaguely familiar voice, but not Brother John Climachus.

"I'm an oblate," I said. "I'm calling to beg for a room the last week of December."

"We get pretty busy," the voice said evenly, "but I can probably find one room for one night."

I held my breath until he came back with a reservation.

"And you are . . . ?" I asked.

"Ed."

I can't quite place the voice—maybe somebody who appeared (or reappeared from an absence that predates my time here) about a month or two ago? A monk named Ed?

I want to ask about Brother John Climachus, but decide not to. Sometimes they are loaned to other places in need. Sometimes they need other places to be for a time. Either way, it is none of my business. I have seen a few go, unexplained, away from this place where we bind ourselves with a vow of stability.

One of the old men came to Abba Theodore of Pherme and said to him, "Look how such and such a brother has returned to the world." The old man said to him, "Does that surprise you? No, rather be astonished when you hear that someone has been able to escape the jaws of the enemy.”[1]

I am grateful for my December reservation, courtesy of somebody named Ed. This day's visit brings me to the monastery filled with absence.

Even stability has shades of meaning here.

~

By noontime, the place is packed and full of life. A group of forty-six Spanish-speaking Catholics from Chula Vista, San Ysidro, and Tijuana have arrived for the weekend.

Abbot Antony finds me at my usual table and brings Pat with him. She faithfully attends Mass every day. A very quiet, obviously devout woman, she is also an oblate. I see that sweetly serene face all the time, but we have never spoken. I take her to be about sixty. At lunch she tells me she is seventy-eight. There is something to be said for sweet serenity as beauty treatment.

"Any news from Washington, D.C.?" Abbot Antony asks. "Have you gone there since the election?"

I bet he knows all about pregnant chads. It is a companionable sort of lunch, and I'm glad to finally know sweet-faced Pat. Abbot Antony is very diligent about trying to get the oblate community to respond to each other "horizontally," not just to him "vertically." It is another of his tools passed along so we can continue in our lifelong conversion after he is gone.

"What are you reading?" he asks suddenly. Pat gets off scot-free, I notice. I hold up *The Way of Catherine of Siena*, one of the books I hauled home from the boxes last visit.

"Very good," he murmurs. I have been reading it since this morning when I packed my bag. The spiritual-lite stuff I left at home.

"He wants me to read St. Augustine," I explain to sweet-faced Pat. "But St. Augustine is too hard for me."

"The *Confessions* is *not* too hard!" says the abbot. "It is his life!"

"Who's Ed?" I ask, wondering if there will be an answer.

Ed was a novice who left and is now back wrestling with a decision about staying. I know the feeling. Routing out the gyratory is sometimes harder than putting down a drink. Perseverance sometimes works in two directions, getting you nowhere.

"He knows about computers, so he's helping on the guest house scheduling while he's deciding," Abbot Antony says. Brother John Climachus inherited a manual scheduling system that he had patiently pieced into a computer application—and thus the retreat house scheduling difficulties since his departure. I am grateful for Ed's return, no matter who he is. I hope he makes the right decision for him.

The prayer walk. Absolutely no good rocks. The one I find is barely passable. Where do they all go?

Chapter 71: Mutual Obedience

Benedict just can't get enough of this! Early on (chapter 5), the Rule discusses obedience, starting with: *The first step of humility is unhesitating obedience.* Two chapters later, the killer chapter on "Humility" brings it out again (as actually the fourth step of humility, but the point is made). Now months later, it returns, this time in mutuality. Obedience is a blessing to be shown by all, not only to the abbot, but also to one another as brothers, since we know that it is by this way of obedience that we go to God.

> Abba Poemen said, "Do not do your own will; you need rather to humble yourself before your brother."[2]

This is the hardest thing to contemplate, as I have stared at it over the last month trying to see where it could apply to an ordinary oblate's life.

It's okay to admit that some part of the Rule has relevance in theory but no practical application, I decided. There's always a first, and it will prove how difficult mutual obedience is in this world if I can't come up with an example of it.

When Felix was in China, I rented videos that interested *me*, rather than *us*. This latest trip of his, I rented *28 Days* starring Sandra Bullock, which had just reached the video rental market. The movie was about a successful professional woman being destroyed unknowingly by her drinking. She enters a detox facility to avoid going to jail for an alcohol-related accident while she is behind the wheel.

I sobered up on tough love during a few days in the infirmary an at AA meetings right after that. I worked at MIT then, and they hau gorgeous benefits, so most of Ron's drunks started their new lives in a twenty-eight-day treatment program at Beach Hill. There were times in the early eighties when MIT could have set up a satellite worksite at Beach Hill.

The question I got over and over in those fuzzy early days was, "Why didn't Ron send you to Beach Hill?"

"I don't know," I'd answer. "You'd have to ask him. "Maybe I wasn't worthy. Maybe I wasn't bad enough a drunk."

"You were bad enough to rate a rehab," Anne argued, adding philo-sophically, "Mysterious are Ron's ways."

"I didn't think you'd leave work for a month," Ron said in exaspera-tion when I finally asked him myself. "You seemed to think your work mattered, and it was the only area of good self-esteem you had left, and I was reluctant to suggest taking it away at that moment."

So I missed out on rehab. *28 Days* was my chance to see what I missed.

Watching the self-centered destruction of an active drunk was hard enough. Watching the numb-faced denial and eventually watching that facade crumble was harder still. "Good identification," as they would have said in AA.

They said a lot of things in AA. "They" were not doctors or nurses or paracounselors like in a rehab center. "They" were not even my social worker Ron at that moment—which was fine, since he seemed to be ignoring me carly in sobriety and since I, for my part, *loathed* him for just about everything. "They" were "us"—drunks like me who'd done every rotten thing I'd ever done drunk plus lots more that I wasn't devious enough to think up. ("You hid the bottles *where?*") And "they," with no more credentials than sobriety longer than mine, which was everybody early on, were more than forthcoming with bossy instructions: "thirty meetings in thirty days," "use the phone," "read the Big Book and don't drink," "get a sponsor," "ask for help."

And I got to obey. "Why do I have to listen to them?" I howled at Ron when I was finally back in his office. "It's bad enough I have to listen to you."

"I'm not a drunk," he said. I'm not sure he made his statement with any pride. It was just a statement.

"Nobody's perfect," I mumbled.

"I don't really know what it's like," he continued. "They do. I'm not available twenty-four hours a day, seven days a week. They are."

It is easier and less humiliating to obey superiors. It is usually good politics and good career practice. It can even be perfected into the art form known as "sucking up." Obedience to each other carries no such distinctions of honor or art. But it taught me humility and kept me sober, in a boot camp, all-or-nothing sort of way. Ron alone, as professional social worker, could not have achieved the results necessary through "vertical" obedience. There had to be this "horizontal obedience" too.

Nearly twenty years later, I see this as Abbot Antony firmly guides us "vertically" to God through Benedict's Rule and also steers us "horizontally" to each other.

~

The Spanish-speaking retreatants, newly arrived, have mobbed the gift shop. One lady has many, many articles to be blessed, and Abbot Antony is found and pressed into service with a prayer sheet, cloth, and holy water tucked behind the cash register for such occasions. I hear his fragile old voice saying the prayers, and suddenly he is gone.

"I told him she still had items to bless," says the bookstore lady. "And he told me, 'You'll find me in the cafeteria taking a rest. I'm all blessed out.'"

So am I. I leave early tonight, before the darkness falls.

November 26, 2000: Feast of Christ the King

It is one of those feasts I label as "odd"—meaning unfamiliar to my plain vanilla Protestant upbringing. I like the odd ones best (Feast of the Immaculate Conception being next up on the list). They are filled with Bible readings I never heard from the pulpit, strange, exotic images, a treasure attic for hide-and-seek thoughts and prayers that would otherwise never see the light of day.

It feels funny not to be going off to the monastery today as I have the last two such feasts. In 1998, it was to make the offering of a novitiate oblate. "This day was made by the Lord," we prayed then. "We rejoice and are glad" (Psalm 118). Words said in uncertain unison with Hildegard and Gregory, and then Vespers with a vivid orange and pink sunset dying all around us.

Last year during this feast, the oblation was made, and each of us individually promised ourselves to this life, and Blessed Joanna Mary became my cloak, my companion for the journey, my namesake. We sang Vespers and Brother Maurius entertained us with magic tricks, and all the salt and pepper shakers disappeared from our table.

After we left, it was Abbot Antony who nearly disappeared, collapsing in a seizure that left his face bruised, his teeth broken, and his ancient heart nearly stopped.

This morning, a year later, we celebrate again that Christ is King. My morning *lectio* was on Proverbs 20:27: "The spirit of man is the candle of the LORD." I thought of the candle I had just lit before saying the Morning Office and how its light flickers and fragments off the statue of Blessed Joanna Mary and the beautiful crystal rosary that hangs from her hands. Would a steady light be as lovely?

I thought of the Lord, coming out of the darkness saying, "Let there be light." And as on Holy Saturday, we stand, illuminated only by candles lit from the one, the flickering faces of hope against the darkness.

The candle on my oratory flickered light onto the little picture of Abbot Antony and me, taken during my novitiate. I am clutching the first book he ever loaned me and smiling into the camera. He is looking to the road to the New Jerusalem. The candle lit us both for a moment.

It is time to leave for church. There are normally two lectors for each service, and I am normally the Saturday evening lector, but God in his delight has watched our scheduler place me at the morning Mass of the Feast of Christ the King. On the anniversary of my oblation, the second reader—no doubt reviewing the difficulty of reading intelligently from the Books of Daniel and Revelation—has declared a "previous engagement," and I am alone on the pulpit.

"His dominion is an everlasting dominion that shall not be taken away," I read from the New American Bible translation that the lectors use. "His kingship shall not be destroyed" (Daniel 7:14).

What has happened since I made the oblation of myself to God— an offering whose words I barely understood, pledging to live a Rule I certainly did not understand. What has happened to the one who sat in the L3 of the lame, lapsed, and late, marveling over her cleverness at naming while she prayed alone, came early, left early, dressed casually, reading during the sermon? Where has that part of my public worship gone?

"Behold, he is coming amid the clouds, and every eye will see him, even those who pierced him. All the people of the earth will lament him. Yes. Amen" (Revelation 1:7). I am standing here, proclaiming the Word to the best of my ability—and the slight amusement of the congregation, as my "proclaiming" seems to draw out the depths of a New England accent. "Ah-mehn." I am so nervous. It is only my second time, and I have all the readings, the intercessions, and the announcements to do.

The Lord showers us all with love and blessings. Like candlelight, his blessings flicker and reflect off us. At some point, do we say yes, amen? Confirmation at twelve years old—an unthinking yes, a social occasion, a new white dress. Ten years ago, Catholic conversion, yes, spare me the isolation that not going to AA meetings might bring. The oblate novice—a yes to life in the spirit, a tentative yes to Father Antony after my father had died before my eyes. The oblation, yes, amen. "The spirit of man is the candle of the Lord." This enormous gift bestowed on this small person, to live reflected in his light, filled with his spirit to shine forth with the light of others.

"Where are you from?" asks Father Don when Mass is over. "I asked visitors to stand, and I wondered, listening to you read: why isn't she standing? She can't be from here."

It's the accent of home he is referring to, of course. And I am glad to bring it here, to the Word, which is bringing me home to the New Jerusalem, yes, amen.

DECEMBER
Prefer Nothing Whatsoever

Let them prefer nothing whatsoever to Christ.
Rule of St. Benedict, chapter 72

December 28, 2000: Feast of the Holy Innocents

While the rest of the country huddles inside or digs itself out of yet another storm, we in San Diego are racing around opening windows as the daytime temperatures approach eighty degrees. By 4:00 P.M., the low winter sun is ready to collapse into the horizon again, and we rush to close up the house before the temperatures drop to freezing.

The roses are all dead on their long, sunflower-like stalks. It is surely winter in San Diego. All you have to do is look at the foliage. The margarita bush is in full yellow flower, and the jade is starting to perk up. The lemon and tangerine trees are marvelous with fruit. There is plenty to compensate for the death of the roses.

It has been a long and frantic month. Roses have their off-season and so do lobbyists. December is normally my party month professionally as well as socially, as legislators return home and mingle with constituents. With the bizarre presidential election, the lame duck congressional session continued until I left for vacation. But I still managed to attend up to seven events a day until the last gasp of legislative 2000. I was in Palm Springs, Long Beach, San Francisco, Tucson, and San Diego this month. My rolling luggage stayed at the foot of my bed when it wasn't rolling off to another destination. My Advent—that glorious pregnant time of waiting—was pretty much reduced to desperately reminding myself that I could at least spend a last few days of this Jubilee Year at the monastery.

This morning, the rolling luggage moved from the edge of the bed to the car again, and I made my way up the hill as the sun dazzled its low-slung journey over the Pacific. Anxious (*who is this Ed, and did they really find a room for me?*), but thrilled in the most honest way to spend these days like a great Christmas gift from God.

"Bonomo?" Brother Maurius, working now as as retreat master, looks doubtful. There are computer lists everywhere. "Do you see yourself here?" he asks, handing me the lists.

I sure do, I think, and point to my name on one list.

"Ah, yes, Bonomo. I am abbot's secretary, and I write the thank-you notes for checks. Felix, right?"

Dear Felix, who has been here exactly once, might be pleased at Brother Maurius's recall. But then, Brother Maurius *is* a magician.

"Check-in is usually 3:30," says Brother Maurius. But he hands me the key to room 26 in case my room is ready. It is—the same quiet, clean room where I spent Easter.

By 9:30 A.M., I am officially here on retreat.

～

In the quiet retreatant cafeteria, I pour myself coffee and go to "my" regular table in the corner. It has a sign on it saying "reserved." How appropriate, I decide. Then I move the "reserved" one table over and sit where *I* sit. It's about making a place for yourself, even here at the monastery.

Abbot Antony comes in as I barely settle down. We have begun to know each other's habits. "I must tell you again how I felt about those meditations you sent me," he says, delighted to be able to tell me in person. "I will admit that I read them through very quickly when I got them. But now I am savoring them very slowly. We say the psalm so quickly in the morning. And I *chastise* myself for not taking the time to appreciate its richness. You must read St. Augustine's *Confessions*."

～

Mass. *Emmanuel Rex Oriens* says one banner hanging left of the altar. *Clavis Radix Adonai Sapientia*, says the other. Past *Emmanuel*, my

Latin is hopeless. I copy it all down to ask the abbot.

The abbey church is decorated simply, and there is none of the pine tree smell that I remember when I started this study in January. It looks like a different decor from last year's decorations too. In January, the Nativity scene filled one corner of the little church where now it is just inside the front doors, but outside the church itself.

It takes me a while to realize that "then" was Epiphany and "now" is the Christmas Octave. No one's reached Bethlehem yet in the tradition of the old stories.

It seems odd, and somewhat fitting, that the end of this calendar year finds us all still outside, still journeying from afar.

～

Two prayer walks so far this retreat. No good rocks at *all*. I do the best I can for the year's end. There are thirty-six rocks at home, plus four shells. Now I have thirty-eight rocks.

Chapter 72: The Good Zeal That Monks Possess

Benedict describes and contrasts bitter zeal from the good zeal that is the goal of his monks. The zeal Benedicts asks for is encapsulated in the most quoted words in the Rule: *Let them prefer nothing whatsoever to Christ.*

While dashing and dancing my way through this holiday season, I entertained my idle thoughts with "zeal" and what it looks like for me, and why *zeal* is a word full of pep and vigor, but *zealot* is bad and without the moderation Benedict so desires for us. *So there is a good zeal which separates from evil and leads to God and everlasting life*, he says early in this chapter.

For me, good zeal comes in words, in writing, I keep thinking, although my career is only superficially about writing. Regardless about what Felix wants me to claim, I am more lobbyist than speechwriter.

My passion is a passion of words, of writing and filling books with words: whether in *lectio*, a prayer journal, a collage diary, or even here in these little notebooks I have dragged around to the monastery. If zeal is about following our bliss, my bliss is in the written words.

I kept a diary for sixteen years. Perhaps I should say it kept me. I called it my diary demon, my calendar sickness, but whatever it was, I d myself into it—forty-seven thick volumes of "it"—for sixteen

I began keeping a diary on January 1, 1980, because I thought writers kept diaries, and I wanted to be a writer. In the years that followed, I learned to write, to observe, to feel, to think by writing in those diaries. No surprise when I began *lectio*, I had to write in an open, empty notebook.

Eventually the diaries seemed to have served whatever purposes they served, and I started to stop keeping them. They were my bliss, but not my joy. They began to stand between me and the world, that enormous pile of self-made books. When I returned to church-going, it became unclear whom I was talking to in those diaries. Immortality? Are we kidding? Finally I began to fill a little prayer journal each morning. At least then I knew who my audience was.

As I say, "I started to stop." I switched to a prayer journal, began a collage diary, working with images and words instead of images *in* words, and did daily "morning pages" as an artist for years. "I don't care what you called it; you never stopped writing," says Felix.

I think it was no accident that God entered my life only when I quit keeping diaries, my third, and hardest, "quit" after drinking and then smoking. *It's about place.* I had to sweep the place clean before God could enter. I had to remove the bliss almost surgically from my life before I could hear God (*Listen* . . .), who answered in the joy of my heart.

Joy is not bliss. You go out and find your bliss. You stay put, and joy is there, where it's been all along, the whisper, the thing you were seeking the whole time.

Zeal is "fervor for a person, cause, or object," says my dictionary this morning when I finally look it up in my *Webster's Encyclopedic Unabridged Dictionary of the English Language*: "eager desire or endeavor, enthusiastic diligence, ardor."

> Abbess Syncletica of holy memory said, "There is labor and great struggle for the impious who are converted to God, but after that comes inexpressible joy. A man who wants to light a fire first is plagued by smoke, and the smoke drives him to tears, yet finally he gets the fire he wants."[1]

When I cleared away the words I was keeping, it was interesting to see what gradually took their place. My church's "Day of Recollection" was held at the monastery last Advent, and Father Stanislaus the conferences that day. Before we began, I had been reviewin 1999 prayer journal—a year's worth of miserable petition, nor seemed, answered.

"Get out of the petition business!" exhorted Father Stanislaus, startling us all, having just gotten us to admit that most of our prayer life consisted of petitions to God. He sounded like a pretty radical Benedictine to me—if there can ever be such a thing. "Petition puts your back to God, facing yourselves and your needs," he continued. "Very limiting. Praise faces God with our backs to ourselves. Yes?"

No. You could see it in our collective body language. Some of the older ones grumbled out loud. We all wanted extra credit for all those prayers we say for others, all those worthy petitions.

Father Stanislaus wasn't giving in an inch. "What is the agenda for such petitions?" he asked. "You are saying that you see all and know what to ask for, that God needs your help to understand what to do. God does not need your help. God does not want your help. All God wants from you is praise. Be like a child. Become child-like."

Praise-prayer is everything Scripture says prayer must be, he informed us. "Praise with the body," he said. "That's where the sin is. Praise through song, through words, not through intellect. Praise through your gifts. Keep your eyes on God."

Nobody was too happy with Father Stanislaus that day, and our Lenten Day of Recollection group went to the Franciscan Mission instead and avoided the abbey completely after that. I probably would have been exactly the same only I had that blasted prayer journal as evidence of a year's worth of the "petition business," and it was enough to make me file for spiritual bankruptcy. I hung around after the conferences for three hours to sing Vespers and think about praising. It seemed to require a complete mental flip-flop in prayer life.

Outside the abbey after Vespers that night of winter solstice, there hung the largest full moon of the entire year, hanging so brightly, praising God in its beingness, reminding us of a star so bright, so long ago, that the wisest of men followed it all the way to a child.

Be like a child. Become child-like, Father Stanislaus encouraged. *Practice,* he said, Fifteen minutes each time, three times a day.

I made resolutions to do so, since we were approaching the millennium and I was making resolutions about everything anyway. I created a fanciful "praise rosary" to say, but the only thing that stuck beyond a day or so was in my prayer journal. In 1999, each day opened with a petition: "For Felix." "For my mother." "For my beloved abbot." "For a greater sense of penance and attrition this Lent than was with me this morning when I failed to get up" (a bad day already, that one). "For a nice day" (a day begun in low expectations). "To know true reward, not those established by men" (work evaluation day). And "I forgot already what I asked for as I began the Divine Office—of the usual platitudes, I guess!"

In 2000, my prayer journal has a sing-songy quality about it that has not always been sincere, but it certainly has been consistent no matter how hard I've had to work at coming up with early morning praising. The prayer journal began clearly enough:

> Praising you always and everywhere at this, the beginning of a new century, new millennium. We want to believe great things with the change of the calendar. Twenty years ago today, I took these changes to mean keeping a diary, and I did so until the diary kept me—and long after that! Now the change is to move from petition to praise. Dopey thing. May I keep that up long after it takes me over and bears me along to the New Jerusalem that Abbot Antony promised.

It continued from that new, fresh start:

> Praising you always and everywhere, especially in these dark, brief, cold days of winter—
> Praising you always and everywhere, in difficulties as well as joy—
> Praising you always and everywhere, in snow-drenched mountains and dry desert floors—
> Praising you always and everywhere, in silence and in noise—
> Praising you always and everywhere, in what I have done and in what I have not done—
> Praising you always and everywhere, in the fog that shrouds us this morning and so much of our lives . . .

It was an awkward turn, this back-to-the-wall/face-to-God stuff. Three months into the year, I began dutifully enough, "Praising you always and everywhere—but in petitions too!" Who knows why St. Casimir's Day (March 4) is so difficult at 5:00 A.M.?

"My fitful efforts at praise leave me feeling distant and lonely from you. I am more suitable as a penitent (although one without any discipline). And yet I cannot go back to the self-indulgence it engendered."

Where does zeal come into play? Surprisingly early in the year, I recognized the path to zeal that praising prayer would bring to me.

> January 19, 2000: Praising you always and everywhere; in the glory of the murderously deep pink skies of winter dawning. Isaiah (today's *lectio*) says: "The zeal of the LORD of Hosts will perform this" (9:7). I have been struggling for over a year now to find and harvest my own zeal. It does not seem to be possible. Isaiah says: "Your zeal shall perform." And so to you I praise and give glory in the morning sky of winter, not to turn inward to my own small worries."

Zeal came into my life by the back door, fitful as a nervous mouse, so obscure I am forced to attribute it to God—even my deviousness is more direct than this. Benedict says of his zealous monks, *Let them prefer nothing whatever to Christ*. I have preferred my words, my cleverness, my penances, my anything to Christ, but these praising prayers turn me outside-in and shake loose at least some of the me-me-mine's. The changes in me are probably subtle, but the entry in the prayer journal was suddenly not subtle at all:

> Praising you always and everywhere, in cheerfulness of heart and voice. I have anxiously wondered about my "call" from you during this Jubilee Year, reading, writing, thinking and studying, trying to "make" it happen (like I tried so hard at Easter). Somehow this week, a series of smaller-than-thoughts came together, and I understood that my way is to be cheerful. It is certainly not a Big-C "Call." But a drop of cheer in a world oddly mixed with prosperity and unpleasantness is useful—and distinctly mine to offer.

I have crossed over into the good zeal. What would have struck me a year ago as an embarrassingly modest resolution is now embraced as my life's work. I can't explain it out of Father Stanislaus's praise

;m (although one led to the other), but it is something, a gift of
)ilee Year.

⁓

My own New England "desert fathers" tell a different kind of
story, the geological kind that helps me understand. Fresh water—
the stuff of life itself—is abundant in the Cape's numerous ponds.
And it comes from the sandy reef of the Cape itself, surrounded by a
salty ocean. The Cape gets about forty inches of rain a year, rain that
gently "percolates" through the sandy soil under the impetus of gravity until it reaches the salt water-filled spaces in the sandy base.
Because it lands so gently, it just sits on top of the salt-water-filled
sand box called Cape Cod.

Think in my own case of God's grace. Think *lectio*. Think Divine
Office. Think Rule. Think about any or all of those things percolat-
ing down so lightly, onto the gyratory soul full of porous grief, frozen
petitions, endless searching. If I stay long enough to let the elements
settle, they will become my eternity. I can go off on a grand quest
seeking answers, or I can stay put and let them percolate.

This year, for once, I stayed still.

Cheerfulness is my work, my prayer, and my good zeal. It is the face
that will each day see Christ's face.

⁓

Father Aloysius is portering when I stomp by to the prayer walk.
(Still no good rocks.) I am always afraid of him for his amazingly deep
voice and fierce looks, but he knows his Latin. I haven't seen Abbot
Antony since this morning, and I'm dying to know what those banners
say.

"Yes?" he looks up over the high pile of liturgical somethings he is
pawing through, and I know I am bothering him.

"Father Aloysius? I'm an oblate here, and I need help with Latin."

"Each word represents one of the 'O antiphons' we sing the week
before Christmas," he explains (not too fiercely). "Did you notice how
the first letter on each banner is red, while the rest of them are black?
We begin them on December 17:

"O Sapientia (O Wisdom)
O Adonai (O Sacred Lord)
O Radix Jesse (O Root of Jesse)
O Clavis David (O Key of David)
O Oriens (O Rising Dawn)
O Rex Gentium (O King of the Gentiles)
O Emmanuel (O God-In-Us)

"In inverse order, the initials of each invocation creates an acrostic: ERO CRAS—Tomorrow I will come. Neat, isn't it?"

Neat indeed, as mysteriously wonderful as any Christmas gift now unwrapped. His gentle "God bless" as I leave is the bow on the package.

～

Vespers. Entirely in Latin. I lose myself, and my place in the hymn-book, in a jumble of unfamiliar, lush words and a watercolor sunset that streaks in pink and orange before expiring in one long red gash. I stand up when Abbot Antony stands and bow when he bows, and feel somehow safe in all those ancient words.

～

Compline at 8:00 P.M. Short and simple. I know Vigils and Vespers, corresponding to my Morning and Evening Offices, are the main offices of the day, but I like Compline best. I say it at home, when Felix is traveling, as an "extra." It reminds me of the Episcopalian camp I went to as a kid where I first heard of Compline. It has a child's faith and trust in the words: "Into your hands, Lord, I commend my spirit," and the Gospel antiphon becomes the blanket I tuck around me: "Protect us, Lord, as we stay awake; watch over us as we sleep; that awake, we may keep watch with Christ, and sleep, rest in his peace."

There are just six cars parked on the retreat side as I head back to my room. I am the only room occupied in the entire renovated building. I am so grateful to close out the year here on this quiet, silent night.

Brother Nicholas is right behind me, turning off the Christmas lights for the night.

PAX.

December 29, 2000: St. Thomas Becket, the Christmas Octave

Lectio: For thou hast found favour with God. (Luke 1:30)

It is not quite 5:00 A.M. If there is anything that finds favor in *my* eyes, it is the discipline required to get up at 5:00 A.M. Of course, the narrow bed and gurgling heater had more to do with my "success" today than any real discipline on my part.

How would I find favor with God? It's easy to roll over and say, "It can't be done; it's all God's grace, God's mercy"—but then I don't have to do anything at all.

I probably can't "do anything at all" anyway that will find favor from God for me, but I would guess that I need to do the things that God has asked, just because he asked and not because they merit favor in themselves. It's like the reason you provide for your children or are faithful to your spouse—because you're *expected* to do those things, not because they earn you favor points.

So perhaps with God. We need to do those things asked of us as the family of God. I could make a long list of such things from the Bible ("feed the hungry," "clothe the naked," "pray without ceasing"), but it's a pretty big list. Not everybody does everything on it. But as the body of Christ, we do what is our body-part to do.

For me, my "assignment" is to follow the Rule of St. Benedict to the best my station in life permits. It is my assignment because I took a vow that made it so, just as I promised to love, honor, and obey my husband. I do those things to the best of my ability and work to grow my capacity to do them. They do not bring me favor from God, but they are what I do anyway, finding God's favor to me in the goodness of my marriage, and the joy of living the Rule.

My hair is flat on the side where I was trying to sleep, and clumpy-sticking-out on the other side. No matter, I tell myself bravely. St. Jane Frances de Chantal, a widow, had St. Francis de Sales as her spiritual director. (The saints travel in packs. No wonder I never get to meet any except poor wanna-be Joanna Mary Bonomo.) Together they founded the Sisters of the Visitation of Holy Mary. At one meeting while she was consulting with him about the possibility of founding an order, he looked at her fine jewelry and asked if she was contemplating remarriage. When she vehemently assured him she was *not*, he suggested, "Why not lower the flag then?"

I am lowering the flag this morning. I look like hell. But based on my Easter experiences here, the entire congregation sports matted or clumpy hair at Vigils.

There are a total of *three* in the congregation this morning. The other two are priests, neatly combed. I sit near the front in my bright yellow sweater, trying to look cheerful, trying to follow the Christmas Vigils. I only yawn once and only get lost in the Vigils book twice.

When we exit at 6:30 A.M., there is the barest backlit glimmer of a cold dawn behind the mountains to the east. The *Benedictus* we just sang comes to mind: "In the tender compassion of our God, the dawn from on high breaks upon us." That one illustrious moment is worth getting up for. Then I dash to the room to shower and declump before Lauds at 7:00 A.M.

～

There are eight of us retreatants at Lauds, including yesterday's rather noisy retreatant who now wears an "I am being silent" badge around her neck, who sits and does not sing or recite any of the Christmas Lauds. (I've had days like that here myself, but always as an unadvertised special.)

In Wheelchair Alley once owned by Brother Robert, Father Stanislaus motors in, still intense and very skinny now since his latest surgery. For all I know, he is using Brother Robert's motorized cart. Father Jerome seems to be able to make it around with a cane and extremely slow, shuffling steps. Brother Barnabas can walk in and out unaided, but has lost nearly fifty pounds and has a huge bandage across one eye.

The oldest ones seem to be fairing the best: Abbot Antony, Father Cornelius, Father Aloysius. Nearly two hundred years of monkhood among the three of them.

Breakfast. I am full of thoughts, many of them dressed in gratitude for this year's opportunity to study the Rule. *It's about place*, I am thinking, without being able to expand my thought yet. I came here so uncomfortable and not fitting in or around everybody, but so desirous to make it my study, and gradually, sometimes painfully or cranky, with a certain amount of stubbornness on my part that I rarely possess, it has become part of my oratory, this abbey. I will miss these regular visits that have been part of my Jubilee Year.

"For you," says Abbot Antony, dropping books into my reverie before getting his cup of coffee. (*Don't these holy ones ever eat?*) Three lovely little black, leather-bound books: *The Way of the Cross* (St. Alphonsus Maria de Liguori), *The Imitation of Christ* (à Kempis), *Introduction to the Devout Life* (St. Frances de Sales). I am pretty sure the only *living* meditationist the abbot has read lately is me. These come from another deceased oblate, he explains on his return, not the one who has filled the oblate library with those boxes.

"I thought you might enjoy them," he says. "They're very pretty, the way they are bound and they seem to go together." He especially enjoys showing me *The Way*, which is done like an illuminated manuscript, plus a modern-day matching walk along *Via Dolorosa*. He tells me of his own journey, alone, into Jerusalem, and how he walked the Stations by himself.

I tell him how I approached Father Aloysius for Latin assistance "even though he scares me to death, he's so fierce."

"Yes, he is," says Abbot Antony, with some perverse delight. "One of ten children, he was. He was with the paratroopers in the war. A chaplain in the army. But a wonderful poet. Marvelous poet. He shows his verses only to me because he says I'm the only one who likes poetry. He was my novice."

It is hard to imagine gruff, fierce Father Aloysius writing poetry or being a humble novice. We talk about Brother Dominic and his feast day celebration last week.

And then my Wise Man, emptied of his gifts, departs from the breakfast room.

Brother Maurius takes his place and tells me of his life as a magician and illusionist, of his family of priests and how his parents were honored by the Pope for so many of their children becoming members of religious orders (nine children became monks or nuns). "I am up before 4:00 A.M.," he tells me. "By 4:00 A.M., I am in the kitchen, drinking my tea. I am in the office working before Abbot Henry gets there at 5:00." He is seventy-one years old, and while he goes to bed right after Compline (8:30 P.M.), that still doesn't add up to eight hours of sleep. Plus he's the abbatial secretary for both abbots, master of ceremonies for Mass, currently retreat master, *and* he walks down this steep hill to get the newspaper every morning and walks back up. "I walk four miles a day," he says. "Good exercise."

And this week he's on kitchen duty too. (*Don't these holy ones ever sleep?*)

Breakfast ends up as an extra-ordinary peephole into these ordinary men trying to live the Rule to the best of their abilities, just like ordinary oblates do. It is with a great sense of peace that I tidy my room and change the linens, not with the sadness I thought I'd have. I'm not of the monastery, but of the world. This is not necessarily a bad thing.

By 8:30 A.M., I am officially checked out as stay-over guest and back in "my" place of study in the oblate library, the place Abbot Antony prepared for me.

~

Mass. Father Jerome is celebrant. Father Jerome embodies perseverance. He holds himself erect with such enormous effort. His cane stands propped against his celebrant chair, ready to serve. Once up, he tends to stay there—the up and down of the Mass is otherwise too difficult for his ruined legs.

But his eyes shine as he fumbles for his glasses to read the Gospel out loud. And for all his priestly solemnity, you can see him mentally leaping up and clicking his heels with joy at being able to celebrate the Mass. *This is what I'm supposed to do*, you can hear his heart sing. *Lord, may I have the strength to do what I am supposed to do*. It makes my own determination to be cheerful in what I do seem pallid in comparison.

After Mass, our oblate mom Nancy hands me another Christmas "present"—*A Guidebook for Confession*.

"Father Ignatius told me to get it for you, remember? In August?"

I don't. I must have a funny look on my face because she hastens to add, "Not to embarrass you, of course! When you came out of confession then, he came out after you and told me to buy this for you. There weren't any at the bookstore and when I told him that, he told me to get Brother Nicholas to order them, and here it is."

My confession must have made quite an impression on the crowd.

"How long's it been?" Nancy asks.

"Confession? That was the last time . . . "

Nancy scrapes the price tag off the back of the book. "Use it!"
I really am getting tidied up for the year ahead.

～

I return to the oblate library, this final, quiet Friday of the year.
Again, I begin to feel a little sad to take my leave with chapter 73 of
the Rule.

Abbot Antony appears, video in hand. "I hate to disturb you, but the
other video player is with Father Stanislaus," he says. "I have had this
for a year and haven't played it yet."

"Okay," I say, agreeably enough, pen still poised above notebook.

"You should watch it too," he says. "It's about *real* history."

I guess I'm listening better than I once did. I put my pen down, close
the notebook, and we watch a video about a 1,200-year-old cathedral
for half an hour together. Chapter 73 must wait a while longer.

Chapter 73: All Perfection Is Not Herein Attained

This rule has been written, says Benedict, to show the beginnings of
monastic life. For those moving beyond beginnings, he offers a reading list to advance in holy life. (I have read none of them but
Scriptures, surprise, surprise.) By keeping the Rule, you will continue
to higher summits in teaching and virtues, *and under God's protection,
you will reach them.*

Benedict goes on to ask the beautiful question Abbot Antony let us
peek at during the oblate meeting a few months ago: *Are you hastening
toward your heavenly home?* His response to your theoretical answer
finishes the book: *Then, with Christ's help, keep this little Rule we have
written for beginners. After that, you can set out for the loftier summits of
the teaching and virtues we mentioned above, and under God's protection,
you will reach them. Amen.*

In every AA meeting I ever attended, somebody would be assigned
to read "How It Works"—chapter 5 of AA's "Big Book," a recovering
alcoholic's equivalent to Scriptures. I haven't seen or heard chapter 5
in fifteen years, but my memory can still trace over those opening
words: "Rarely have we seen a person fail who has thoroughly followed our path. Those who do not recover are people who cannot or

will not completely give themselves to this simple program."[2] Bill W,
Alcoholic Anonymous' founder, could be writing about the Rule.

And there in chapter 5 and How It Works is the encapsulation of
chapter 73 of the Rule: *We seek spiritual progress, rather than spiritual
perfection.* I can almost see my old sponsor Lucille putting down her
reading glasses and her twelve-step book and saying, "I'm so glad
we're at the end because it means we can start over again."

The Benedictines would call that *conversatio morum suorum*—a conversion of manners, a continuing and unsparing assessment and
reassessment of one's self and what is important and valuable in life—
and would be mighty pleased by it. It's all I need to remember about
chapter 73: spiritual progress, not spiritual perfection.

> As he was dying, Abba Benjamin said to his sons, "If you
> observe the following, you can be saved: Be joyful at all
> times, pray without ceasing, and give thanks for all things."[3]

I've been trying to study and understand a bit of Benedict's Rule
this year, but sometimes I wonder if all I did was write about Abbot
Antony. Come to think of it, probably anything I learned about the
Rule has not come from reading it or even my hard-pressed study this
year. What I know of the Rule has come from watching Abbot
Antony, from following his suggestions, from *listening* to him—a very
Benedictine thing to do after all. He is my old abbot, and I love him
as dearly as I can love anyone or anything on this earth. Way back in
chapter 2 ("Qualities of an Abbot"), Benedict says the abbot *holds the
place of Christ in the monastery, since is he addressed by a title of Christ.*

If Abbot Antony is even just one-millionth part Christ, I have found
the Christ in him, and followed and obeyed and loved the Christ in
him. If this is what it looks like and feels like, then there's hope for my
redemption yet. Plus, he prays for my redemption and my destination
of the New Jerusalem. Even if I fail in my own failings, there will be
the Divine Assistance to guide me when Abbot Antony is no longer
here. He promised.

It's about place. I've been thinking that for the last two days without
understanding what I'm trying to get at. It's about place, the oratory

of the heart, this whole Benedictine way. When my parents' Episcopal priest heard I was an oblate novice, she said, "You'll like it. It's very Episcopalian in its sense of place."

I didn't understand then. I almost understand now. I am making a beginning of understanding, the way Abbot Antony said he was beginning at the seventieth-year anniversary of his vows.

It's about place, the place made within, the "inner monastery" of obedience, silence, and listening that invites God to enter and shows true hospitality by making him welcome. *It's about place*, the outer stability Benedictines pledge themselves to, that gives rise to the inner place, made ready for God. God will work with a moving target, a gyratory, but until that person stops moving, there's no place ready for God to settle, no room at the inn.

Here is where I found the place of moderation that Benedict wants for me. Not in hard-line AA or parish politics, or the drifting sands of the artist's life, not even in the plain, sandy shores of my native New England. Here, this place, St. Augustine's Abbey, high on the canyons where ocean and desert meet is where I came to find my way home.

> They came from almost every place.
> For almost every reason.
> They came out of loneliness and love and desire and hate . . .
> They came because it was a new beginning, or a last chance,
> or because
> there was nowhere else to go.[4]

My father died. It was the last buoy keeping me afloat, however adrift I was. Abbot Antony answered the call. "Come to lunch. Come early for Mass." He knew where I needed to go, and he had some tools to share for the journey.

And having come to lunch—and early for Mass—I am here with this Rule, here for good, coming home at last.

Listen . . .

~

A final meander around the prayer walk. Never did see a snake there (don't intend to start now). Vespers shortly with the sunset. And then what?

The rest of my life.

The Rule.

I'm so glad I'm at the end because it means I can start over again.

And maybe make that rock garden.

Maybe read St. Augustine.

APPENDIX

NOTES:
"WHAT ARE YOU READING?"

January: If Ye Will Hear His Voice

1.   Robert Frost, "Into My Own," verse three, from *Complete Poems of Robert Frost* (New York: Holt, Rinehart and Winston, 1962), p. 5.

2.   Commentaries on the Rule of St. Benedict: there are quite a few such "Cliff Notes." I count at least eight on my own bookshelf. For this study, I used two:

Joan Chittister, OSB, *The Rule of Benedict: Insights for the Ages* (New York: Crossroad, 1992). This commentary takes the Rule in its daily "chunks" equal to three readings a year, and makes modern day exhortations after each small section. The Rule is rewritten into a non-gendered translation, which could read awkwardly at times, but was also helpful for its inclusionary assistance.

Benet Tvedten, OSB, *A Share in the Kingdom: A Commentary on the Rule of St. Benedict for Oblates* (Collegeville, Minn: Liturgical Press, 1989). Brother Benet takes the Rule chapter by chapter, explaining Benedict's perspective, adding notes from his own experience as a monk, and finally making suggestions for oblate experience. This is a cheerful, enjoyable book.

I used these commentaries because they explained the Rule in linear fashion as I was doing. Most of the other commentaries in my collection followed the major themes of Benedict's Rule (silence, humility, obedience, and so on), and I was not ready to see the overarching themes yet. All were written by clerics and other "professional religious." The one exception to both of these statements is Esther de Waal's *A Life-Giving Way*. A lay writer from the Anglican Church tradition, she takes each chapter as it comes in the Rule, writing little homilies for each. The writing is more academic than personal, and by the time I came upon this, late in my study, I wanted my own experience of the Rule itself.

3. *The Rule of St. Benedict.* All quotations and references use the 1975 version translated by Anthony C. Mersel and M. L. del Mastro (New York: Doubleday Image Books).

4. The old desert fathers (and a few mothers) have a tradition of stories that go back to earliest Christianity. I used three wonderful collections/translations of such stories. Many are duplicated across collections, and sometimes the choice of reference came down to which one contained what I was looking for.

Thomas Merton, trans., *The Wisdom of the Desert: Sayings from the Desert Fathers of the Fourth Century* (New York: New Directions, 1960).

Helen Waddell, trans., *The Desert Fathers* (New York: Vintage Spiritual Classics/Random House, 1998).

Benedicta Ward, SLG, trans., *The Sayings of the Desert Fathers* (Kalamazoo, Mich.: Cistercian Publications, 1975).

5. Ward, p. 185.

6. Ward, p. 231.

7. Merton, p. 54.

8. Thomas à Kempis, *The Imitation of Christ*, Clare L. Fitzpatrick, ed. (New York: Catholic Book Publishing Co., 1977), p. 26.

9. Ward, p. 4

February: Your Goal Is Jerusalem

1. Walter Hilton, *The Ladder of Perfection*, Leo Sherley-Price, trans. (London: Penguin Books, 1988), p. 151.

2. Merton, p. 50.

3. Ward, p. 239.

4. Ward, p. 98.

5. Merton, p. 55.

6. Ward, p. 178.

7. Anonymous (Bill Wilson), *The Twelve Steps of Alcoholics Anonymous* (New York: Alcoholics Anonymous World Services, Inc., 1987), p. 75.

8. Merton, p. 53.

9. Merton, pp. 53–54.

March: For Discipline You Endure

1. Ward, p. 193.

2. Thomas Spidlik, *Drinking from The Hidden Fountain: A Patristic Breviary* (Kalamazoo, Mich.: Cistercian Publications), reading for February 11.

3. Norvene Vest, *No Moment Too Small: Rhythms of Silence, Prayer and Holy Reading* (Cambridge, Mass.: Cowley Publications, 1994).

4. Ward, p. 173.

5. Spidlik, reading for February 26.

6. Ward, p. 11.

7. Waddell, p. 102.

8. à Kempis, p. 70.

9. Waddell, p. 145.

10. Thomas Moore, *The Re-Enchantment of Everyday Life* (New York: Harper Collins, 1996), pp. 213–214.

11. Merton, p. 51.

12. Waddell, p. 58.

13. Waddell, p. 72.

14. Waddell, p. 143.

15. Merton, p. 62

April: The Parched Ground Shall Become a Pool

1. Ward, p. 171.

2. Ward, p. 169.

3. Waddell, pp. 114–115.

4. Waddell, p. 115.

5. Ward, p. 30.

6. Ward, p. 80.

7. Ward, p. 121.

8. Ward, pp. 106–107.

9. Merton, p. 49.

10. Tvedten, p. 94.

11. Joseph Holzner, *Paul of Tarsus*, Eckhoff, Frederic, trans. (St. Louis: Herder, 1945), p. 261.
12. Ward, p. 234.
13. Tvedten, p. 97.
14. Merton, p. 51.

May: And Blossom as the Rose

1. Ward, p. 65–66.
2. Chittister, p. 146.
3. Chittister, p. 147.
4. Ward, p. 78.
5. Ward, p. 101
6. Merton, p. 70.
7. Merton, p. 61.

June: I Am the Door

1. Ward, p. 188.
2. St. Ephrem, "Song on the Ascetic Life," lines 36–45, private translation.
3. Merton, p. 65.

July: Search and Ye Shall Find

1. Merton, p. 59.
2. Ward, p. 68.

August: Bring Forth Fruit

1. Divine Office, vol. III (New York: Catholic Book Publishing Co., 1975), p. 1573.
2. Ward, p. 148.
3. Romano Guardini, *The Lord*, (New York: Regnery Publishing, Inc., 1996), p. 236.
4. Divine Office, vol. IV, from a sermon by Anastasius of Sinai, Bishop, p. 1286.

5. "Ceremonies for Oblates of St. Benedict," pamphlet (Collegeville, Minn.: Liturgical Press).

6. Waddell, p. 68

September: Under the Fig Tree

1. Chittister, p. 170.
2. Ward, p. 154.

October: Entertained Angels Unawares

1. V. Rachel, ed., *A Woman Like You: Life Stories of Women Recovering from Alcoholism and Addiction* (San Francisco: Harper and Row, 1984), Malinda P's story, pp. 73–74.

2. Chittister, p. 174.
3. Tvedten, p. 128.
4. Ward, p. 90.
5. The story is used in Tvedten, p. 127, to illustrate the Rule, chapter 68.

6. St. Francis de Sales, *Philothea, or, An Introduction to the Devout Life* (Rockford, Ill.: Tan Books, 1994), pp. 75–76.

7. St. Francis de Sales, p. 85.

8. Woodeene Koenig-Bricker, *365 Saints: Your Daily Guide to the Wisdom and Wonder of Their Lives* (San Francisco: Harper, 1995), reading for November 1.

9. St. Francis de Sales, p. 88.

November: Candle of the Lord

1. Ward, p. 75.
2. Ward, p. 189.

December: Prefer Nothing Whatsoever

1. Merton, p. 55.
2. Anonymous (Bill Wilson), *Alcoholics Anonymous* ("The Big Book") (New York: Alcoholics Anonymous World Services, 1976), p. 58.

3. Ward, p. 44.

4. Curt Gentry, "The Last Days of the Late, Great State of California," quoted in Peter H. King, "Welcome to the Elusive State," *Los Angeles Times Magazine*, (17 December 2000), p. 15.

And Beyond . . .

The Confessions of St. Augustine, Edward Pusey, trans. (New York: The Modern Library, 1999).